THE RIGHT TO SAY
NO

JUDITH TODD

The Right to Say No

THE THIRD PRESS
JOSEPH OKPAKU PUBLISHING COMPANY, INC.
444 CENTRAL PARK WEST
NEW YORK N.Y. 10025

Published in the U.S. by
The Third Press, 1973
Copyright © 1972 by Judith Todd

Library of Congress Catalogue Card Number: 72–93680

SBN 89388–066–3

First printing, 1973

Printed in Great Britain

For my brave mother

Contents

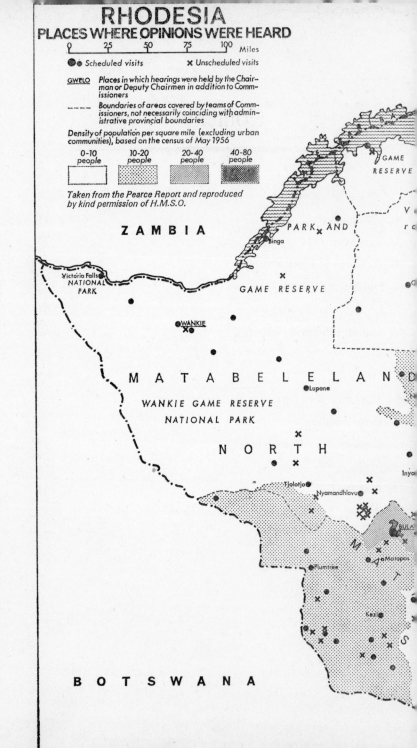

RHODESIA
PLACES WHERE OPINIONS WERE HEARD

0   25   50   75   100   Miles

●○ Scheduled visits   ✕ Unscheduled visits

GWELO   Places in which hearings were held by the Chair-
         man or Deputy Chairmen in addition to Comm-
         issioners

- - - -   Boundaries of areas covered by teams of Comm-
         issioners, not necessarily coinciding with admin-
         istrative provincial boundaries

Density of population per square mile (excluding urban
communities), based on the census of May 1956

0-10   10-20   20-40   40-80
people   people   people   people

Taken from the Pearce Report and reproduced
by kind permission of H.M.S.O.

ZAMBIA

PARK ✕ AND

GAME RESERVE

Binga

Victoria Falls
NATIONAL
PARK

GAME RESERVE ✕

✕ WANKIE

MATABELELAND

WANKIE GAME RESERVE
NATIONAL PARK

Lupane

✕
NORTH
✕

Inya

Tjolotjo

Nyamandhlovu ✕

BULA

Plumtree

Matopos

Kezi

BOTSWANA

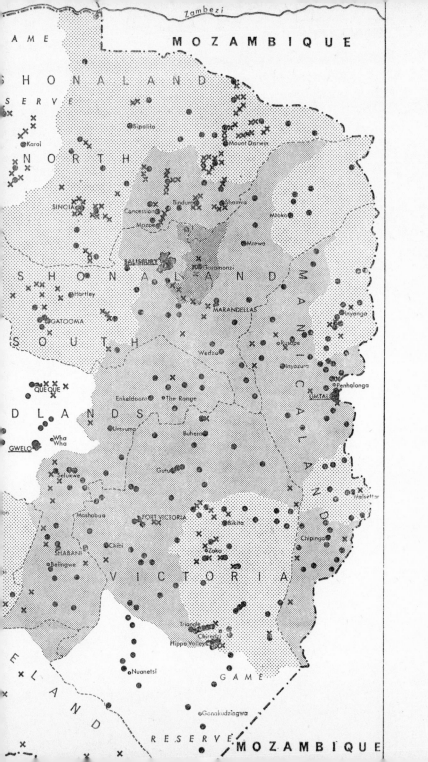

Introduction

RHODESIA is a British colony in southern Africa named after Cecil John Rhodes. Her neighbours are the white-ruled apartheid Republic of South Africa and the Portuguese colony of Mozambique, and the black-ruled countries of Botswana and Zambia.

Before Zambia was granted independence from Britain she was known as Northern Rhodesia and this country was called Southern Rhodesia. We are today ruled by a tiny white minority, but it is already known that when African majority rule is eventually established Rhodesia will be re-named Zimbabwe.

The African population of Rhodesia outnumbers the whites by twenty to one. But the government of Rhodesia is in the hands of the Rhodesian Front, a political party dedicated to the maintenance and perpetuation of White minority rule.

There are approximately 5,310,000 Africans in Rhodesia; 255,000 Whites; 17,200 Coloureds (mixed race) and 9,400 Asians. The African population has one of the highest birth-rates in the world and every year more African babies than there are White inhabitants are born. In 1970 279,000 African babies were born.*

The land is divided approximately equally between the five million Africans on the one hand, and the 275,000 non-Africans on the other.

The average annual wage of an African is R$307.** The average annual wage of a white is R$3,104.

In an attempt, so far successful, to ensure that wealth and power would remain in the hands of the whites, Mr Ian Smith, Prime Minister of Rhodesia, unilaterally declared Rhodesia independent of Britain (U.D.I.) on 11 November 1965. He took this action as Britain had not been prepared to grant independence to Rhodesia while her government showed no intention of moving forward democratically to the establishment of majority rule. In his declaration of Rhodesia's independence Mr Smith had borrowed heavily from the wording of the American Declaration of Independence but it was significant that he had discarded its soul.

* December 1971. Central Statistical Office, Salisbury.
** 58p is roughly equivalent to the new Rhodesian dollar.

'We hold these truths to be self-evident, that all men are created equal, that they are endowed by their Creator with certain inalienable Rights, that among these are Life, Liberty and the pursuit of Happiness. That to secure these rights, Governments are instituted among Men, deriving their just powers from the consent of the governed . . .'

The Rhodesian declaration of independence was regarded as an act of high treason, and Her Majesty's Governor of Rhodesia, Sir Humphrey Gibbs, dismissed Mr Smith and all other members of the Rhodesian cabinet from office. Britain imposed a policy of economic sanctions against Rhodesia. It was hoped that within 'weeks rather than months' sanctions would effectively split the white population of Rhodesia and that a new group would then step forward with whom Britain could negotiate. This did not happen. However the economic effect of the policy was significant.

The Rhodesian Front remained in power, ruling Rhodesia under stringent emergency regulations which had been imposed just before U.D.I. These regulations effectively turned Rhodesia into a full-blooded police state. The authorities skimmed off the cream of African leadership and kept hundreds of people restricted to certain areas or detained in prison cells and detention camps. No political activity which threatened the continued dominance of the white group was permitted.

Over the years which followed U.D.I. the British position steadily weakened in will, intent and principle. By November 1971 the British Foreign and Commonwealth Secretary had flown to Salisbury, capital of Rhodesia, to sign a document with Mr Ian Smith which was intended to clear the way for the recognition of Rhodesia as a legally independent country which would continue to be governed for the foreseeable future by the Rhodesian Front.

There were a number of obstacles to surmount before Her Majesty's Government could confer sovereignty on Rhodesia. Successive British governments had repeatedly stated that any settlement of the independence dispute would have to be found within the framework of the famous five principles which had been formulated by Sir Alec Douglas-Home in the years 1963-4 when the Rhodesian Government was demanding independence from Britain.

The five principles are:

1. The principle and intention of unimpeded progress to majority rule, already enshrined in the 1961 constitution [which Mr Smith had torn up], would have to be maintained and guaranteed.

12

2. There would also have to be guarantees against retrogressive amendment of the constitution.

3. There would have to be immediate improvement in the political status of the African population.

4. There would have to be progress towards ending racial discrimination.

5. The British Government would need to be satisfied that any basis proposed for independence was acceptable to the people of Rhodesia as a whole.

During 1971 British negotiators managed to hammer out proposals with the Rhodesian authorities which dealt with the first four principles, but the fifth principle remained a problem. Any thought of a democratically conducted referendum to assess whether Rhodesians accepted the settlement proposals was ruled out from the beginning. The settlement proposals had been devised by two white parties, Britain attempting to represent the 'best interests' of the Africans. Africans were not consulted on the proposed settlement terms and their participation in reaching an agreement was not invited.

Whatever advantages the proposals for a settlement provided, such as the British offer of up to £5 million a year for ten years for the development of African areas, it was most unlikely that Africans would approve a document which conferred respectability on what they regarded as a rebel regime; which left political power in the hands of the white minority in Rhodesia; which did not provide for the release from detention and imprisonment of the leaders of the African people. There was no guarantee that the document signed by Mr Smith and Sir Alec Douglas-Home would not be torn up once legal independence had been granted and sanctions lifted and Africans were well aware of this.

It was decided that a British Commission under Lord Pearce would canvass all sections of Rhodesian opinion and report on whether the settlement proposals were acceptable. The commission arrived in Rhodesia on 11 January 1972 and both Her Majesty's Government and the Smith regime gave the impression that they confidently awaited a verdict that the proposals were acceptable.

The Pearce Commission found that the proposals were acceptable to most Whites, Asians and Coloureds, but as they were unacceptable to Africans they were not, therefore, acceptable to the people of Rhodesia as a whole.

Despite the findings of the commission, Sir Alec Douglas-Home stated that the proposals were still on the table and that he still thought it could not be difficult to reach an agreement with Mr Smith.

He did not accept that the Africans should have rejected the proposed terms, and hinted that perhaps the terms had not been understood. He urged Africans to think again and he took note of, rather than accepted, the findings of the Pearce Commission. He asked members of the British House of Commons to study, once more, the rejected settlement terms. He said that in any future settlement bid the method of testing Rhodesian opinion would have to be re-examined.

He did not seem to appreciate the fact that if the same proposals were once more presented any honest test of acceptability would find that the Africans would reject these terms again and again. As Lord Pearce had reported, in discussing the rejection by Africans of the terms:

Although statements by British ministers expressly disclaimed all hopes of any improvement in the terms or any future help if this settlement fell through (and we never gave anybody any reason to doubt this), some clearly persisted in the hope that some time, somehow, something better would turn up. It may well be that such hopes were fallacious and that it was unwise to abandon some present advancement for the sake of them. But if people genuinely prefer hope to present realities they are entitled to do so. And if they reject on that score one cannot invalidate their rejection or even less turn it into an acceptance on the grounds that their hopes were likely to prove vain.

CHAPTER TWO

Rhodesia, 1971

RHODESIA entered her sixth year of an unhappy, unrecognized 'independence' with a broadcast to the nation by Mr Ian Smith for the New Year, 1971. Mr Smith said that although there was no more than an outside chance that sanctions would be lifted in the forthcoming year, Rhodesia would enjoy another quiet year of progress and consolidation.

'As the great majority of you know, especially those of you who have travelled outside our borders, in spite of all the criticism you hear and read against us, there is no better place in which to live than our Rhodesia. Let us try to preserve it. If we conduct ourselves in our traditional manner, showing kindness, tolerance and consideration for the other man's point of view, then with our well-known Rhodesian resourcefulness and with God's continuing guidance, we will succeed.'

As Mr Smith was speaking so Mr Guy Clutton-Brock, treasurer of the non-racial co-operative Cold Comfort Farm Society on the outskirts of Salisbury, was being deprived of his citizenship. Mr Clutton-Brock had been a Rhodesian citizen for over twenty years. No charges were laid against him and he was not taken before any court. On 6 January two immigration officials presented him with a document which read: 'Ministers have the honour to recommend that the President may be pleased in terms of the Immigration Act to deem Arthur Guy Clutton-Brock to be an undesirable inhabitant of or undesirable visitor to Rhodesia.'

On 15 January a statement published by the Smith regime read:

By proclamation in the Gazette today, the President has declared the Cold Comfort Farm Society to be an unlawful organization in terms of the Unlawful Organizations Act. This action has been taken because the President is satisfied that the activities of the Society and some of its members are likely to endanger public safety, to disturb or interfere with public order, or to prejudice the tranquillity or security of Rhodesia, or are dangerous or prejudicial to peace, good order or constitutional government . . .

'The Government is satisfied that, over a period of years, under the cover of an organization whose aims are ostensibly to promote understanding, friendship and co-operation among people, in reality officials and members of the Society not only sympathize with, but actively support the terrorist cause as a means of overcoming the Constitution and the Government which they describe as oppressive and illegal . . .

Armed police sealed off the farm and notices were erected declaring the area to be a 'Protected Place'. No-one without a permit from the authorities could enter. Signs warned any would-be visitors that trespassers faced a R $2,000 fine.

On 17 January it was reported that Mr Clutton-Brock and his colleagues were shocked and angry at the allegations against society members. 'All of us were and still are opposed to violence in any form. We have never supported terrorism.' The *Rhodesia Herald* had commented the previous day that 'what we cannot understand is why the action was not taken in a court of law.' But the workings of courts of law in Rhodesia had become a formality which the Smith regime was increasingly content to evade. All allegations about Mr Clutton-Brock and the Cold Comfort Farm Society were made under the cloak of parliamentary privilege.

The farm was closed down and sold for over R $50,000. The money from the sale was appropriated by the Smith regime. Mr Clutton-Brock was taken from his home, physically placed on an outward bound aeroplane and deported.

'I am being abducted from my wife, home and friends in Rhodesia,' he said. 'Countless Africans have been hounded from their homes here throughout the years. I am glad to share in the fellowship of the dispossessed. I take nothing with me beyond my love for many friends. I have little to go to beyond more friends.

'I leave Rhodesia regretting no significant thing I have done or said, only not saying more and doing better . . . I regard the present regime as only temporary and myself as a continuing citizen of Rhodesia, so expect to see Zimbabwe again before long. I therefore say goodbye to nobody.'

The same month the Smith regime received a request from the Fort Victoria Town Council that the town's four parks be declared 'For Europeans Only'. The request was made after a resident had complained that the parks were developing 'into a play-ground for

Africans'. But on 11 February Rhodesia's Minister of Mines, Mr Ian Dillon, pled for 'subtlety' on the matter.

A lot of damage had been done to Rhodesia's cause by the world headlines that had followed the proposed banning of Africans from Fort Victoria's parks, he said. If action such as that contemplated by Fort Victoria was taken – and he didn't think it would be – then European families would be deprived of the 'nannies' who looked after their children in the parks. 'In removing these pin-pricks we must be more subtle and not make it known by world headlines,' he said.

The previous November the Residential Property Owners' (Protection) Bill had been published in draft form and was due to be brought before Parliament in March, for enactment as law. The bill provided for the eviction of 'infiltrators' from areas predominantly occupied by residents of a race different from that of the 'infiltrators'. The basic purpose of the bill was to make possible the removal of Asians and people of mixed race from 'White areas'. Africans had already been dealt with under the Land Tenure Act which forbade them to live in white areas and which laid down, amongst many, many other strictures that any white wishing to offer hospitality to an African overnight must first apply for a permit.

The Residential Property Owners' (Protection) Bill, soon dubbed the POP Bill for the sake of convenience, provided for the establishment of a tribunal to determine the racial classification of people. The bill provided that fifteen people could anonymously petition for the removal of any 'infiltrators' in their area. The tribunal was also to act as a board of appeal. Evictees could appeal to the tribunal, denying, if they so wished, that they were of the racial group alleged.

The press, the Asian and Coloured communities and a few Whites protested about the proposed legislation. On 6 January the Bulawayo Town Council decided that it wanted no part in financing or administering the bill when it became law, on the grounds that as the proposed bill would be a matter of national policy, so it should be financed and administered by the national government.

During the year an anonymous booklet, *A Guide To The Thoughts Of Ian Smith*, started circulating within the country. The police, despite continuing investigations, have not as yet discovered the writer or the publisher. Using the vehicle of the proposed POP Bill the booklet lampooned Mr Smith and his colleagues and its effectiveness lay in that much of the dialogue comprised actual quotations taken from *Hansard* or newspaper reports. For instance the discussion by Mr Smith and his colleagues of the POP Bill was based on the actual wording of the draft.

Partridge: (Minister of Local Government and responsible for the Bill) ' "Asian" means an individual – (a) who is a member of a race or tribe which is indigenous to – (i) India, Pakistan or Ceylon; or . . .'

Smith: Inadequate!

Partridge: I beg your pardon?

Smith: You haven't put down enough countries. I mean just think of all the races and tribes of Israel and Ethiopia and Egypt and all those countries to the north. How do we keep them off of our property?

Partridge: Well, I think that situation is adequately covered under the definition of an Asian. You see it goes on to say 'or (ii) such other country or state as the Minister may, in accordance with a resolution passed by the House of Assembly, specify by notice in the Gazette . . .' So you see, sir, there's nothing to worry about. If any wogs, I mean Egyptians, come sliding in down here, we just declare Egypt an Asian country, and that fixes them.

While the South African press reported that the 'Thoughts' was 'the most sought-after book in Rhodesia at present', Mrs Barbara Gadd, an eloquent and tireless exponent of the views of the far right, was extremely upset to find herself the recipient of a copy.

As an interested observer of the international struggle for political power [she wrote to the *Rhodesia Herald*] I have read some pretty foul stuff, and I consider that this so-called 'play' is quite on a par with the best efforts of the Kremlin itself. As with all Communist-inspired subversion it would have an appeal for the ignorant, particularly since it is laced with what would pass for satire in the minds of the perverted.

The only good thing that may be said of this pamphlet is that it should serve to remind us not to await the sound of snow-covered Russian boots or the Yellow Peril crossing our borders but to be on the alert for the Communist vanguard living right in our midst.

The draft of the proposed POP Bill was not submitted to Parliament during 1971. The Rhodesian authorities quietly dropped the Bill until negotiations with Britain on a proposed settlement had been finalized. After Lord Pearce had reported that the proposals were not acceptable to the people of Rhodesia as a whole, Mr Ian Smith admitted that his government had been considering other ways of implementing the POP Bill had there been a settlement. It was quite clear that the Rhodesian Front had never seriously contemplated deviating from its policy of white supremacy. Once a settlement had been safely arrived at all assurances of reducing racial discrimination would have been scrapped.

That year the Smith regime redoubled its efforts to evict the Tangwena tribe from their land. The 10 square miles of land in the Inyanga area which the Tangwena people regarded as their home, having lived there since before the advent of the white man to Rhodesia, had been declared a European area under the Land Tenure Act. The Tangwena had taken their case to the courts and the courts had found that the Tangwena could not lawfully be moved.

The government then issued a proclamation which effectively changed the law and ordered the Tangwena to move to another area known as Bende.

The Tangwena steadfastly refused to move.

Then the authorities moved in, burnt down the huts, arrested men and women, drove the cattle away, closed down the school for the Tangwena children and charged Chief Tangwena with making subversive statements.

In an interview with *Struggle* the previous November, Chief Rekayi Tangwena had spoken freely as he watched his cattle being driven away.

'We are angry with what is happening,' said Tangwena. 'This land is ours and now they say that it does not belong to Africans. They arrested my people. They beat a pregnant woman – she is still in hospital up to this day. The government will have to build a jail large enough to take all my people. We do not want to go to Bende. We want our cattle back on this land . . .

'It is the Europeans who have come to disturb us, to destroy our property, to deprive us of the wealth of this land. This is unforgiveable. My people are heartsick. These cattle that they are driving away . . . they are trying to provoke my people so that they may shoot us with their guns, because we are defenceless.'

'Do you see yourself, chief, as a politician, and do you see yourself playing a more prominent political role in the country?' asked *Struggle*.

'I am not a politician. I simply want my rights.

'I think that this country should be freed so that every individual would have a say in his government. If the Europeans were less cruel and oppressive in their government we could determine our lives in consultation with one another. This would be good. The Europeans should not ill-treat us; kick us; say this belongs to me; that belongs to me; everything belongs to me. Where was the African living when the Europeans first came? They found us here. Should we live in trees today? Every place that they find to be good they say belongs to them. Good and fertile land they want for themselves. As Africans we have been driven into the mountains. What is there for us to eat? Is this not destructive? It is.

'We fear. We fear because they threaten to shoot us with guns. Where can we go? They arrest us and toast us on fires; they hit us with the butts of their guns. How can you say anything? If you open your mouth you are hit with the butt of a gun. They show you the gun and threaten to shoot. Where can we go? You have no option but to fear the gun that you can see . . .

'The people must tell the government to stop their cruelty. We want a better system; we want a situation of love.'

Chief Tangwena wrote to the British Government, pleading for help. On 5 May 1971, the contents of a letter to him from the Foreign and Commonwealth Office were published in Rhodesia. The letter was signed by the Marquess of Lothian.

'The British Government has observed with concern the position of your tribesmen and this has been made clear on several occasions in the British Parliament.

'I realize that this does not fully meet your present request, but I can assure you that we are not indifferent to your situation. The fact is, however, that we are not in the position to intervene in internal affairs in Rhodesia.'

The letter said the British Government was now trying to establish whether a basis existed for negotiating a settlement of the Rhodesian issue within the Five Principles.

'I cannot say whether we shall be successful in our efforts to find a just settlement, but the British Government believes that such a settlement would be the best way to foster racial harmony among the people of Rhodesia and improve the conditions of all who live there.'

Meanwhile *Struggle* was banned. The editors, Mr Anthony McAdam, a former lecturer at the University of Rhodesia, and Mr Charles Perrings, had their passports seized and were warned that they faced charges under the Law and Order (Maintenance) Act. The two men eventually fled from Rhodesia without their passports.

The offices of *Umbowo*, a newspaper run by the United Methodist Church, were raided by police and the editor informed that he would face charges relating to material he had published on the Tangwena. He was eventually convicted on one count under the Law and Order (Maintenance) Act for publishing a poem about the eviction of the Tangwena people from their land. The magistrate, Mr H. P. Duncan, referring to the poem, said: 'This is basically an attack on the whites as a group.'

The question, said Mr Duncan, was: 'Were the verses likely to engender feelings of hostility?'

Some of the lines read:

'We are hunted down like klip-springers with dogs on our scent . . .
'We get locked up . . .
'Our homes have been destroyed . . . our cattle have been grabbed . . .
our schools have been grabbed . . .'

Mr Duncan said that according to the poem these were all actions which had been attributed to the whites. Use of the word 'grab', he said, strongly suggested an unjustifiable and dishonest taking away. He sentenced the editor, Mr Everson Chikwanha, to six months' hard labour conditionally suspended for three years. The poet, an American missionary, was deported.

1971 celebrated Rhodesia's first pop festival held in the Glamis Stadium in Salisbury where over 15,000 people disregarded the rain to watch and listen to South African and Rhodesian pop groups. The press reported that sheer weight of numbers had made it impossible to enforce 'Europeans Only' signs and police orders were treated with good-humoured contempt, expressed in announcements from the stage like: 'The fuzz wants you to put your shirts back on. But it's your party and your clothing so you do exactly as you please.'

The organizer and promoter, South African Mr Ralph Simon (twenty-four), said later that the festival had been a resounding success.

'There were no racial barriers at all,' he said. 'When you see people of different races walking hand in hand out of friendship, it's great.'

White Members of Parliament and sections of the public howled their disagreement. There were calls for pop-festivals, pop-music, beards, long hair and 'permissiveness' to be banned. Deportations of white immigrants who consorted with non-white girls in Rhodesia were speeded up. Many of the immigrants were themselves discovering that Rhodesia was not such a happy country to live in and a young Irish immigrant, silently pleading for deportation, drew a large hammer and sickle on the cab of the Rhodesia Railways train he was working on.

Rhodesia's book of the decade was published that April. Copies of *The Silent War* were stacked in the display windows of every bookshop in the country. In the foreground of the dust-jacket two soldiers, one black, one white, lay peering down their gunsights. In the background white soldiers leapt from their chopper, machine guns at the ready. On the back of the jacket were quotes from the book: ' "They threw matches on my husband but I think he was too wet with blood. They would not ignite . . ." '. 'The bombing was accurate and intensive. The R.R.A.F. screamed in . . . When they had finished . . . weapons, limbs and food were scattered all around the once-tidy camp.'

The book was described as a 'documentary account of the fight for Southern Africa' and was written by two journalists, one Rhodesian, the other South African. It was designed for the white southern-African market and the feelings of Africans were ignored in the advertising techniques used. Huge reproductions of a notice dropped by the armed forces to guerillas were on display with the books in the show windows. The fact that these guerillas are not vermin who crawl out of holes in the ground but are the sons, brothers, fathers, lovers and friends of countless Rhodesian Africans was not appreciated.

NOTICE TO TERRORISTS

You are far from your home. Do you want to die? You have been sent by your leaders in Lusaka to fight against us in Rhodesia. These men refuse to come themselves because they know our strength and do not want to die. They have sent you to die for them. You will die if you do not obey the orders which we are now giving you. You will save your life if you do as we tell you. To refuse is death. You will never be seen or heard of again . . .

. . . You will shout so that our soldiers know who you are and where you are. Remain silent and you will be shot as one who creeps about with evil in his heart . . .

WHEN YOU SEE THE SOLDIERS COMING YOU WILL SHOW YOUR-SELVES WITH YOUR ARMS HELD HIGH . . . If they see your hands are down they will think you are carrying arms and they will kill you dead . . .

The only concession made to the passing public was that the photograph of a dead guerilla's face, captioned 'Why wait for this?' had been omitted.

Top security officials from Portugal and South Africa arrived in Rhodesia on Sunday, 14 February 1971. Major-General Hendrik J. van den Bergh, South Africa's security chief was said to be on a 'private visit'. Major Silva Pais, Portugal's security chief, was said to be on a trip 'to see some old friends'.

The two men were among seven top security officials who booked into the Jameson Hotel, Salisbury. The block booking was made by the Rhodesian Prime Minister's office. The seven officials were:

Major-General van den Bergh:	Head of South Africa's Bureau of State Security (BOSS)
Colonel Michael C. Gerdenhuys:	Assistant to Gen. van den Bergh
Mr A. F. R. Vervey:	BOSS
Major Silva Pais:	Head of the Portuguese Security Directorate (D.G.S.)
Dr Antonio Lopes:	Chief security officer of Angola
Mr Antonio Vaz:	Chief security officer of Mozambique
Mr Gomes Lopes:	An inspector in Mozambique's security organization

Shortly after the visit of these men Sir Alec Douglas-Home announced in the House of Commons (22 February) that there were no South African armed forces in Rhodesia but only South African policemen. This announcement gave the impression that Sir Alec believed that the South Africans, brought in to kill Rhodesian and South African guerillas in Rhodesia's Zambezi Valley, were exact reproductions of blue-uniformed, unarmed London bobbies. In fact, as he must have been aware, the men are 'police' in name only. They are highly trained commandos, equipped with helicopters and sophisticated armaments.

Later, in the same debate, when asked if Britain would try to end the guerilla raids into Rhodesia, Sir Alec replied: 'What we can do is try to get a settlement in Rhodesia which will remove the cause of these incursions and, therefore, *the need for* South African police in Rhodesia.'

One was left wondering whose need Sir Alec was concerned with: that of the illegal Smith regime, forced to rely on South African military might in containing the repressed people in the British colony of Rhodesia, or the need of those who, in a mixture of despair and hope, had reached the stage of being willing to lay down their lives for their people and their country. Earlier it had been announced that the Conservative government of the United Kingdom was willing to sell certain categories of arms to South Africa and orders were invited for what British Westland Wasp helicopters South Africa required. It was, of course, as fallacious to argue that South Africa was arming against Communism as it was to argue that the way of life in South Africa was Christian. The Anglican Dean of Johannesburg was being charged under the Suppression of Communism Act. The willingness of the British Government to sell any military equipment to South Africa revealed that the protestations Sir Alec Douglas-Home had made about his abhorrence of apartheid weighed as little, in reality, as the seconds it took to make them. South Africa's arms and helicopters are for use against black South Africans and black Rhodesians. The British Government was in grave danger of becoming identified with the South African Government and the Smith regime in their continued, enforced, savage policy of white supremacy in southern Africa.

Rhodesia's censorship board was as busy as ever, delighting in banning Norman Mailer, James Baldwin and even a book by Dr Havelock Ellis M.D. Predictably books on such people as Martin Luther King Jnr and Malcolm X were banned as were, less predictably, the German recording of 'Hair', a record entitled 'The Irish Sing Rugby Songs' and Joan Baez singing 'We Shall Overcome'. In January 1971, the censorship board banned sixty-one publications in one fell stroke, including *South Africa's Rule of Violence* by Patrick Duncan published in 1964. That May the censorship board published an up-to-date list of the 450 books, various issues of 125 different periodicals and eleven records it had so far banned. The banned books included two by President Kaunda, the *Kama Sutra* and *My Life and Loves* by Frank Harris, published in 1925.

The censorship board is not the sole censoring authority in Rhodesia. Newspapers reluctantly exercise self-censorship and when the United Nations seized a shipment of ammonia to Rhodesia, newspaper editors were informed by the regime that it would not be in the national interest to allow the story to be published. The press thereupon printed an official government handout stating that there was a shortage of fertilizer (for which the ammonia had been needed) because of labour problems in South Africa, no doubt hoping that the report would not be drawn to Mr Vorster's attention as he had recently said that, unlike other countries, South Africa had no labour problems.

On 6 May a four-line paragraph was blacked out of the current edition of *Newsweek*. The deleted paragraph carried 'derogatory remarks about the Prime Minister, Mr Ian Smith', according to the manager of Kingstons, the Rhodesian publisher of *Newsweek*, and he was afraid of prosecution.

The Rhodesia Broadcasting Corporation, a model propaganda vehicle, scuttled along with the censorship board, ever eager to be ahead of the times, at least in Rhodesia. In mid-1971 it managed, rather breathlessly, to beat the censorship board at its own game, and it was announced that the R.B.C. had banned 'A Summer Prayer For Peace', an innocuous record by The Archies which was playing happily over every other radio network in southern Africa. The song listed the populations of various countries and totalled them in the chorus.

> *Three billion people, together, for ever;*
> *Three billion people sing a summer prayer for peace . . .*
>
> *Oh look, look around you,*
> *See what we have done.*
> *Where's the world that God intended, with love for everyone?*
>
> *Sing, oh sing of freedom,*
> *Sing a song of joy,*
> *All together, make it better, what some would destroy.*

The Chronicle, Bulawayo's daily paper, asked the Director-General of the R.B.C., Mr James Neill, three questions. Here they are, with his answers.

Q. Has the R.B.C. restricted the record?
A. Yes.
Q. Why?
A. No comment.
Q. What is meant by restricting a record? Will it be broadcast at all?
A. Restricting a record means the R.B.C. restricts a record in its use.

While discussion of 'A Summer Prayer For Peace' continued, John Lennon's 'Power To The People' continuously throbbed, unnoticed, over the R.B.C.

The courts of Rhodesia were as busy as ever handing out judgements and sentences on those accused who were fortunate enough not to be incarcerated in prisons or detention camps without trial. On 23 February 1971, Gideon Edward Becking (twenty-seven) of Surrey Farm, Gwelo, shot and killed one of his employees, Amon Nyoni. The following account of Becking's trial is from the *Rhodesia Herald*, 28 May 1971.

Mr J. C. Andersen, for the defence, said yesterday that Becking should not be found guilty of murder. The proper verdict, he said, would be one of guilty of culpable homicide.

Becking continued his evidence yesterday and said Amon, who had been an unsatisfactory employee, had made him angry. He had had a provocative smile and tried to annoy him by the way he spoke.

THE RIGHT TO SAY NO

Becking said his idea had been to frighten Amon by getting the rifle. Asked if he was in complete control of the rifle he said he was not, because his wife had bumped into him.

Mr Justice Beck asked Becking how he could explain the fact that if he were aiming overhead one shot struck Amon in the left foot.

Becking replied: 'It could have happened when my wife bumped me.' Becking said that the purpose of bringing out a ·303 rifle after he had used a ·22 rifle was that it would make more noise and frighten Amon more.

Mrs Irene Becking said Amon had been 'cheeky' in the way he had answered her husband. She agreed it was possible she might have told Amon 'to run' because she was afraid her husband might hit him.

Mr St J. A. Bruce-Brand, for the state, said a reasonable man would have stopped shooting after using the ·22 rifle. He asked the jury to return a verdict of murder.

Mr Andersen, in his closing address, said Beck had never intended to kill. He admittedly had wished to 'donder' Amon: had he wished to kill him he would have used a stronger Afrikaans word. All Becking had intended was to frighten an unsatisfactory employee who had angered him by his conduct. Unfortunately Amon was hit. Afterwards Becking had been solicitous for Amon's welfare. 'If he had intended to kill why should he have been so upset?' asked Mr Andersen.

The jury of five white men found Becking guilty of culpable homicide. Mr Justice Beck then sentenced him to three-and-a-half years' hard labour of which nine months was conditionally suspended for three years.

On 4 June the *Chronicle* reported that

two Africans who broke into Macey's Store in Abercorn Street on 29 April and stole two crates of empty bottles were jailed by Bulawayo magistrate Mr J. Redgement yesterday.

Lovemore Sibanda and Nimos Elliot Matemba, both of whom had previous convictions for theft, pleaded not guilty.

Sibanda was jailed for four months and ordered to be placed in solitary confinement and on a reduced diet for the first, third, fifth and seventh fortnights of his sentence. A suspended sentence of three months for a previous offence was also brought into effect.

Matemba was jailed for eight months and a suspended sentence of six months was brought into effect.

26

March 2nd marked Rhodesia's first anniversary as an illegal, un-recognized republic. There were no celebrations.

Sport continued to hold its leading position in Rhodesian life. There were many protestations, when it was thought possible that Rhodesia might be able to compete in the next Olympic games or that FIFA might re-embrace Rhodesian football, that sport in Rhodesia was a completely non-racial activity, open to all. While it was difficult for observers of the Rhodesian scene to avert their attention from the all-white sports clubs throughout the country few commentators seemed to realize that by government edict, no non-European child in Rhodesia is allowed to take part, either as a contestant or a spectator, in any sporting or athletic event within the grounds of a European government school. As all major sporting functions are held on 'European ground' this naturally has an adverse effect on the chances of any non-white child.

But so what? argued Rhodesia's major financial journal, *Property & Finance* in May 1971.

It is in no way racialistic to record that 'sport' is an entirely Western (i.e. European) concept. Like other particular charac-teristics, it has grown from the environment, history and socio-logical development of the white man, a competitive individualist: But sport is now being used as part of 'a struggle for power'.

The Negro, for instance, may lack the mental and organizational capacity of his white equivalent; but if, as a result of sheer physical strength or by virtue of the particular ethnic bone-structure of his heel, he becomes a world champion in boxing or athletics, his prowess is hailed as proof of racial equality if not of actual superiority.

The article ended by warning of what would happen were sport to be integrated.

Not least . . . is the destruction of the social basis of sport, the friendly get-togethers after the game, the convivial drink, the banter of comradeship, all based on common outlooks, common history, and shared community experiences. That that aspect, part of the life of every European community for many centuries, cannot apply, was one of the reasons for the limited ban on multi-racial sport in Rhodesian schools: there was no point of contact, there never is, and there never can be.

In April 1971 Lord Goodman and a small team of senior British officials arrived in Salisbury for discussions with the Rhodesian authorities. The British White Paper, *Proposals For A Settlement*, reports: 'These visits continued at intervals throughout the summer and were concluded by a final round of talks at official level in October 1971. In the light of these discussions the British Government decided that a basis for negotiations with the Rhodesians had been established.' 'The Rhodesians' of course meant the *white* Rhodesians.

Towards the end of 1970 I returned to Rhodesia after nearly five years abroad. In those years I had visited a number of countries on speaking tours about Rhodesia, and had written a certain amount of material on my country and the Smith regime. In the earlier years I had hoped for a major contribution from outside but now it seemed to me that if there was to be any change in the Rhodesian situation, it would have to come from within Rhodesia.

I was, and am, fully aware that any significant change will eventually be brought about by the African population of Rhodesia, but I do not find this fact an adequate excuse for white Rhodesians opposed to racism and the Smith regime to sit back and helplessly observe events in the field. Each individual has a certain amount of responsibility for what has happened and what will happen. The overriding problem is to find something one can effectively do oneself. Some concerned individuals, because of their personal situations, can do nothing. Others can and won't. The only role I can attempt to fulfil is to inform people, inside and outside Rhodesia, of events here.

In April 1971, I wrote to the *Rhodesia Herald* and the *Chronicle* pointing out that 1971 was being observed as international year against racism. I wondered what we in Rhodesia could do to mark the year.

I was immediately and decisively informed what could be done in a number of obscene letters from whites. One was signed: 'from one of the many who look forward to your imprisonment'. But a stream of longing letters started arriving from Africans, full of suggestions.

My joy was full and overflowing to know that 1971 is international year against racism. Personally, I strongly detest racial discrimination, especially in this country. We should fight like Trojans. Racism and racial discrimination is just as evil as the slave trade of long back. Let us denounce it like Abraham Lincoln and William Wilberforce. They moved everywhere preaching strongly against it. The government is detaining and imprisoning freedom-fighters. Their families are going hungry. They are not going to school. They don't have sufficient clothes. So ourselves, as freedom-fighters, let us do contrary to the government. We must educate, clothe and feed these unfortunate families.

One of the most moving was from an inmate of Ingutsheni Mental Hospital, near Bulawayo.

Racism is inhumane, a violation of human rights, an abomination and a mockery of God's creation of the people. Even if I have never held a thermometer in my hands or worn a white jacket I know that disease kills and because many people have lost their lives because of racism I declare it a dangerous disease. I hope those who contribute to its existence will regret it in future. Ironically enough, racism is in the hands of those people who claim to be civilized. It is in top gear in Rhodesia and South Africa where the objects of the governments there are solely to subjugate those who sinned by being born black, to deny them their fundamental rights of citizenship and to impose upon them terrible and unbearable legislation . . .

I was very glad when I read that 1971 is a year of fighting against racism. I am also very glad that you have given us the chance of expressing our feelings . . . I think it would be a wonderful thing if all people unite now to fight racialism and racial discrimination. But I wonder how these practices shall be fought in countries like Rhodesia and South Africa where acts of racism are under practice by the governments themselves? We can fight for 100 years to end this race problem but as long as the government in power supports racial policies we cannot expect ourselves to win. I, as other Africans, will spare no effort or strength in attempting to bring down the Vorster and Smith regimes.

In the end nothing much was done, at least publicly, to mark anti-racism year in Rhodesia. A few meetings were organized and a number of people were arrested and questioned. Some people started collecting goods and money for the Tangwena as their contrib tion. Others started withdrawing their custom from shops where the personnel in charge were openly racist in their behaviour towards customers. A few articles appeared in the press and some anonymous, threatening letters arrived for me from South Africa, where it had been reported that I was attempting to find ways of celebrating the year in Rhodesia. Hostile letters started appearing in the Rhodesian newspapers and *Property & Finance* called for action to be taken against me.

Far from becoming more amenable to a settlement with Her Majesty's Government, within the letter and the spirit of the five principles, Rhodesia was, under the Rhodesian Front, steadily becoming more racist, more authoritarian, more intolerant.

It was against this background that the British Government went full steam ahead, with the help of the brilliant negotiator Lord Goodman, to reach a settlement with the Smith regime. On 24 November 1971, Mr Ian Smith signed an agreement with Sir Alec Douglas-Home (who flew to Salisbury for this purpose) which would, it was thought, clear the way for the recognition of Rhodesia as an independent, sovereign republic, outside the Commonwealth and under the continuing government of the Rhodesian Front.

CHAPTER THREE

Welcome to Britain

WHEN the plane landed at Heathrow on Friday, 24 September 1971, I felt as though I had arrived back home. I was delighted to be visiting Britain again and as the plane taxied to a halt I realized how much I had been missing friends and freedom during the past year in Rhodesia.

I joined the immigration queue under the United Kingdom passports sign. An officer contemplated my passport while my fellow passengers were dealt with, one by one. Before long I was the only new arrival standing at the counter. When I asked the reason for the delay and said that so far as I knew my passport was in order I was told that that was not the point.

After a long wait I was informed that I would have to be questioned and was led to a small booth where I met the chief immigration officer, an old and courteous gentleman. He wanted to know why I had come to Britain. I explained that I had come to try once again to get a full British passport instead of the temporary one I now held.

He grunted.

'Do you know that there is a likelihood of a settlement between Mr Ian Smith and Sir Alec Douglas-Home?'

I replied that I was aware of the possibility but didn't really think there could be a settlement.

'Have you come to be a thorn in the side of the British Government?'

'No,' I answered, both astonished and amused by the question.

'Are you planning to address any meetings?'

I was increasingly perplexed. These were the kind of questions I might expect to be asked at Salisbury airport but not at Heathrow. 'No,' I replied. 'Only about four people in Britain know that I'm visiting the country. But if by any chance I am asked to speak at any meeting, I'll certainly consider the invitation.'

'I see.' He smiled. 'Of course you are aware that if I have any political feelings I'm not allowed to express them. However we wouldn't want you stirring up any trouble, would we?'

31

After being delayed at the airport for an hour I was allowed into Britain for one month, provided I neither sought nor accepted paid employment. A young plainclothes policeman who had been chatting to me while the immigration department was trying to get instructions about what to do with me, grinned sympathetically. 'It would be *much* easier if your name was Miss Smith, wouldn't it?'

The following day Mr Justice Julius Greenfield, a Rhodesian judge appointed to the Rhodesian Bench by the Smith regime after U.D.I. and whose rulings are therefore not recognized by courts outside Rhodesia, was admitted to Britain without any difficulty. Journalists, attempting to check the story that he was now in Britain, were politely refused any information by the Home Office. Amongst others on his visiting list was Sir Alec Douglas-Home.

Seven months later two of Mr Ian Smith's top officials, Mr E. A. T. Smith, the Rhodesian Attorney-General, and Mr Jack Gaylard, Secretary to the Rhodesian Cabinet, visited London on intergovernmental business. They were entertained at the country residence of Mr Philip Mansfield, head of the Rhodesia Department at the Foreign and Commonwealth Office. The British Government and their officials seem to regard long-standing opponents of the Smith regime with more antagonism than they regard members of the Smith regime.

At the end of 1969, after having lived in Britain for over three years, I applied for a British passport. Officials at the Passport Office said it would be impossible to give me one but that they would consider giving me the six-month British passport available for 'loyal Rhodesians'. I had to answer a few questions by an official and when our interview was over and I had assured him that I was not contemplating embarking on any sanctions-busting exercises on behalf of the Smith regime he excused himself for a few minutes, explaining that it was necessary to ring the Rhodesia Department to get clearance for the granting of a temporary passport. I was glad that the British were taking such precautions.

When he came back he was less formal.

'They seem to know you and they say that since your father, mother and sister all travel on New Zealand passports perhaps you would like to apply for a New Zealand passport too. You can get one quite easily. Your parents were born in New Zealand.'

'You are the legal government of Rhodesia, you know,' I said. 'I'm *your* responsibility, not New Zealand's.'

He sighed. 'Oh dear,' he said. 'Mr Allison thought you'd say that.'

The difficulty about the passport I was given is that it expires every six months. In March 1971, my father applied on my behalf to the British Embassy in Pretoria to have my passport extended. Sir Hugh Beadle P.C., Chief Justice of Rhodesia, who betrayed his country, his Queen and his friend, Sir Humphrey Gibbs, by suddenly switching sides and attempting to legalize the Smith regime, had recently had his British passport extended for a further ten years. The British Vice-Consul replied to my father: 'May I explain that your daughter ceases to be eligible for the renewal of her concessionary passport for further six monthly periods once she is no longer ordinarily resident outside Rhodesia. However, we are prepared to consider whether she is eligible for travel facilities on grounds other than residence but before we can do so we shall need to know the object and itinerary of the proposed journey.'

I then wrote to the British Vice-Consul myself and explained that I was a journalist and that a passport was of vital importance to me. I said that I had spent the past five and a half years of my life doing what I could to oppose the Smith regime. I had visited a number of countries on speaking tours and I had done my best to inform opinion about the realities of the Rhodesian situation. 'I would therefore have hoped to be regarded as a friend of Her Majesty's Government rather than as an appendage of the present illegal situation within Rhodesia . . . I do not regard myself as a resident of Rhodesia any more than I am a resident of New Zealand, Australia or countries other than Britain where I have spent any time since U.D.I. and free access to and from Rhodesia is of the utmost importance to me. I would not be surprised if I was frustrated in this by the Smith regime, but I would be saddened as well as surprised if my movements were restricted by Her Majesty's Government.'

My passport was sent from South Africa to the Home Office who then referred the matter to Mr Philip Mansfield, head of the Rhodesia Desk. An extension of my passport was granted.

When I arrived in London everything seemed to happen at once. I immediately realized that I had been paying far too little attention to the negotiations which Lord Goodman had been conducting on behalf of the British Government with the Smith regime. I knew that there was no possibility of an honourable agreement being reached with Mr Smith but I had not suspected how far the British Government had been prepared to go to accommodate Mr Smith. London was clearly far more hopeful of an agreement than were most people in Salisbury. I managed to get a further extension on my passport and prepared to stay in London longer than I had planned. Both the Labour and Conservative Party Conferences were coming up and it was obvious that Rhodesia was once more an issue in British politics.

My passport was a continuing problem. In my dealings with British officials in preceding years I had found them friendly and co-operative. Now they were civil but not in the least helpful.

At length I managed to get an appointment to see Mr A. R. M. Barber of the Rhodesia Department in the Foreign and Commonwealth Office on 26 November. It was an unsatisfactory interview. A friend and adviser of mine came with me. He is a fellow Rhodesian now working in London and his Rhodesian-born sister had been given full British passport rights within a short time of her departure from Rhodesia and arrival in Britain.

After the interview my friend wrote to Mr Barber to place what had been said on record. The letter read:

Dear Mr Barber,
Passports For Loyal Rhodesians
I write by way of confirmation of the interview which Miss Todd and I had with you this morning on the above-mentioned subject.

. . . Miss Todd pointed out that she had been born in a British colony which, subsequent to the Illegal Declaration of Independence, had once again been claimed by the British Government as a Colony. She stated that she had, to the best of her ability, for six years followed the British Government's wish that Loyal Rhodesians should oppose the Illegal Regime and, as such, considered herself and her passport rights the responsibility of the British Government.

You stated that with a settlement no doubt she would revert to being the responsibility of a legal Rhodesian Government.

I then asked you what would be the status of this hypothetical legal Government. To this you replied that you thought it would be a Republic outside the Commonwealth.

I then said that although it seemed clear from reports from Salisbury that the leaders of the African and Coloured people were opposed to the document which had been initialled by Sir Alec Douglas-Home, it was, of course, possible that the proposed Commission of Enquiry would somehow find that the document was acceptable to the People as a whole. In which case it seemed to me that the only historical analogy in Africa to this situation of the founding of a Republic outside the Commonwealth would be the case of South Africa in 1961 where, as far as I could remember, Loyalists to the Crown were given a period in which to claim their British passport rights. You said that you had no knowledge of this subject.

34

You once again suggested that Miss Todd claim a New Zealand passport, and she reiterated that her passport status was the responsibility of the British Government.

We then considered the analogy of my sister . . . where she had been granted a full British passport having been in England for a shorter period than Miss Todd. Having examined her file you could find no answer to this.

You went on to say that this was a question of law and that Miss Todd quite simply could not be granted a United Kingdom and Colonies passport. I said this was extremely strange as your Department had in fact given her just such a passport, but of only six months' duration.

You then said that this stemmed from a decision announced by Ministers in Parliament in June 1968 and I said that it was, therefore, a question of Ministerial decision rather than law.

Miss Todd then explained to you that the reason for her concern was that it would give her a minute measure of protection on her return to her home. She explained that at the last political meeting conducted by Mr Smith in Salisbury, the night before the Mabelreign by-election in August, a questioner had asked why no action was taken against Miss Judith Todd. To which Mr Smith replied: 'I am confident that our police are capable of doing their duty.'

I then attempted to summarize the position by stating that in the event of a settlement the Rhodesia Political Department would doubtless advise Ministers to consider the South African analogy. At this point you stated that people in other independent African countries, such as Zambia, did not have this British passport option. At this point I mentioned to you that Zambia, unlike your prediction about Rhodesia, was, as far as I knew, still in the Commonwealth.

I went on to say that if there were no settlement Loyal Rhodesians continued to be your responsibility, which you seemed to accept. That Miss Todd had been born British in a British Colony and had suffered considerably in the name of loyalty to the Mother Country. This also you appeared to accept.

I then said that a decision by Ministers could obviously be reversed by a new decision by Ministers who, as is the way of the world, would no doubt act on the advice of their Officials. You seemed to accept this.

I then mentioned to you the conversation you had had by telephone with Miss Todd this week in which she told you that the Earl of Longford wished to discuss with the Parliamentary Under-Secretary of State for Foreign and Commonwealth Affairs, the Marquess of Lothian, the issue of Miss Todd's passport, and that you had replied that the Under-Secretary of State would, of course, refer to the Rhodesia Political Department for advice. If I recall my words correctly I then said: 'Good, in that case you will, no doubt, give him the advice which, from this conversation, is clearly just and equitable.'

The interview concluded by our thanking you for giving us your time and by my explaining to you how appallingly let down we Loyal Rhodesians have been by successive British Governments.

At the beginning of December I left Britain without a full British passport and returned to Rhodesia. In the months that followed I was arrested by armed Rhodesian police, jailed without charge or trial, then released from jail into detention at home. As I write I am still detained.

My passport expired the following April. As all my letters to people outside Rhodesia have to be censored by the Rhodesian police before they are posted my mother wrote on my behalf to the British Embassy in Pretoria. She enclosed my passport and asked that it be renewed for a further six months so that when I was released from detention I could leave Rhodesia immediately. Her letter was delivered by hand and the friend who took the letter informed us that he was sorry there seemed to be such a delay but the British officials in Pretoria were seeking advice from the Foreign and Commonwealth Office in London.

Over a month later she received a letter from the British Embassy in Pretoria dated 4 June 1972. It read:

Thank you for your letter of 3 May about the renewal of the concessionary passport of your daughter, Miss Judith Todd.

Concessionary United Kingdom passports for Rhodesians resident in Rhodesia are issued or renewed in order to enable the applicant to make a particular journey or visit. I suggest, therefore, that as soon as your daughter is released from detention and has the permission of the Rhodesian authorities to leave the country you re-apply for the renewal of her passport.

We shall handle consideration of her application with all possible despatch.

Meanwhile, I have retained your daughter's concessionary passport.

Yours sincerely,
I. J. Towner
Second Secretary & Vice-Consul

My mother was so hurt, and so unexpectedly angry, when she received this letter that she wrote immediately to the Foreign and Commonwealth Secretary, Sir Alec Douglas-Home. She asked that attention be given to the following points arising from the letter she had received:

1. The tone of paragraph 2 suggests that the British authorities accept and condone the detention imposed upon my daughter by the Rhodesian Minister of Law and Order.

2. This, despite the fact that Judith has not been charged or convicted of any crime: not even accused or interrogated. Also despite the fact that in 1965 Her Majesty dismissed Mr Smith and his Ministers and has not, to date, re-instated them. It is well known that my daughter has consistently opposed the illegal regime, working with others for a continuing British presence in Rhodesia. It is also well known that certain supporters of the regime who have taken an active part in advising the Rhodesian administration have had no difficulty in renewing their British passports.

3. It is repugnant to me to receive advice from the British authorities that they and we should wait upon the will or whim of the Rhodesian Minister of Law and Order, and that only when he has expressed his will can consideration be given to the application.

4. I had asked and expected that in view of all that has happened between Britain and Rhodesia, and of what has happened to our family in particular, this request would have been met with sympathy and the immediate action which the British authority could have taken. My request was simply for an extension of six months.

5. Reports from the United Kingdom have from time to time stressed your statements that Britain lacks power to take effective action in the Rhodesian dispute. In the matter of granting passport facilities to my daughter Britain undoubtedly has the power but appears to lack the will.

CHAPTER FOUR

Swallowing Camels

Ye blind guides, which strain at a gnat, and swallow a camel.
                                                            Matthew 23:24

THE attempt to reach a settlement with 'Rhodesia' which, in reality, meant the Smith regime, was at its height. 'Sir Alec Douglas-Home flew off to Rhodesia last night, diplomatically choosing a roundabout way,' reported the *Daily Express* on 5 November 1971. 'The R.A.F. VC 10 was flying an extra 2,000 miles to avoid black African states opposed to talks with Rhodesian leader Ian Smith. After a refuelling stop at Bahrain, in the Persian Gulf, the peace-mission jet goes south over the Indian Ocean, crossing the African coastline at Portuguese Mozambique, Rhodesia's neighbour and ally.'

The carefully planned flight was as significantly and determinedly devious as the settlement proposals hammered out in Salisbury. The 'peace-mission jet' flew round all the Africans who could express their opposition to the proposed settlement, flew into Rhodesia where Africans could not as yet express their opposition and eventually flew out again, the Foreign Secretary reputedly sure that Rhodesian Africans, unconsulted, indeed mocked, would be found to support the proposed settlement. Her Majesty's Government and their partner in the settlement bid, the illegal Smith regime, were in for a profound shock. 'No! No! No!' Rhodesian Africans roared when the Pearce Commission eventually asked whether the settlement proposals were acceptable.

It would be interesting to know what Lord Goodman's thoughts on the whole exercise are today. He cannot say that he was not warned. One evening in London, before his final trip to Rhodesia and before the settlement terms were finalized, I handed him a clipping from the *Rhodesia Herald* headed 'Africans calling him Lord Badman'. The clipping referred to the fact that Africans were angry and disappointed that the British negotiating team had failed to consult African opinion on their proposed settlement bid. Lord

Goodman skimmed through the story, grunted and said he would have been prepared to see any African. I do not doubt him but his comment wasn't relevant. Africans had not been invited to the negotiating table and the negotiators, therefore, had no idea what African opinion was. They found that out far too late.

Lord Goodman was, no doubt, chosen for his role, because of his previous and spectacular successes in negotiating. It should perhaps have been noted that in his previous triumphs he was able to meet representatives of all parties involved in a dispute and therefore was able to assess accurately the facts presented and the feelings involved.

The major aggrieved party in the Rhodesian dispute was the Africans who were not represented in the negotiations. Lord Goodman should have been aware that this fact in itself augured ill for any proposed settlement, but sections of British public opinion, from late 1966 onwards, had seemed to assume that any deal arrived at by the British Government would be accepted by grateful Africans as an agreement on their behalf.

The Labour government, under Mr Harold Wilson, had led the way to negotiating with the Smith regime without African participation. Indeed it was Mr Wilson who first introduced Lord Goodman to the Rhodesian scene. At the time I remember not paying much attention to Lord Goodman as I had never heard of him, but of being seriously alarmed that Mr Wilson had asked Sir Max Aitken of the *Daily Express*, a friend of Mr Ian Smith, to assist. Lord Wigg in his memoirs later revealed that it was Lord Goodman who had suggested the involvement of Sir Max.

If the Labour party had been in power in 1971 and had sought a deal with Mr Ian Smith they would have been supported by the Conservative party. With the Labour party in opposition it was natural that their front bench should oppose the settlement terms. It would probably have been better for Rhodesia had the Conservatives been in power at the time of U.D.I. It would probably have reacted strongly against treason and the assumption of independence and would have received the full support of the Labour party. It is possible that in these circumstances force would have been used and the Smith regime would by now be a remnant of history. It is argued that if force had been used, this would have been evil and would have resulted in massive bloodshed. That argument is not supported by the facts. At the time of U.D.I. Rhodesia's military power was dispersed throughout the country to quell any possible African uprising. If there had been a possibility of military intervention from outside, Rhodesia's forces would have had to be grouped in preparation, leaving Africans the opportunity to rise.

Rhodesia would not have taken this risk. In addition, Mr Ian Smith was in so much doubt about the loyalty of his forces that a year before U.D.I. he sacked the head of the army, Major-General John Anderson. After his 'retirement on grounds of age', General Anderson told the press that he had been called in by Mr Smith and sounded about his attitude to a unilateral declaration of independence.

I told him I would not support it. I told him of my attitude to any unconstitutional action. Recently I have had two interviews with the Prime Minister (Mr Smith) and he told me that accusations had been made against me that I was anti-Government.

I asked to be confronted with my accusers, as I have given twenty-six years of service during the war and after to the Rhodesian Army. I have not been confronted but there is possible evidence that I am not sympathetic towards the present Government.

My stand has always been that as a soldier I cannot change my loyalty with any change of government. I was subsequently accused of being anti-Government and I admitted that I am naturally anti a Government that has hinted at any unconstitutional action. I have been represented politically as being the only stumbling block. But I do not believe that this is so. I think I have the support of some members of the other services and security forces in my attitude . . .

His successor Maj.-Gen. Putterill, when he retired, joined the Centre Party in protest against the Rhodesian Front 1969 Constitution which he said, in effect was an invitation to violence. Sir Alec Douglas-Home subsequently ratified an amended 1969 constitution which was little altered from the original.

It can be said that these conclusions are easy to arrive at in retrospect, and that, in retrospect, some would agree with them. My conclusions, in fact, remain exactly as they were at the time of U.D.I. A few hours after Mr Smith declared his illegal independence I fulfilled an appointment to address the Overseas Press Club in New York, where I was studying at the time. I said that the British Government should embark on a short, swift, surgical action to remove the Smith regime. The longer they delay, I thought, the more difficult it would be for them to cope with Rhodesia. By the time Mr Wilson announced that sanctions would be applied to Rhodesia I was flying to Toronto having been invited to appear on a television programme. I was given details of what Mr Wilson had said and my response was that the British Government should recognize that no sanctions policy could succeed in the way it was intended while Rhodesia could expect help from two powers, Portugal and South Africa. The Portuguese colony of Mozambique borders Rhodesia, as does South Africa. These facts would frustrate the sanctions policy.

The point of this digression is that while it was of little comfort to find that my gloomy predictions were correct, their accuracy gave me confidence that I was also right to predict in 1971 that no settlement with the Smith regime would be honourable and that therefore the whole exercise should be attacked even before the details were known.

This I did and in an article requested by the National Union of Students, before the settlement terms were announced, I wrote on 16 November:

Sir Alec Douglas-Home, the British Foreign Secretary, has been spending time in Rhodesia in the company of men who, for the large part, make Governor Wallace of Alabama look like a liberal. There have been so many protestations about Sir Alec's 'honour' during the past weeks in Britain, so many affirmations that a man of his integrity would not sell out to Mr Smith and his friends, that it is difficult not to feel a little uneasy.

Whatever the words any settlement may be cloaked in, it will nevertheless be a disaster for the majority of Rhodesians. So far the British negotiating teams that have visited Salisbury have not included any Africans in their talks, apart from the occasional individual. Even if the negotiators had been available, Africans would have been too frightened to go and see them.

You don't have to live in Rhodesia to be aware that the Smith regime is based on the use of police and army and that the actions of the police are based on the constant flow of reports from police informers. But it is perhaps necessary to have lived in Rhodesia to appreciate how afraid the people are – afraid that their own relatives and friends may be taking note of what they are saying or doing; afraid of a summons by the local chief; afraid of the sound of a police jeep chugging up your road. Anyone wanting to see Lord Goodman, Sir Philip Adams or Mr Philip Mansfield would have had their names taken and at some future time – be it weeks, months or even years hence – they would have been asked *why* they had seen the British and why, by so doing, they had given outsiders the impression that they were not satisfied with life as it is today in Rhodesia.

I then analysed the five principles and found they could be twisted

41

by unscrupulous people into almost any settlement. Then I ended on the fifth principle:

> The British Government must be satisfied that any basis proposed for independence was acceptable to the people as a whole.
>
> The British Government have made it perfectly clear that they *do not* have to be satisfied . . . Any forthcoming 'honourable settlement with Rhodesia' will be one of the most dishonourable events in British colonial history. It will be a declaration of peace between Her Majesty's Government and the Rhodesian Front – nothing more, and nothing less.

The British Government and the Rhodesian authorities were badly let down by their civil servants – unless, as is possible, Mr Heath and Sir Alec Douglas-Home took no note of information placed at their disposal by the Rhodesia Department of the Foreign and Commonwealth Office (whose philosophy anyway appeared to be one of trusting the other side). It is more likely though that those officials had themselves gathered information from others who had no real contact with Rhodesian African opinion. The betrayal of the Rhodesian regime by their civil service was quite clear and quite unintentional. A vast network, the Ministry of Internal Affairs, was established to maintain white rule over the Africans in rural areas through the government-paid chiefs. The district commissioners told the chiefs what to tell their people which the chiefs obligingly did. When, or if, the district commissioners asked the chiefs what the people were thinking, the chiefs faithfully reported back that the people were thinking what they ought to be thinking. And so the fantasy that Africans supported Mr Smith eventually became translated into what was thought to be fact. 'The district commissioners tell us that the chiefs and their people support us. Therefore the Africans do support us, and therefore they want a settlement.'

Most of the credit lavished on the British team of negotiators was given to Lord Goodman. On 1 December 1971, he dived into a sea of print to explain himself (in the context of Rhodesia) to the readers of the *Observer*. The heading was: 'My case for settling with Smith'. The case was unconvincing.

The argument was 'though we had not sold out the African, the African had been sold out long before . . . It is against this background of constant moral capitulation by every shade of government that the terms we negotiated, scratched out of a wall with bare fingers, have to be set.'

It was soon seen that though Lord Goodman may have judged his efforts honourable, set against 'a background of constant moral capitulation', the Africans of Rhodesia judged his efforts dishonourable, set against their background of suffering and consequent unwavering rejection of the illegal Smith regime. Lord Goodman, after having observed that the Africans had been sold out, devised or at least collaborated in the device of offering them up to £5 million a year (£1 each) for ten years to assuage their hurt feelings. The Africans came back, as soon as an opportunity presented itself with a burning statement that though they had been betrayed, only they could sell themselves out and this they had not done, nor would they do, even for 'up to' £50 million. It is said that every man has his price but it was unrealistic to offer money to Africans in return for the eager abandonment of Rhodesia to the Smith regime by Her Majesty's Government. The Africans were not thinking in terms of money. They were concerned with land and with political power. They were not for sale.

Lord Goodman observed that those 'who, throughout the period of the negotiations, were assuring Mr Smith that he need not bother about agreements since the Conservative party could be relied upon not to reimpose sanctions' were, happily, proved wrong. He went on to say that 'their activities will redound in shame for generations'. I agree, but it must be recognized that their activities were responsible for the attempts to settle with Smith, and should not be underestimated. Furthermore I believe that Lord Goodman's role in the negotiations, however vehemently he may disagree, will be placed in the same category as those who assured Mr Smith that he need not bother about agreements.

Lord Goodman himself was well aware that there was little likelihood that the Smith regime would honour any agreement. He was well aware once a full settlement, on his terms, had been reached, once sovereignty had been granted to the Smith regime and economic sanctions removed, Britain would have no authority left even to try to enforce the honouring of the settlement. Mr Harold Wilson once said that he would not 'legalize the swag'. He did not but Sir Alec Douglas-Home and Lord Goodman were prepared to do so. 'It is not for me', he wrote, 'to act as a guarantor for Mr Smith and his friends, nor should I be prepared to do so. They have to live down a record of malfeasance that will live in history.'

The proposed settlement bid, the machinations which led up to it, the eventual attempt to test opinion, but far more important the combined responsibility of the white racist Rhodesian authorities and their friends in the Conservative party (exemplified by the hopefully untypical Monday Club), led eventually to grief, destruction and the murder of blacks by whites in Rhodesia. It led to the arrest of many people, including my father and myself. Few good things came out of it but those which did may yet prove worth the suffering. Firstly, the wise, dispassionate Pearce Report was presented to the British House of Commons. It provided information which people had lacked, or had not been prepared to accept as true, since U.D.I. Secondly, and of equal importance, the African people of Rhodesia – for whom the British Government had purported to be acting – had been given the opportunity to express their own views. Their own views, expressed, were that they would not sell themselves out and that they believed the British Government was attempting to betray them. Nonetheless they were prepared to give the British Government the benefit of the doubt. This they did by asking that British authority including the sanctions policy be maintained, and that any new settlement proposals be first discussed with the African people of Rhodesia who form 95 per cent of the population.

Anthony Sampson, in his *New Anatomy of Britain*, says that Lord Goodman 'calls for a special digression from anyone concerned with analysing the British Establishment. He is a phenomenon not only interesting in himself, but throwing light on the whole power-structure; and he crops up in many chapters (more than anyone else) of this book – in the Law, in Corporations, in the Press, in the City. For he is a kind of universal joint, always able to join one bit of scaffolding to another; a broker who understands better than anyone how to conciliate between two sides. He is primarily a very shrewd lawyer, in the American rather than the British pattern, who has become indispensable as an adviser and settler of disputes, cajoling, defining and settling. But he has come to be a conciliator not only between people but between institutions, and hence as a kind of benign prophet of the neo-capitalist consensus.

'His presence in any gathering is unmistakable. He is large and hirsute, shaped like something between a bear and a gorilla, with an expressive face that seems lost in the middle of an indefinite head and thick black eyebrows coming half-way round his dark eyes. When he sits down in a chair, it is hard not to catch one's breath.

'Encountering him is like encountering a physical object, a great rock or tree; and from the middle of it there emerges a voice which is equally unique, a kind of soft growl, firm but subtle, and infinitely articulate, full of elaborate ironies, parentheses, double negatives and understatements, as if it came from the Delphic oracle itself. He talks of the world of power with tolerant amusement, so that he seems to be right outside the arena, simply enjoying a spectator sport. But he is himself in the middle of it; and the ability to keep

44

his detachment in the midst of the fray is a large ingredient of his success and his strength . . .

'It was not till Harold Wilson came to power in 1964 that he hit the headlines. At first he was "Mr X" who settled the commercial television strike, but by the next year he was transformed with a few waves of Wilson's wand into Baron Goodman, Chairman of the Arts Council, and Lord High Everything-else for the new Government. From then on he appeared much more openly as the chief troubleshooter; and he even emerged from his shyness to be a gruff kind of social lion. "Send for Lord Goodman" became the first thought of any top person in difficulties; and often it seemed that the mere mention of his name would make the other side collapse. It was part of Goodman's approach that there was nothing that could not be settled between intelligent men; and he took this to its extreme when in 1968 he flew out to Rhodesia (with Sir Max Aitken) to try to reach a settlement between Ian Smith and Harold Wilson.'*

I did not meet Lord Goodman by design, but as far as I am concerned it was one of the most interesting events I associate with the proposed settlement deal with the Smith regime. One evening during my stay in London, I was talking to a friend of his who is a journalist deeply concerned with Africa. I was speaking to her about Rhodesia and she appeared alarmed at some of the things I was saying. Eventually she asked if I knew Lord Goodman, or had spoken to any members of the British negotiating team. When I said that I didn't know Lord Goodman and that I hadn't spoken to any members of the negotiating team she said that I should. 'I'm sure that no-one is telling Lord Goodman the things you are telling me.'

I replied that I would be delighted to meet Lord Goodman but did not see how this was possible.

'Lord Goodman is a very kind man,' she said. 'I'm sure he would see you if he has time. I'll try to arrange it.'

Arrange it she did. An appointment was made for me to see Lord Goodman at his home at 6.30 p.m., 30 September.

I knew that Lord Goodman, deep in negotiations as he still was at the time, would not be prepared to tell me anything so I went prepared to meet a listener. I was grateful that he had been prepared to see me and was not at all surprised when he initially seemed suspicious and withdrawn. He said that the interview was private. I agreed and went ahead to give him all the obvious reasons for not attempting to settle with the Rhodesian Front regime.

It seemed to me that as the few minutes he could spare sped by he

* By permission of A. D. Peters and Co.

45

became increasingly interested in what I had to say. He asked if I would meet some of his fellow-negotiators and I said that nothing would please me more. Anthony Sampson says that he is known as 'the late Lord Goodman' and he was certainly late on the two occasions I met him. Perhaps this is due to his generosity. At the end of the first interview he said that he was rushing for another appointment. Then he paused and asked where I was going. I told him and he said he would take me there. We went down to his car and he gave my address to his chauffeur – near Piccadilly Circus – just about the worst place to have to drive to in London. He took me there, dropped me and went on his way, late, because of a kindness to me.

A few days later I received a telephone call from Lord Goodman, asking if I could see him and two other people at 6 p.m. that day, 6 October.

Lord Goodman wasn't very late that evening but the other men were. Emperor Hirohito had arrived for his state visit and there were traffic jams right through the West End.

As we sat waiting for his colleagues a plate of tomatoes was brought in and I was invited to have one. He had already provided me with a drink, but was not drinking himself. I accepted a tomato and was enjoying it when he asked unexpectedly:

'Why haven't you married, Miss Todd?'

'That's a very personal question, Lord Goodman,' I countered. 'Why haven't you?'

He lowered his head over another tomato.

'Oh, wars and calamities,' he said.

I remembered an Englishman who would have counted himself kindly and liberal referring to 'that Jew Goodman'. I hadn't thought of Lord Goodman in this context before and felt very unhappy when I remembered what 'wars and calamities' had meant to people of Lord Goodman's age. He could remember, as could his generation. But Hitler, his actions and his philosophy were things I had learnt about, never experienced. We changed the subject but I do remember thinking that Lord Goodman would know so much more than I did about racial oppression that I really had no right to be there for the express purpose of warning him and his colleagues about what would happen if we were abandoned to Mr Ian Smith and his Rhodesian Front.

His two friends eventually joined us. They were Mr Philip Mansfield and Sir Philip Adams, fellow-negotiators with the Smith regime. I was once more anxious to assure the British negotiators that I hadn't come to learn, but to give. I had prepared a statement

46

for them with copies for each. But there was some conversation during which I said: 'If there's a settlement all it will mean is that you are leaving us alone, at the mercy of the Smith regime,' to which, with great frankness, Sir Philip Adams replied: 'Miss Todd, you should have realized that we left you alone a long time ago.'

The next and last time I saw Lord Goodman was in the House of Lords. The proposed settlement terms had just been announced and I had been given a ticket to listen to the debates in the Lords and the Commons. Lord Goodman sits on the cross-benches and he was almost directly in front of me when he rose to defend the settlement proposals.

I had not thought I could ever, in my life, have felt as outraged as I did when the terms were announced. I had very carefully listened to Sir Alec Douglas-Home announcing them in the Commons and while Mr Healey, speaking for the opposition, had said that he defied anyone who had listened to the announcement to be able to work out the mathematical intricacies of the proposals immediately, I knew enough about Rhodesia, as did Mr Healey, to know instantly that these terms were, to use the grossly over-worked but painfully apt phrase, a sell-out.

But when Lord Goodman started speaking I listened with even greater disbelief and anger.

He made an admirable speech. The speech was brilliant and so was the delivery. He bounced physically within the shining bubble of his words. He had triumphed and so great was his triumph that he excluded those right-wing Tories who had always wanted a settlement from the victory that he, the Conservative government, the Foreign and Commonwealth Office and the proprietor of the *Daily Express* had achieved – a settlement with Mr Ian Smith and the Rhodesian Front regime.

The following morning the newspapers echoed his triumph. Under the headline, 'Lord Goodman attacks "pious hypocrisy" by critics of settlement', Hugh Noyes of *The Times* wrote:

Lord Goodman, Britain's chief negotiator on Rhodesia under both Labour and Conservative Governments, today cut through the party political squabbling and feuding over the terms brought back by Sir Alec Douglas-Home, the Foreign Secretary, like a razor going through a doughnut.

Speaking clearly and with realism today he swept aside scornfully all the legal outpourings that had come from Lord Gardiner, Labour's former Lord Chancellor, in a preceding speech. He could have done a better job of criticizing the terms than Lord

Gardiner had done, he remarked, but that operation was largely irrelevant because the issue that had to be decided was what was the alternative.' [This was the one issue never seriously dealt with, at least in public.]

Referring bitterly to the pious hypocrisy that often surrounded this issue Lord Goodman said that much of this moral gesturing was no more than an act of personal indulgence. It would be hypocrisy, he went on, to say that they had set out on this mission to reform Mr Ian Smith and his friends. If they had, they had returned with a total lack of success. What they had done was to persuade Mr Smith that the world would no longer accept a regime which imposed an inhuman despotism by 250,000 on five million.

Lord Goodman said that the negotiators were prepared to take certain political risks which offered the only hope for emancipation of Rhodesia from the certainty of the most horrible and violent insurrection. The alternative to the present proposals was bloodshed and massacre.

He reminded the House that the opportunities for slaughter and massacre were as available to the African today as they were before this agreement. But the greatest advantage was to the white Rhodesians, not for the cynical reason that this provided them with the opportunity to remain in power for several lifetimes, but for the far more important reason that they would be able to relinquish control peaceably and without danger of violence . . .

There were times during Lord Goodman's speech when it took an overwhelming amount of self-discipline not to stand up and shout that this was not true as some of the unrealistic things he was now saying in public so blatantly contradicted the hard realism of what he was saying to some people in private.

At length Lord Goodman sank to his seat in the applause of his peers. I scribbled a note to the effect that I was in the House and would be very grateful to see him, signed it and gave it to a messenger. I watched it being delivered and saw Lord Goodman reading it. He didn't respond. It didn't take me many minutes to regret my impulsiveness and presumption. This was a moment of glory for him and naturally he would want to listen to the reactions his speech aroused without being disturbed. Naturally he wouldn't want to see me.

I sat on in the House of Lords for some time wondering what could be done. The terms were disgraceful, a betrayal, no matter how many soothing, dishonest, intentionally misleading phrases they were bandaged in. Within a few days I would be on an aeroplane bound for Rhodesia. If the essence of the terms, the deception so carefully camouflaged in legalistic phrases, was not clearly seen for what it was in Britain, what chance was there of it being revealed and recognized in Rhodesia?

I remembered all that had been said during my first interview with Lord Goodman. I remembered that the second interview had not been conducted under a seal of secrecy. And anyway, what really mattered was the ultimate effect on Rhodesia of the terms of this proposed settlement. This was far more important than the feelings of Lord Goodman, Sir Alec Douglas-Home or any other gentleman comfortably reclining on the benches in the Lords or Commons or less comfortably perched on chairs in the great warren of the Foreign and Commonwealth Office. I went back to my lodgings and drafted a statement which I took to the *Sunday Times*.

What I had to say was a repetition of what had already, in essence, been printed in the *New Statesman* and in the Rhodesian *Sunday Mail*. This was that Lord Goodman had said in private to a group of people that there was no alternative to violence in Rhodesia. He did not believe that bloodshed could be avoided and neither did I if these terms were to be implemented. But now Lord Goodman was publicly affirming that the settlement proposals of his devising would save Rhodesia from bloodshed and the spectre of babies shattered by bombs. Lord Goodman had lashed out at the 'pious hypocrisy' of those who opposed the terms. Who in fact was the hypocrite? In private Lord Goodman spoke with realism but now, in public, he proclaimed himself the saviour of Rhodesia. The brutal truth was that the proposals he had produced were, in the words of Lord Caradon, a 'cunning fraud . . . a monstrosity of impediments . . . a plain lie'.

The journalists I saw at the *Sunday Times* told me that my statement was a front page story and would be treated as such. They then checked my statement with Lord Goodman and subsequently told me that he had been very angry and had denied what I had said. When the Saturday deadline was approaching they said they would not be publishing my statement. Lord Goodman had given them a comment to print under the statement. In essence this said that he was sorry that Miss Todd, 'whose opinions I respect', should be the only person in the world to think that he relished the prospect of bloodshed. He invited the readers of the *Sunday Times* who were interested in the truth to read his account ('My case for settling with Smith') in that day's *Observer*.

The *Sunday Times* would not print this advertisement for the *Observer*. It was suggested that I take my statement to the *Sunday Telegraph*, which I did.

I had never thought, and did not say, that Lord Goodman relished the prospect of bloodshed. I am quite sure that he does not and could not advocate violence. The fact remained that he had said that there was no alternative to blacks killing whites in Rhodesia and under the terms of the proposed settlement, I agreed with him.

My statement was accepted with excitement and interest by a senior journalist on the *Sunday Telegraph*. He asked me to wait while he checked it with the editor. When he came back, some time later, he appeared very angry.

'Mention the name Lord Goodman,' he said, 'and everyone takes fright.'

The *Sunday Telegraph* did not use the story.

I rang a friend who is a prominent writer on *The Guardian* and discussed the matter with him.

'What you have to realize,' he said, 'is that Lord Goodman is one of the most powerful people in Britain. I don't think even *The Guardian* would print your statement.'

I was amazed.

'You do realize,' he said, when I expressed my surprise, 'that Lord Goodman is chairman of the Newspaper Publishers' Association?'

I hadn't.

So I left Britain with my side of the story unprinted. After I had gone a friend sent the statement to the editor of the *Observer*. He received a stiff note in reply. 'The letter is, I imagine, the same document which was offered to the *Sunday Times* a week ago. They decided not to publish it because they were told by Lord Goodman that it was plainly libellous and he would sue. The same consideration would oblige me to give you the same negative reply.'

The *Sunday Times*, as far as I know, was not informed that my statement was libellous. Eventually *Private Eye* published it and they were not sued for libel. Had Lord Goodman sued, which is extremely doubtful, I had witnesses to support my statement. I was not the only person Lord Goodman had spoken to about Rhodesia.

Questions remained unanswered. If the *Sunday Times* had been told by Lord Goodman that my statement was libellous and he would sue if it were published, why were they given the statement I was shown which was to be published as a footnote to mine? Again, why did Lord Goodman not object to reports carried by the *New Statesman* and *Private Eye*? Who told the editor of the *Observer* that Lord Goodman had told the editor of the *Sunday Times* that my statement was 'plainly libellous' and he would sue 'if it were published'?

On Tuesday, 30 November, I spoke at a meeting at the Westminster Central Hall.

The *Tribune* headed its quotes from my speech 'Home's Declaration of a Police State'.

Her Majesty's White Paper, *Rhodesia: Proposals for a Settlement*, is in itself a racist paper in which white people are generally referred to as 'the Rhodesians' and others are termed Africans. Asians and Coloureds, who form 10 per cent of the non-African population are not mentioned and therefore do not, presumably, exist any longer in the eyes of Her Majesty's Government.

It is a disgraceful paper in that it is an attempt to legalize a regime which has committed treason; which perpetuates racism; which has broken innumerable laws – including those of Rhodesia herself. Having been presented as 'honourable' it reveals that the honour of Sir Alec Douglas-Home, Lord Goodman, the Conservative party and the Foreign and Commonwealth Office is, at least in the Rhodesian context, as insubstantial as Salome's seventh veil.

Instead of bringing hope to the African people of Rhodesia it has simply provided Smith and his men with an occasion to celebrate and drink champagne. They know that under these terms white supremacy will not only be maintained, it will be reinforced with the assent of Her Majesty's Government.

The Declaration of Rights which fills the final sixteen pages of the White Paper should be the heart and soul of any Settlement which purports to be in the best interests of the people of Rhodesia. Instead it can only be described as the regulations governing a penal colony. This declaration authorizes detention without fair and open trial for unlimited periods. It declares that no-one should be obliged to suffer slavery, servitude, forced labour, torture, inhuman or degrading punishment *except in certain circumstances* (Paras. 3 and 4). These circumstances make it lawful for Smith's armed forces to shoot and/or kill people in reasonably justifiable circumstances (Para. 1, sect. 2) 'for the purpose of suppressing a riot . . . or of dispersing an unlawful gathering'.

As the two major African leaders are to remain incarcerated and their parties are to remain banned, this presumably means that the Smith regime is given carte blanche to continue using the methods it has used to date in silencing the voice of the African majority. Rhodesia is, in theory and in fact, a police state, governed by statutes such as the Law and Order (Maintenance) Act under which it is a crime to do such things as cause alarm and/or despondency; to mock the Smith regime; to bring people such as the chiefs and police into disesteem and disrepute.

'The White Paper's Declaration of Rights actually reinforces the police state by specifically laying down that nothing done under the authority of any (present) written law in Rhodesia shall be held to be in contravention of the Declaration of Rights (Para. 13). The Declaration lays down that a person can be deprived of his life intentionally: that any person may be deprived of his liberty: that organizations declared unlawful (such as Cold Comfort Farm) may have their property seized; that people's homes may be arbitrarily searched. When the Declaration touches on tribal law, we read that "a tribal court shall not be regarded as not being an independent and impartial court by reason of . . . the fact that a member of the court has an interest in the proceedings because of his position in tribal society . . ."

'Then there is a section which claims to lay down protection from discrimination. This section, Para. 11, after laying down the protection, goes on to state that these provisions shall not apply "to any law to the extent that it makes provision whereby persons of a particular description are subjected to any condition, restriction or disability or are accorded any privilege or advantage which . . . is reasonably justifiable . . ." In other words, long live White Supremacy! Long live Black subjugation!

'This is a document which should surely outrage any person having any respect for the concept of law and human rights. It reflects gravely on the integrity of Sir Peter Rawlinson (the Attorney-General) and all other members of the British negotiating team to Rhodesia and shows all too clearly that they did little more than collaborate with the racists in Salisbury.

'The deliberate lie perpetuated by the Smith regime, that there are only two restrictees in Rhodesia, as distinct from detainees, is compounded by its repetition in this document. There are in fact hundreds of restrictees in Rhodesia, unknown, uncared for. And as Sir Alec Douglas-Home has stated that he has no immediate hope for the release of Mr Nkomo, what hope could he have for the release from restriction of all the people whose existence he does not seem to be aware of?

'Often ordinary prisoners are detained on the day they are to be released from imprisonment. These men are not mentioned. Furthermore, and ominously, it is stated on page 15 that it is the intention of the regime to release a further thirty-one detainees "as soon as necessary arrangements can be made". This simply means that they will be released from detention as soon as arrangements are made for them to be restricted elsewhere.

'The promise that others may be released after the test of acceptability is in fact an implied threat. "If you go along with us, during this test, then you may be released . . ." '

I thought that many of us who opposed the settlement proposals would be in grave danger after the Pearce team had left Rhodesia. It did not cross my mind that some of us would be imprisoned before the commission had properly started testing opinion.

In the long days and nights of solitary confinement that lay ahead I often remembered the cocktail party held by the Primrose League at the 1971 Conservative Party Conference in Brighton. Towards the end of the party a waiter came to me and asked if I would mind seeing the head waiter? 'He would like to speak to you,' he said. By this stage the party had thinned considerably and I followed the waiter towards the back of the room. The head waiter greeted me with friendliness. 'I've got an idea that you are Miss Todd. Are you? I suppose you're here to try to stop the sell-out of your country? Miss Todd, I just wanted to tell you that I'm doing my best too.'

My second vivid recollection concerns the people who bade farewell to their guests. At the end of the party I was introduced to Lady Tweedsmuir and we spoke of Rhodesia for a few moments. Lady Tweedsmuir is now Minister of State for Foreign and Commonwealth Relations. She took my hand in hers and as I looked at her lovely, tranquil face she said, 'Oh, Judy, the trouble with you is that you won't trust people. Do give Mr Smith a chance.'

CHAPTER FIVE

In the Sweet By and By

BEFORE the violence and the shootings started the days were like a spiritual spring-time throughout Rhodesia. Material on the White Paper proliferated and at a performance of traditional music in the Belingwe Tribal Trust Lands (T.T.L.s) I saw young men dancing with copies of the White Paper flaunting from their trouser pockets. The girls held theirs in their hands and the copies swayed in the music like paper flowers. Often I saw construction workers on the roads taking a break over a copy of the White Paper. Everywhere Africans were discussing the terms and, so far as I could judge, rejecting them in language which ranged from tired despondency to profane, fiery anger. Very few whites seemed to be bothering to read the document. It took some time for them to realize that there was any possibility of the proposals being rejected.

My father and I, sometimes separately and sometimes together, were invited to a number of meetings to help explain the terms. At one meeting I attended in a remote rural area about four hundred people, the majority of them old, illiterate and poor, listened in heavy silence as a variety of speakers interpreted sections of the White Paper. The old men dominated the meeting. They rose up with their questions and their statements, some of them acting, some miming, many enticing sustained laughter at the expense of both the British and Rhodesian governments.

'Oh yes!' one of them said. 'Britain! Britain! She says she has come in to stop us hurting one another. She is like a man who comes in and says: "Please stop raping that woman. I don't agree with this. If you stop fighting and listen to me then I will *give* you that woman." '

My father had quite wrongly been reported by a small Bulawayo weekly as urging that the proposals be accepted. What in fact he had said was that everyone wanted a settlement, but not *any* settlement. He had advised people to study the White Paper carefully and not to reject the proposals out of hand. 'This is a time for consultation. If there are matters which make acceptance impossible perhaps they could be altered.'

Unfortunately the local stringers of the London *Times* and *Evening Standard* relayed the report that he had accepted the terms, without first checking with him. This led to such embarrassing incidents as the Conservative peer, Lord Blake, quoting my father's supposed acceptance as a significant reason for supporting the proposals. In fact, in the *Sunday Mail* sayings of the year for 1971 my father is quoted as saying, in response to a request for a comment on the Smith–Home agreement which had just been announced: 'First, I would like to know which survived: the five principles or Mr Ian Smith.'

At the first Belingwe meeting to which we were invited my father's clear rejection of the terms seemed to cause some embarrassment. At the close of the meeting we discovered why. Three men who had read the Bulawayo report that my father urged acceptance of the terms had formed a local committee and had written, cyclostyled and widely distributed an open letter to my father which they had planned to give him at the end of the meeting.

It was the first written rejection of the terms that we had seen, and was probably the first to be drawn up within the country. It read:

Dear Sir,

Sensible of the fact that you are morally and spiritually affiliated to the wishes and demands of the African people of Zimbabwe, any statements emanating from your mouth receive great positive attention. We are astounded by your recent statements which have appeared in the press.

You have publicly urged the PEOPLE to accept these racialistic, oppressive, inhuman and utterly undemocratic proposals. After a thorough study of this diabolical sell-out of the Africans by the opportunist, imperialist, self-seeking demagogues we have found to our great exasperation that the African cause of human dignity and equality which you as a churchman preach is nowhere represented. The settlement proposals do entrench division between African and European, Ndebele and Shona, Coloured and Asian. This is a degradation of human values, based on colour and tribe.

The provisions of the proposals are abhorrent to human dignity in that 5,000,000 people are represented by eighteen puppets, while less than one-quarter of a million are represented by fifty men of their own choice. Simple arithmetic illustrates how many Africans are equal to one white.

Majority rule is already impeded if not dismissed by high,

unrealistic voting qualifications. Chances of African advancement are at the mercy of the white, racist regime.

Discrimination remains firmly unprovoked in the proposals. How do you reconcile the fact that the same people who entrenched discrimination are left alone to revoke it?

There are no guarantees that the same irresponsible gang which usurped power cannot overthrow a mere paper.

It is very well known internationally that the Smith regime claims to rule with the mandate of the African people as a whole. We wish to show the vanity of this distorted, unjustified claim, but we know we shall not be given freedom of expression to air our views . . .

We feel we must register our profound disgust at these unilateral white proposals made without the representatives of the PEOPLE. The proposals are utterly unacceptable to the PEOPLE. They undermine the aspirations of the PEOPLE.

We unreservedly reject them.

You have deviated from the PEOPLE with whom you have identified yourself for so long. We call upon you to apologize in public and stop misleading the PEOPLE.

My father, and the eminent former Rhodesian, Lord Acton, ad in fact signed a letter to *The Times* which was published on 10 November 1971, stating that 'in a 1971 white Rhodesian context no settlement, tragically, could be honourable. But it would have made no difference to African opinion whether we had rejected the proposals or not. They were unacceptable to the Africans and so, even in the most remote parts of the country, they were rejected. The reason we were invited to meetings was because the people were hungry for information – nothing more nor less. They hoped for information from us and we did our best to provide it.

One of the happiest days I spent during that period was towards the end of December 1971, and once again it revolved around a meeting called to discuss the White Paper. The reason I found so much pleasure in the day was because it combined so many elements of the Rhodesia I love.

That morning I set my alarm clock for five and was away by six. The meeting was to be held in a remote part of the Belingwe District at a place called Mavorovonde which I hadn't visited before. It was a wet, cloudy morning, warm and shining with the beauty of a generous rainy season. The roads were decorated with sparkling pools of water and blanketed with mud. On the way to Mavorovonde I picked up a friend, Mr Lot Dewa, who is headmaster of a primary

school. He was happy and expected a good meeting. As we drove
the bucking Peugeot truck over the slippery, rutted roads which
wind through the Tribal Trust Lands we watched streams of people
walking in the direction we were going. At one point we stopped
and half a dozen or more men jumped on the back, smiling, friendly
and very excited about the forthcoming meeting.

'It's going to be a good meeting,' Lot said joyfully. 'Beautiful.'

We reached Mavorovonde at nine and had tea with the local
Lutheran pastor, the Rev. Isaiah Gumbo. We were seated in the
room of honour with its carefully shrouded chairs, polished table
and a piece of Christmas wrapping paper propped decoratively on
the mantelpiece. As Mrs Gumbo, the minister's wife, brought tea
in to us I saw through the kitchen door that a lot of old men were
propped up round the stove, smoking clay pipes and looking sternly
contemplative. In our room the atmosphere was lighter. There were
a couple of university students, whose homes were in the area,
Mr Gumbo, Lot and me. One of the students was in fits of
laughter telling me of an encounter with an old man from his village.

'And he said to me: "So it's called the White Paper. But if it's
about a settlement why is it not called the White and Black Paper?" '

The Rev. Gumbo had made his church available for the meeting
and when tea was over we drove up to it. When we drew near my
heart fell as I saw people walking away from the church. 'The police
are there,' I thought, but Lot was as cheerful as ever.

'They are going to get more benches from the school,' he said.
'Look at the people coming . . .'

So I looked and wandering over the hills towards us came the
people. It was a sight I had never before seen and will probably
never see again. Against the warm, misty backdrop of the morning
the people emerged over the tops of the little hills and flowed down
through the trees to the church.

'It is a multitude,' said Lot laughing with pleasure, and indeed
the scene was as unreal and moving to me as the New Testament
multitude scenes.

The word 'multitude' is of course relative. When the meeting
started there were 335 people crammed into the tiny church sitting
on benches facing each other. As the morning sped towards the
afternoon more people flocked in and so eventually there was no
central aisle and the knees of people facing each other in the central
aisle were soon interlocking. The meeting went on all day and when
I left, shortly after noon, people were standing five or six deep round
the entrance to the church, craving any crumb of knowledge or
information. Notice of meetings like that travels on foot and by

word of mouth from village to village and some of the people there had walked through the night to be able to attend.

The meeting started with a hymn, a Bible reading and a passionate prayer. Mr Smith, had he been present, would have referred to the people present in Rhodesian Front language as 'tribesmen'. This term is, in my opinion, calculated, dangerous and part of the old divide-and-rule mentality. There were many solemn peasants, dressed in their best rags. There were teachers, university students, evangelists and, no doubt, plainclothes C.I.D. and police informers. It was a mixed meeting but predominantly it was a gathering of the old, the poor, the humble, the forgotten and, so far as most whites were concerned, the unknown. Halfway through the morning a man at the back of the hall started singing softly. The audience joined in and harmonized their way through a song. It sounded like a hymn but in contrast to the hymn which opened the meeting in loud and confident terms, this was soft and secretive. It sounded like a very private supplication and the people sang with their eyes lowered as though they were indeed praying.

> 'This is our land . . .
> We are fighting for our land . . .
> Nkomo,* we are crying to you;
> Freedom, we are crying for you . . .'

Soon I was asked to speak and I told the gathering that I had been in the House of Commons in London when Sir Alec Douglas-Home had first announced the terms of the proposed settlement. There was a physical ripple of interest throughout the church. I said that the British Parliament looked rather like this church as the Members of Parliament also sat on benches facing in from the walls on to each other.

'On this side,' I said, gesturing to my left as though I was in the Visitors' Gallery, 'sit the Conservative party who are the government. They seemed very happy when Sir Alec announced his terms. On *this* side,' gesturing to my right, 'sit the opposition and they did not seem happy. Some of them said that the proposals were shameful.'

The Secretary of State for Foreign and Commonwealth Affairs (Sir Alec Douglas-Home): *With your permission, Mr Speaker, and that of the House, I wish to make a statement about my recent visit to Rhodesia.*

Following my statement on 9 November, I have been in Salisbury and have held talks with Mr Smith. I had the opportunity also to meet

* Joshua Nkomo is the acknowledged leader of the Africans in Rhodesia and has been in detention since April 1964.

many Rhodesians of all races and opinions, including a number of detainees and ex-detainees. As the House will be aware, Mr Smith and I have signed a document setting out certain proposals for a settlement which are fully within the five principles to which the governments have constantly adhered. These proposals will now be put before the people of Rhodesia as a whole in a test of acceptability, according to principle five. For this result I am greatly indebted to the Lord Goodman and to the team of negotiators, who have worked so hard and have made my visit possible.

The proposals have the following main features. First, amendments will be introduced into the present Constitution of Rhodesia to remove the provision which precludes any possibility of progress beyond parity of representation in the House of Assembly between Europeans and Africans. This will be replaced by arrangements providing for unimpeded progress to majority rule. The present number of lower African roll voters will be increased by a reduction of the franchise qualifications.

Secondly, in order to proceed to this end, changes in the present franchise conditions will be made and the present income tax regulator abolished. The present number of directly and indirectly elected Africans in Parliament will continue but there will be created a new higher African roll with the same qualifications as the European roll. New African seats will be added as the proportion of voters on the higher African roll increases in relation to the numbers of voters on the European roll. On the present estimates, it seems likely that four new African seats will be due to be created when the procedures for registration are completed and in that case they will be filled by by-elections in advance of a general election. These new seats will be filled, the first two by direct election by the higher African rolls, and the next two by indirect election on the same lines as the present indirectly elected members, until parity is achieved.

At parity, ten new seats will be created and filled through election on a common roll consisting of the European and higher African rolls. At that stage, the numbers on each roll would be approximately equal. Throughout this period up to parity, the blocking mechanism for the specially entrenched clauses of the Constitution will be two-thirds of the Assembly and the Senate voting separately plus majorities of the European and African members of the Lower House, again voting separately.

At the parity stage where there are fifty African members of the House of Assembly, a referendum will be held amongst voters on both African rolls to determine whether all the African members should in future be directly elected.

Following that referendum and any consequential elections, the ten common roll seats will be filled, unless the Assembly determines, on the recommendation of a commission to be set up at that stage, that some more acceptable alternative arrangements should be made. Any such decision, however, would be subject to the blocking mechanism I have described. Thereafter the blocking mechanism will revert to a simple two-thirds majority. This would mean that at least seventeen African members of the Lower House would have to approve any change to the specially entrenched clauses, and at that stage the Africans would be represented by directly elected members if that had been their choice. So much for the constitutional arrangements.

The proposals also involve other important changes designed to reduce discrimination and to promote racial harmony. There will be a Declaration of Rights that will be justiciable in the courts. This is a major advance on the present Constitution. In particular, on discrimination, the Declaration will re-enact the safeguard relating to discrimination contained in Section 67 (4) of the 1961 Constitution.

Secondly, there will be a three-man Commission, whose membership, to be agreed with us, will include an African, the task of which will be to review the question of racial discrimination throughout the whole field, but with particular regard to the Land Tenure Act and to certain of its effects. Mr Smith has put it clearly on record in the proposals that it is his Administration's intention to reduce racial discrimination and that he will recommend to his Parliament legislation to give effect to the commission's recommendations, except where there are considerations which any government would regard as overriding——

Mr Faulds: *This is shameful. It is an absolute betrayal, and the Right Hon. Gentleman knows it.*

Sir Alec Douglas-Home: *I think that the House will wish to hear the whole of my statement.*

Thirdly, there will be no further evictions of established communities from Epworth or other areas, until the recommendations of the commission have been considered.

Mr Kaufman: *Until? This is monstrous.*

Sir Alec Douglas-Home: *Fourthly, further land is now available for African settlement, and, as the need arises, more will be allocated. Fifthly, when sanctions have been lifted, the State of Emergency will be revoked, unless unforeseen circumstances intervene.*

Fifty-four detainees out of 116 have been released or will be shortly. For the remainder, there will be a special review, at which a British observer will be present. Rhodesians living abroad will be free to return save only where criminal charges lie against them. The Rhodesian Government have undertaken to encourage African recruitment to the public service. As a further important part of the settlement, the British Government will provide £50 million in aid over ten years for economic and educational development in African areas, such aid to be matched appropriately by the Rhodesians with money additional to their present planned expenditure.

Finally, the whole complex of these proposals is to be submitted to the Rhodesian people for approval. This test will be conducted by a Commission appointed by Her Majesty's Government, of which Lord Pearce, a former Lord of Appeal in Ordinary, has agreed to be Chairman, and will report to Her Majesty's Government. The Rhodesian authorities have agreed to allow a full and fair test, and to permit normal political activity to the Commission's satisfaction. Thereafter, if the proposals are acceptable to the Rhodesian Parliament it will be asked to enact the necessary legislation to give effect to them; and the Government will ask this House, once they are satisfied on that score, to enact the amended Constitution and to give independence to Rhodesia. This will clear the way for the lifting of sanctions.

Hon. Members will wish to study the proposals in detail. I am publishing the text in a White Paper which I hope will be available tomorrow at two o'clock. Meanwhile I am arranging to make available in the Vote Office today, in advance of the White Paper, the text of the 'Proposals for a Settlement' which Mr Smith and I signed yesterday. This – with the addition of its most important appendix 111 containing the full text of the revised Declaration of Rights – will of course form part of the full White Paper. The House will also want to debate the issue; for their part the Government will be ready to make time available. I will therefore confine myself to saying that I believe these proposals are fair and honourable; and that they provide an opportunity to set a new course in Rhodesia, which can lead to the greater harmony of all races there and to the partnership and prosperity of all Rhodesians.

This is a complicated matter, and I have kept the House already too long. Hon. Members will wish to study the documents and to make up their own minds. I would only ask them to do so fairly, considering past history and the present realities of power. Whatever Hon. Members may feel about the proposals now put forward I believe that they will agree that the Rhodesian people should certainly be given the chance to judge these for themselves. And let us be in no doubt that the price that will be paid if we fail in this attempt, will be paid, not by us but by others.

I gave the audience in that tiny Mavorovonde church extracts of what had been said in the House of Commons and they entered into the spirit of the occasion magnificently, with those on my right looking eminently satisfied with the interjections by Her Majesty's Opposition, and those on my left rather gloomy and embarrassed. Then, I said, when Sir Alec had finished speaking someone from the opposition side stood up and asked about Mr Nkomo and the other detainees. The Mavorovonde church hardly breathed as they waited for what Sir Alec had said.

Mr Thorpe: . . . *May I ask him, first, since only fifty-four of the 116 detainees are to be released . . . whether he gathered from Mr Smith that it was his intention that the natural leaders of African opinion, like Mr Joshua Nkomo, who has been detained without trial for more than six years – people of this calibre – would be released?*
Sir Alec Douglas-Home: *On the tribunal looking into the detainees, as the Right Hon. Gentleman said, fifty-four are to be released and the others examined. I myself saw Mr Nkomo and had a long conversation with him. Whether he would be in the numbers to be released or the numbers to be considered, I cannot say——*
Mr Faulds: *Why not?*
Sir Alec Douglas-Home: *If the Hon. Gentleman could control himself for a little, what I can say is that, of course, he will be able to be seen by the Commission.*

'Ahhhh!' the assembly at Mavorovonde groaned. An old man, fighting for footspace amongst the legs and feet that pressed his own, rose and faced me as sternly as if I had been Sir Alec Douglas-Home himself.

'Miss Todd. How can we say "yes" or "no" to the commission when our leaders are locked up and unable to advise us?'

A young man leapt up and answered the question for me. 'We can now see that if we say YES to these proposals, so we are saying YES to proposals which allow for our leaders to be kept in detention for ever.'

'NO!' said a number of the audience loudly while whispered Noes scurried around the assembly.

So far the questions had been relatively straightforward and simple to deal with. The next query almost floored me.

'You have said that the Conservative government sits on this side of the House, and the Labour/Liberal opposition sits on the other side. Miss Todd, what we would like to know from you is from which side of the House have the members of the Pearce Commission been chosen?'

I thought rapidly in the few seconds I had to get to my feet. The question was superficially simple. In reality it was profound. I stood in silence for a few seconds, considering my reply.

My questioner grinned at me. He seemed well aware that a ready answer would miss the point he was trying to make, or would have to be an admission that judging by all available reports the majority of the members of the Pearce Commission would have to be placed in the Conservative party, government side of the House context. At that stage I had little faith that the commission would, as they were human and not divine, be able to assess the opinions of the people of Rhodesia in the short time allotted for the exercise. But I was afraid that people might decide to boycott the commission which would, I believed, be disastrous. So I answered the question as diplomatically and carefully as possible.

I said that it appeared that the majority of the members of the commission were Conservative people. But I hoped and believed they would report honestly on their findings, however much they individually might favour the proposals. The people were restless, gloomy and dissatisfied. Nonetheless, when a proposal was made that they boycott the commission, they rejected it.

An ancient woman swayed to her feet and told the assembly that the time had come for the truth to be told. There was agreement. The truth must be told whatever the consequences. NO! to these proposals.

If some all-knowing deity had kindly stooped from the clouds one day and breathed into my soul the knowledge that if I continued participating in African meetings, if I persisted in rejecting the settlement proposals, then I would be imprisoned and detained without trial or charge for an indefinite period, I would have continued attending the meetings. These gatherings were exciting and impressive and they were also profoundly important. The Test of Acceptability was the most effective exercise in adult education – consciencization, as current terminology has it – that Rhodesia has ever seen. The meetings called to discuss the proposals were illumined by an awakening spirit in oppressed people who, for the moment, felt within themselves the stirrings of a possible freedom, and saw it and heard it in their brothers. They were discussing their future and, moreover, according to the White Paper they were *permitted* to discuss their future. There was an element too, in these meetings, which should have interested and comforted my fellow-whites. Usually I was the only white present and I was invited and accepted as a friend, a sister, an honoured guest. I know that if any number of whites had gone as friends, they too would have been equally welcome. But today's rulers of Rhodesia do not and will not seek friendship and acceptance. It hurts and offends the whites to see any members of their own tribe discover a basis for a courteous comradeship with African people whom they appear to consider to be their enemies.

The police began arriving at meetings carrying guns and riding in armoured Land-Rovers. I went alone, safe in the friendship of the people, which is the only true safety that exists for whites in this land of Rhodesia.

Many attempts were made to hold meetings in Shabani, an asbestos-mining town fifteen miles from my home. All attempts were frustrated by the authorities. Eventually, one week in December, I received a message that the newly formed local branch of the African National Council had arranged a meeting. Would I attend? 'With pleasure,' I replied.

The meeting was in fact the normal Sunday service in the tiny Baptist church in the African 'location', a township on the outskirts of the white town of Shabani. The sermon would be on the White Paper. Would I help to preach it? It was the only possible way to get the White Paper discussed in Shabani.

I met my hosts a few miles from the church and as I drove behind them towards the location we were surrounded by young people running, running. Word had spread through the various African townships that there was to be a discussion on the White Paper. People were running, running, walking to rest, then running again. It suddenly struck me that there had been no opportunity for at least fourteen years, if there really ever had been an opportunity, to share in normal political activity. This would be the first semi-political meeting that most of the people, running, running, had ever attended.

We arrived twenty minutes early and the church was already full to overflowing. There were no aisles, no corridors, no floor-space; simply benches of people who had spilled off to cover every inch of space in that little building. It was a hot, humid morning and the service was restricted to two hours. There were hymns and prayers and Bible readings and then the White Paper was to be discussed.

There were half a dozen speakers. The congregation, the speakers, the people hanging through open windows, the people packed behind them (unable to see the speakers, unable to hear unless the speakers shouted but waiting, packed together on the off-chance of hearing something) were all shining and dripping with sweat. Inside the church, copies of the White Paper were being put to good use as fans except when a reference was made and then there would be shouts of 'What page?' and pages would be turned to a paragraph on the vote, or land, or the Bill of Rights, or to the offer of financial aid from Britain.

'If we say NO, we'll still cling ourselves to Britain,' the simplest speaker roared. 'If we say NO, sanctions will still continue. Now who is bitten by sanctions?'

'We are,' the people called.

'And who else is bitten by sanctions?'

'THEY are!'

'Are they prepared to suffer sanctions?'

'NO!'

'Are we prepared to suffer sanctions?'

'YES!'

'Yes,' said the speaker. 'We are prepared to suffer sanctions. We are prepared to sacrifice for our freedom.

'The Labour party used to insist on NIBMAR – no independence before majority rule——', he continued. 'But the old man Douglas has forgotten this. Look at these franchise qualifications! They are set to exclude us, the African people. The whites are able to continue ruling us. These immigrants, these Greeks and Portuguese and other people, are they highly learned gentlemen?'

'NO!'

'No. They come in and take our jobs. They get the vote. They rule us. They can't even speak English.'

I saw young men at the back of the church lifting themselves up on the door-frames, their muscles straining, to catch a momentary glimpse of the speakers. Someone outside who could hear us was trying to repeat what was being said for the people behind him who could not hear. The main elements of the White Paper were covered and then questions were invited.

The church immediately became a forest of arms. Everyone present seemed to be quivering with questions. The speakers sat on a tiny platform, a curtain behind us. While the chairman was rapidly deciding who might have had his hand up first I nearly fell off my chair as a loud, completely unexpected voice shouted from the curtain behind us: 'HERE! HERE!'

I moved round and parted the curtains. They screened a baptistry, a kind of mini-swimming-pool in the floor with steps going down into it for baptisms. During the meeting people had silently flowed into the baptistry and they stood there, packed below us, physically apart from the body of the church but equally anxious to ask questions. Only a few of the hundreds of questions were dealt with. Then, all too soon, the meeting had to close.

Those in favour of the proposals were invited to raise their hands.

No-one moved.

'Those against the proposals?' the chairman asked.

There was a roar of 'NO – we don't want them!' and the church surged with waves of hands and arms, signifying their disapproval of the settlement proposals.

'Look!' said the man sitting next to me, half-laughing, half-crying. 'Look at that little girl!' A child of about ten stood behind us on the steps of the baptistry, her hand solemnly upraised for a NO.

'She doesn't understand what she is doing,' he said, 'but when she is old she will remember this meeting and she will be proud then that she said NO.'

I remembered attending my first political meeting when I was nine and when Mr Lardner-Burke* and my father shared a platform. Mr Lardner-Burke, who imprisoned us not long after, had said disapprovingly all those years ago: 'Political meetings are no place for little girls!' I remembered how hurt I had felt then, all the excitement of going to my first meeting momentarily deflated, and looking at the little girl with her serious face and unwavering hand I said to my friend: 'I think she understands what she is doing.'

Now the meeting had to end. I had hoped it would close with the singing of the African national anthem – 'God Save Africa' – and had suggested it. But it was felt that a revivalist hymn would be more in keeping with the Baptist tradition and that we should be kind to the Baptists who had so kindly allowed the White Paper to be discussed at their service.

The hymn that was sung has words which are really quite banal, but the singing might have moved the hearts of the Monday Club. The sweet, high tenors and sopranos lifted the tune over the whole location, while the throbbing bass rocked the physical foundation of the tiny church. It was tremendous.

> *'There's a land that is fairer than day,*
> *And by faith we can see it afar;*
> *For the Father waits over the way,*
> *To prepare us a dwelling place there.*
>> *In the sweet* . . . (soared the sopranos and tenors)
>>> IN THE SWEET (the bass drummed in echoing harmony)
>> *By and by* . . .
>>> BY AND BY
>> *We shall meet – on that beautiful shore* . . .
>>> BY AND BY

* The Rhodesian Minister of Law, Order and Justice.

66

In the sweet . . .
IN THE SWEET
By and by . . .
BY AND BY
We shall meet on that beau – ti – ful shore!
BEAUTIFUL SHORE!'

The music was an expression of a tentative liberty ('in the period before and during the test of acceptability normal political activities will be permitted to the satisfaction of the commission . . .') that many of the assembled had never before tasted, and the soaring voices of the people lifted and held aloft their hearts.

CHAPTER SIX

'Normal Political Activities'

Dear Judy,

We, the undersigned, invite you to a meeting of four chiefs at Mataruse Council. The meeting is to be held on 30 December (1971) for the sole purpose of explaining the White Paper. Chief Mataruse, who was interviewed on our behalf and is the organizer and chairman of the meeting, expressed a wish to have the White Paper thoroughly explained at this meeting and permitted us to invite whomever we can. With this permission and an issue of such national importance, the White Paper, before us, we are sure we can value from your presence and contribution. The undersigned will all attend, to give you a backing. Thanks, Judy, and welcome.

This letter was signed by nineteen people and was a formal gesture as I had already accepted a telephoned invitation to attend the Mataruse meeting. But the bearer explained that it was thought I should have a written invitation with me in case any government officials asked by what authority I was in the Tribal Trust Lands, attending a chiefs' meeting. In the event the letter didn't help. When the police came and stopped me speaking I felt that I could not show the letter to them when they asked for it as the nineteen signatories would immediately have been placed under their scrutiny.

Mr J. B. Hove, the local Member of Parliament, had also been invited. He is elected by the chiefs and their councils and is, therefore, their special representative. The night before the meeting he phoned me and asked for a lift to the meeting which was to be held near his home. Mataruse Council is about 50 miles from my home and en route to Mr Hove I picked up a number of the young men who had signed the letter.

We arrived at his place just after 8 a.m. and were warmly and courteously welcomed. But Mr Hove, who is known to his friends as J.B., was unhappy and agitated. The Belingwe District Commissioner, Mr I. C. Bissett, had telephoned him minutes before I arrived to say that he was not allowed to speak at the meeting. The meeting was not properly constituted, Mr Bissett had said, as he had not been given seven days' notice of Mr Hove's intention to speak. It was, he said, to be a meeting consisting solely of the chiefs and their people.

I could hardly believe my ears. Besides the White Paper's promise of normal political activity Mr Hove was a Member of Parliament and if anyone should be telling anyone else what to do, Mr Hove should be telling his District Commissioner. But Mr Hove is an African and Mr Bissett is white and that is all that matters. The white man is the boss and if the African concerned happens to be a Member of Parliament, or a chief, that is just too bad.

We were all very sorry about J.B's obvious distress, but I told him that I would still go on to the meeting and intended to speak, as I had accepted an invitation to do so. After a few minutes of indecision he changed his mind and said that he would come too. So we all set off for Mataruse Council.

J.B. is a very solidly built gentleman with an almost shaven head of white hair, and white eyebrows. On the way we spoke of his son, who is a scholar in the United States. Eneas Hove, a relative of his who is at present studying at the Rhodesian University, sat between J.B. and myself in the cab of the truck I was driving and at one point asked J.B. respectfully if it was true that his son had been invited to join the space programme in the United States. J.B. said he had heard that this was so, but wasn't sure. On the way to Mataruse Eneas pointed over the hills to a house we could see in the distance. He said that that was Byron's home. Byron is another Hove and an old friend of mine. We were at university together but he fled Rhodesia some years ago and now practises as a barrister in London. So many of the people that our country desperately needs have been forced into exile.

There is no council hall and although it was early in the morning Chief Mataruse emerged smiling and friendly from a fairly new-looking bar that has been built near the council offices. It is a matter of policy to provide each chief with a bar or a beer hall. The sale of liquor increases the income of chiefs and is meant to keep the men in their areas content and undemanding. A radio blared cheerfully from inside and the bar was packed with people but it seemed as though J.B. thought it would be improper for me to enter. He pulled the chief and myself round a corner of the building and proceeded to tell Chief Mataruse that the D.C. had forbidden him to attend the meeting, let alone speak.

The chief immediately and almost physically started oozing concern. 'But I *did* tell the D.C. you were coming,' he said. This seemed to cheer J.B. greatly.

'Well,' he said, 'this is a chiefs' meeting and if the four chiefs present give me permission to speak then I will do so.' Many people had already assembled. The young men were grouped in serious conversations. Others were chatting in the shade of trees and a number of cars, packed to the number plates, were pulling in. There were a few women present, smartly dressed and carrying brilliantly coloured sunshades. I was taken to the office of the council secretary and he was asked to look after me until the meeting started. A limp, Rhodesian flag drooped down a pole outside the office. Someone had torn its heart out and when, now and again, it stirred in a breeze, its identity was only just discernible. In the office a copy of the famous White Paper lay on the table and in a corner a pile of brand-new, uninflated footballs climbed on top of each other up the wall. A calendar on the wall advertised

Castle Beer

True-Brew   True-Brew
Beer   Taste

There was little else in the office and the secretary, round and saturnine, looked as though he would be more comfortable with a Castle beer than with a football which was perhaps why they had remained so new and uninflated. The secretary brought in chairs – most were outside in preparation for the meeting – and then he brought men to fill the chairs. 'You may be lonely,' he said, 'so I have brought friends to talk to you.' He then disappeared and I wondered what was happening with the chiefs.

The men who joined me were worried and unhappy about the proposals. One of them said glumly: 'We're all right in this area. We've studied the White Paper and set up committees to draw up memoranda for Lord Pearce in case we can't see his commission. But I wonder what is happening in the north of the country?'

A pastor who was sitting with us hastened to give comfort. 'Everything seems fine,' he said. 'I had a guest over Christmas from Enkeldoorn and he made me wish that we were as active against the proposals as the people in his area seem to be.'

The first speaker did not, as yet, wish to be reassured. 'I was thinking of *further* north,' he said, and relapsed into his gloom. I found this attitude wherever I went. In Salisbury people would say: 'We're all right here, but nothing seems to be happening in Bulawayo.' In the rural areas people would say that they were organizing against the proposals, but were worried about the urban areas – and vice versa. No organization of itself could have generated the massive 'NO!' which reverberated around the country. It was a groundswell from the hearts of the people which took everyone by surprise, including the people concerned.

Eventually Eneas Hove, cool, calm and academic, came in and told us that it had been decided that J.B., Chief Mataruse and myself would drive back to J.B's house where there was a telephone. Chief Mataruse would ring the District Commissioner, tell him that J.B and myself had been invited to the meeting which was about to start and seek authorization for it to go ahead.

'But Eneas,' I said. 'I'm not going to ask permission from the D.C. to be here. We're surely acting on the promise of normal political activities given in the White Paper?'

'The chief knows that,' he said.

So I went outside to my car. J.B. climbed in and we waited for the chief. As I started the engine people surrounded the car. 'Why are you going? . . . Where are you going? . . . Please do not leave before you have explained the White Paper . . .' Some of the young men were getting angry. We had been there for well over an hour and there was no indication when the meeting would start. Then Eneas came to the window and spoke quite sternly to his uncle. 'You are going to get permission from the D.C. to hold this meeting,' he said. 'But you know perfectly well that he will not give permission. You must stay and hold this meeting. Chief Mataruse agreed that we could have the meeting. You are the Member of Parliament. You represent the people here. You do not represent the D.C.'

Once again J.B. changed his mind. 'You are quite right,' he said, and climbed heavily out of the car. 'I will tell the chief.' I went back to the office and met a new group of people – the 'Settlement Proposals Committee chosen by Chingoma, Mataga and Mposi Councils'. They told me they were afraid that the mails were being tampered with and asked that I should take a letter from them to the advance party of the Pearce Commission now in Salisbury. I said I would do my best. The letter read:

Dear Commissioners,
In the light of events here that the chiefs and councillors alone . . . are the only people likely to be visited by your commission at the District Commissioner's confidentially private place, we, the people of Chingoma, Mataga and Mposi Chiefdoms wish to request Her Majesty's Pearce Commission to visit, in accordance with the provision in the Settlement Proposals, the following centres in the aforesaid chiefdoms: Chiefs' courts, Council centres

71

(where such exist), Mission Stations, Mining centres and some headman kraals to meet as many members of the public as possible, and that the respective centres and possible dates and times of visiting be made known to members of the public through the local Press and Radio media.

Signed by,
Members of the Settlement Proposals Committee . . .

Having delivered their letter to me, the committee members left Mataruse Council. They had studied the terms fully and needed no further explanations. Their great anxiety was that they did not know how to contact the Pearce Commission or where to present memoranda which had already been prepared. The District Commissioner had spread the word around that no-one would be allowed to see the commission, unless those wishing to do so first registered with him.

I was told that at a meeting held by the D.C. it had been requested that Mr Garfield Todd and Mr J. B. Hove be allowed to explain the terms, and that the D.C. Mr Bissett had replied that Mr Hove was welcome to explain the terms, but that he would never allow Mr Todd into his Tribal Trust Lands. The teacher who had made the request was, a few days later, arrested by the D.C's policemen, who are known as district messengers, taken to Belingwe and conducted into the presence of Mr Bissett. Mr Bissett had then allegedly said that the man had better watch his step or else he would be restricted to the detention camp at Gonakudzingwa. He was then released and allowed to walk all the miles home. At other chiefs' meetings the D.C's interpreter, Mr Chinamora, read the White Paper without explanations. Many people alleged that when he read the section promising normal political activities he had translated 'normal' as 'no more'.

Eventually the chiefs decided to go ahead with the meeting and we were summoned to attend.

We walked out of the office into a sweltering world. It was noon and the sun blazed directly overhead.

The people had assembled on an enormous ant-hill which, growing up to the sky between trees which flourished on the rich ant-soil, had become a living, moving stadium. It looked as though the inhabitants of a vast ant-kingdom beneath the earth had suddenly been transformed into humans and had climbed out on their earthy castle to get a breath of fresh air. They were packed, shoulder to shoulder, knee to back, on the ant-hill and people were even sitting in the trees, all facing towards the sloping ground. At the foot of, and facing the ant-hill, chairs were arranged in a semi-circle, two deep.

A table stood astride between the chairs and the ant-hill and the guests of honour were placed around the table.

Chief Mataruse opened the meeting and then handed over to a local Lutheran pastor, the Rev. Shire. The meeting opened with a lusty hymn, a profound prayer (which obviously touched the hearts of the assembled judging by the swelling 'AMEN! AMEN! AMEN!' thundering from the ant-hill) Bible reading and then a short sermon. 'Ezekiel, chapter 33, verse 6,' ordered the Rev. Shire, and read it in Shona. I looked it up in English later.

But if the watchman see the sword come, and blow not the trumpet, and the people be not warned; if the sword come, and takes any person from among them, he is taken away in his iniquity; but his blood will I require at the watchman's hand.

The four chiefs sat in attentive silence. Chief Mataruse was dressed in khaki – a long-sleeved shirt and trousers – wearing the badge of office that proclaimed him 'Chief Mataruse'. They all wore their badges which, I suppose, are the proud symbols of an honourable position but which obviously cost the Rhodesian authorities a very few cents each. They resemble an inferior brand of bottle opener. Chief Ngungubane, an old, old man with a flowing white beard, sat like an embalmed Old Testament prophet, unmoving. Then there were Chiefs Mazivofa and Negove who became more and more thoughtful as the sermon proceeded. Negove, who looked like a hard-bitten businessman whom nobody could take for a ride, started gazing at the ground with the same passion that John of Revelation must have looked at heaven. Ezekiel 33, verse 6 was being aimed in all its horror at the chiefs.

'It is a time of great decision,' Rev. Shire said, 'and our children's children will hold you Chiefs, our watchmen, responsible for the decisions that are taken.' 'AH-MEN! AH-MEN!' the ant-hill responded. 'Amen,' murmured decorously the ladies and gentlemen of the semi-circle of chairs.

Chief Mataruse had gladly yielded the chair to someone else and as the chairman rose to take the Rev. Shire's place the audience was as still as the air often is before a storm breaks. There was an atmosphere of foreboding as the chairman said that this was a discussion on the White Paper to which all were invited to contribute; as he asked for questions; as a young man rose and said it would be more helpful if I spoke first before any questions; so a spiral of dust swung around a distant hill behind the stadium facing me and grew larger as it swept at great speed up the road.

Other cars had still been arriving, travelling gently and self-interestedly over the bad road. But this vehicle was travelling so fast that the driver was obviously not the owner or else he, mindful of the vehicle's well-being, would not be hammering it up the road.

'Police,' J.B. murmured to me. I knew already. People at the top of the ant-hill had turned to look and they had not turned back as they would have, had whoever approaching been a friend. The police Land-Rover swung into a clearing and a man on the right of the ant-hill who had not been able to see it coming now saw it, and clapped his hands together five times in a sharp, staccato warning.

'SssssH!' breathed the people and a determination to continue with the meeting grew in an invisible cloud over the assembly. The chairman, a round and tiny man, was shaking. But he too ignored the Land-Rover.

'We shall now read the White Paper,' he said.

The police climbed out of their vehicle. There were only two of them, one white, one black, both unarmed.

They walked around the gathering, keeping a distance of about five yards. Chief Mataruse rose from his chair and went to greet them. Almost immediately he came back walking quiet and bent like a messenger-boy, as so many African men are termed in Rhodesia. I looked up into his old, deeply-lined face.

'Miss Todd, you are wanted.'

I got to my feet and started moving towards the police slowly as I was hemmed in by the many people who had no chairs, no room on the ant-hill and who were carpeting the ground around us in an almost uninterrupted mass. As I made my way out a young man leapt to his feet on the ant-hill.

'I now read Section 1 of the White Paper,' he shouted in a high, tremulous voice. ' "In the period before and during the test of acceptability normal political activities will be permitted to the satisfaction of the commission provided they are conducted in a peaceful and democratic manner." ' I sent him my silent thanks and as I reached the police his short speech was greeted with a storm of applause.

I found to my irritation that I was trembling. I wrapped my hands round my waist and greeted the police. The African policeman was very young and looked away as though he wished he wasn't there. 'Miss Todd, I presume?' said the white policeman.

My reactions were slow and it took me some seconds to appreciate the humour of the situation. Amongst the hundreds of people present I was the only white, with the exception of this policeman. I wished I had murmured: 'Oh. Inspector Stanley!' but by the time

74

I wished that, I had already said: 'Yes, I am. But I don't know who you are, I'm afraid.'

The policeman looked slightly pained. He was, after all, a policeman and that was, after all, what mattered.

'Member in Charge, Belingwe,' he said.

'But I don't know your name.'

'Stephens.'

'Hullo, Mr Stephens.'

There followed a long and complicated conversation. The meeting continued behind us and it was obviously becoming emotional. Mr Stephens increasingly divided his attention between me and the meeting.

'Have you got a permit to be here?'

'No. I haven't.'

'Why not?'

'Because I don't recognize racial laws; because I won't agree to get a permit to visit my friends (and neither does the Anglican Bishop of Mashonaland) and because, even if I did, the District Commissioner probably wouldn't give me one.'

'It's not a racial law,' he said. 'It's to keep whites out of African areas and is designed for the protection of Africans.'

'Well,' I said, 'I was born in an African area and a permit wasn't required for that.'

'That doesn't make you an African,' he said, and looked pleased with his observation. He was a pleasant-looking man of about forty and he sounded as though he was originally from England. He was obviously getting worried about the meeting which seemed to be going well, in that it was lively and there seemed to be no lack of speakers. But a number of people had detached themselves from it and were hovering around me anxiously.

'What about the Pearce Commission?' I asked. 'Will you have to chase *them* around and see if *they* have permits to enter African areas?'

He looked thoughtful.

'I presume,' he said, 'that they'll be issued with a blanket permit from the Ministry of Internal Affairs.' I grinned, and he teetered on the verge of grinning back. Then he issued me with a long series of conflicting orders.

'Do I take it that I'm under arrest?' I asked.

He reacted strongly.

'No. You are not!'

I stood quietly listening, and he floundered in the midst of another rising grin.

'If you are arrested that will be the Attorney-General's decision. I might charge you today or tomorrow.'

'I'll be at home today and tomorrow,' I said. 'But then I'll be in Salisbury for a couple of days.'

Despite his increasing interest in the meeting, Mr Stephens was becoming quite friendly. He was falling into the same state I have observed amongst a number of whites who, when they first meet me, expect to see signs of horns and a tail, but when they don't, seem to want to talk to me about what they have heard I am. They all know I am meant to be a monster and seem to be rather disarmed by the reality of an innocuous human-being.

Then, obviously wanting to be free to deal with the meeting, he started issuing me a long and conflicting series of orders. First he said that I must leave immediately and report at the police station in Belingwe. He said he would follow behind me to ensure that I didn't go to any more meetings en route. Then he said he would have to stay, and that I must report to the District Commissioner at Belingwe. Then he said I must get into my car and wait for him. Then he said I must go immediately, he didn't care where, so long as I left the Tribal Trust Land.

I got into my car and started the engine. Changing his mind again he leant through the window.

'Go and park under that tree,' he said, pointing out some shade. 'Wait for me.'

I started rolling the car down the slope towards the shade. A mass of people left the meeting and came running over, surrounding the car.

'Don't go; *please* don't go! Don't *you* be afraid.' A young man turned on Stephens, almost crying. 'You people say we are stupid. All right, we *are* stupid. That's why we've asked Miss Todd to explain the White Paper to us. *Please* let her stay.'

Stephens was now quite obviously afraid. 'GO!' he shouted at me, but the people pressed around the car, trying to restrain it with their bodies.

'Mr Stephens,' I said to him, as he pushed people away from my window. 'It would be much easier if you allowed the meeting to continue. There really wouldn't be any trouble.'

'Go!' he repeated. I felt terrible, but knew I must leave. If I stayed in these circumstances it would mean a direct confrontation with Stephens; he might start arresting people and this might lead to violence. I doubted that it would, but there was the possibility, and the police were hopelessly outnumbered. Stephens was shouldering the unresisting people away from the car roughly, and I edged away slowly through the crowd, touching the hands of friends in farewell as I went past apologizing.

The Rev. Shire, old and gentle, apologized back. 'Don't worry, Judy. Thank you for coming.'

I left that meeting, obeying the orders of the police, to avoid any possibility of conflict. A few days later the London *Daily Telegraph* reported that I had refused to leave the meeting and that violence had ensued.

(*Telegraph* quote: 8/1/72): 'First violence in the campaign to discuss the terms of the settlement is understood to have involved Miss Judith Todd . . .' The day after my father and I were arrested the *Daily Telegraph* again reported that I had been involved in a violent incident. 'In one (violent incident) Miss Todd was asked to leave a meeting in the Belingwe tribal trust land. When she refused, police and Africans clashed.'

This was very serious misreporting as at every meeting I attended there were calls for peace and calmness. On several occasions I had myself warned of the possibility of *agents provocateurs* being used to stir up trouble which would have rebounded gravely on those who wished simply to make their views on the proposals known.

I learnt, a few days later, what actually had happened after I had left. The secretary of the meeting sent me a copy of the minutes, extracts of which read:

After the meeting had hardly proceeded a quarter way, the Member in Charge, Belingwe, and an African police constable arrived and pulled Miss Todd out of the meeting for questioning . . . It was later learnt by the meeting that Miss Todd had been ordered to leave the meeting by the Member in Charge, much to the indignation of the audience. At this moment the audience was in confusion since they disliked the Member in Charge's interference. The Member in Charge threatened to close the meeting if the confusion continued. Most members of the audience said the Member in Charge should close the meeting, if he so wished, since his interference was the cause of the confusion . . . Mr Loyas Moyo, one of the members of the audience, asked the Member in Charge to issue a statement of closure of the meeting with his signature. This the Member in Charge refused to do and consequently the meeting was resumed but Mr L. Moyo's particulars were taken down and noted by the Member in Charge . . .

There followed a closely-typed foolscap page of arguments given by members of the audience against the proposals which showed clearly that there never really was any need for my presence. The proposals were well understood. The arguments against them were well reasoned and detailed. Provisions relating to franchise and the land were dismissed as racist and unrealistic.

On the 'up to £50 million' bait for the Development programme, which Britain promises to send in the event of a settlement, speakers pointed to the tricky phrase 'up to' which only states the maximum that can be sent, without stipulating the exact amount or stating the minimum . . . One speaker pointed out that the government is exploiting the ignorance of the chiefs, their headmen and kraalheads to achieve a 'Yes' answer. These are the people who are likely to be called out and claimed to be representing the opinion of Africans when the commission arrives. Such likely treachery was jeered at and booed by the meeting . . . After much explanation and discussion it was suggested that the chiefs should now have the chance to say what they felt.

Chief Negove who spoke first among the chiefs said that he and his colleagues had called the general meeting because they were ignorant of the meaning of the White Paper. He was thankful that explanations had now been given. He emphasized that the general meeting was called because chiefs love their people and therefore he (Negove) would not deviate from the opinion of his people and the meeting – e.g. a 'NO' answer to the proposals. To sum up, Chief Negove said that what had been said at the meeting is what he wanted to hear.

Headman Zijena (former Chief Mataruse) said: 'We cannot throw away our people by deciding something contrary to their opinion. We stand with them for a NO!'

Chief Mataruse said that in the Council of Chiefs held in Salisbury shortly after the publication of the Anglo-Rhodesian proposals for a settlement 'no chief agreed to them' and, he said, 'we were promised that the White Paper would be translated for us in Shona to read and understand. Since then no such thing has been done. What we refused before we still refuse . . .'

Chief Ngungubane: Chief Mataruse who interpreted for Chief Ngungubane (since the former spoke in Ndebele) said that Chief Ngungubane was for a 'NO', only that he could not stand up to speak . . .

In the end it was decided that in view of what had been discussed on that day, committees would be set up – four members from each chiefdom. These would join forces to construct a letter inviting the commission to the areas of the four chiefs who met on

30 December at Mataruse Council, and to draft a memorandum which will be handed to the Pearce Commission when it visits each of the four chiefdoms. This was done. To prove their support for the opinions of the meeting the chiefs agreed to endorse their signatures and to put their official stamps to both the letter and the memorandum.

The meeting, which started at about 12.00 ended at about 5 p.m.

CHAPTER SEVEN

Violence

THE first violence that was reported flared in the Belingwe District and then in Shabani. People travelled during the day and through past midnight, skirting police and army road-blocks, to come and tell me what was happening and who had been arrested. I transmitted the news to fellow-journalists and to the Pearce Commission, an advance party of which was setting up their headquarters in Salisbury.

On my return from Britain at the beginning of December 1971 I had been asked what I thought of the settlement proposals and I had replied that I would do all in my power, as an individual, to make sure that the proposals were rejected. 'My main reason for opposing this settlement is that it demonstrates that the principle of unimpeded progress to majority rule is irrelevant and the British first principle has been abandoned, no matter what nice words have been used to cloak it.' But individuals can play only a very small part in any national exercise and what I was concerned with was to ensure that accurate information about what was happening in the African rural areas was gathered and broadcast. What I could do in this field was very limited, but when people in the areas surrounding my home heard that I was gathering news and, more important, heard or saw some of it being relayed back to them, many appointed themselves as news gatherers. Everywhere I went people would come to me with reports, verbal and written. Initially the stories were too vague and insubstantial to use, but as soon as I explained that reports should give the names of people involved and if possible witnesses, background information if relevant, place-names, dates and so on, the reports became so concrete that at times they were difficult to digest. If normal political activities had been permitted and freedom of discussion allowed I would have become one of the most contented journalists in the country. People were coming to me with dozens of stories and their reports proved marvellously accurate and detailed.

We were appalled by the eventual violence, but not surprised. Police and officials from the Ministry of Internal Affairs were acting with the greatest provocation. Whether the provocation was intentional or unwitting is a matter for speculation. Many district commissioners in particular were attempting to force the people to accept the settlement proposals. One of the many reports I received gave the flavour of a meeting called at the end of December in the Belingwe area. It was headed: 'Chief Mudavanhu Is Refused By His People' and read:

The people of Chief Mudavanhu of Belingwe District had long asked their chief to allow them to meet and be read and explained the White Paper, but the chief refused. He told his people that it was unnecessary to do so, and he emphasized that the people were not concerned with the settlement but that it was going to be decided by the white inhabitants of the district including the District Commissioner who had told the chiefs that he was in favour of the settlement proposals.

But after some days the chief called all his people to a gathering at Chabengwa Primary School on 29 December 1971 to discuss the settlement proposals. People all over his T.T.L., headmen and kraalheads, women and men and also people of the neighbouring chiefdoms who had had a chance of discussing the proposals with their own chiefs, came. The D.C. who had been invited to the meeting arrived at exactly 10.00 a.m. Before the arrival of the D.C. the chief called his Community Adviser and his Agricultural Demonstrator and told them it was not going to be a meeting to discuss the proposals but to form up a Council.*

Some of his kraalheads suggested that it was more necessary to ask the chief and the D.C. to allow them to discuss the proposals and that they also wished to meet the Royal Commission in their area. The chief said that Africans had no right to say anything but to say YES! to the Commission. People overheard this talk and were grumbling.

The 600 people were waiting very patiently for the D.C. to come and there he arrived, and was met by the chief with his two advisers who greeted the D.C. and had a short discussion about the attendance. What was said or advised by the D.C. no one knows.

Seats had been arranged for them. They took their seats.

* In Rhodesia the authorities are forcing the pace in the establishment of local government. In 1962 there were thirty-three councils in the country. Now there are 146. If the political philosophy of the rulers was acceptable there would be no objection to the establishment of councils, but people are now fighting against their imposition for it is believed that this is simply another way through which the District Commissioners and the chiefs will exert their authority.

'Stand up and greet Mambo' (the King – i.e. the D.C.), the chief said.

The people remained seated. He said that three times and no one stood to greet the so-called Mambo.

A prayer was conducted by an Evangelist, after which the D.C. and the so-called Community Adviser stood up to address the 600 listening audience.

'Have the people of Mudavanhu all come?' Very few voices answered 'yes!' or 'no!'

'Any persons who do not belong to this area must stand up and go. I have come, and I would like to form a council for the Mudavanhu T.T. Area with them alone. We will not discuss the White Paper or the settlement proposals because they are beyond Africans' understanding,' the D.C. said.

This statement in itself was provocative but the people were doubly incensed because they had no wish to discuss the establishment of a council having previously refused to have one in their area. They had been enticed to the gathering under false pretences.

The statement concluded:

As soon as he finished saying this all the people stood up and went away. Some drove their cars homewards, including his closest friends. What remained on the spot was the D.C. with his big book in hand, the Community Adviser, the Agricultural Demonstrator, two messengers and two dogs from the villages fighting near the officials. The people of Mudavanhu allowed a great dislike for their chief and what he is ever advised to do or to say. So the meeting was on for five minutes only.

The District Commissioner for the Belingwe area, Mr I. C. Bissett, had had a busy month. At the beginning of December he had called a meeting of all chiefs and their councillors to his office in Belingwe. At the meeting he said that there was no need to explain the terms as they were in favour of the Africans. He told the chiefs to make sure that their people gave a unanimous YES to the terms.

At a meeting of the Mataga-Chingoma Council on 8 December Mr Bissett again urged those present to accept the proposals. When the councillors asked what was to happen to their detained leaders Mr Bissett said that these detained men could now be forgotten. They had no further part to play in the political life of Rhodesia.

On 10 December at Mataruse Council Mr Bissett repeated that it was not necessary to have the proposals explained. Africans would not understand them 'as even I myself cannot understand much that is in them'. One of the reports I had on this meeting read: 'In spite of his awareness of the complexity of the White Paper the D.C. was presumptuous enough to urge his audience to endorse it without scrutiny. He said: "The proposals are in your favour. If you say YES you will no longer suffer the troubles you have had so far." The D.C. claimed that it was useless to reject the proposals because the Pearce Commission would not change anything in the proposals. He gave the impression that the commission was coming to announce what had already been agreed and finalized. He further said that anyone wishing to see the Pearce Commission would first have to register with him at the D.C's office.'

By this time African members of the police were saying to people that it would be useless to oppose the terms. One Sunday, at Keyara bus station two plainclothes C.I.D. openly warned people that anyone organizing meetings to discuss the White Paper would be arrested.

So against this background of increasing fear, anger and frustration the probability of eventual violence loomed fearfully. It broke on 5 January at Humbani in the Belingwe area.

The Smith regime eventually attributed the violence to 'a carefully planned programme' to 'spark off political and national emotionalism'. It was alleged that 'known agitators' at the Humbani meeting had used 'intimidatory tactics' to break the meeting up.

This was all a lot of nonsense, as I well knew. The truth became even more apparent when I received reports detailing what had happened at the meeting and the background to the meeting. The main report started off with a daunting amount of detail.

The source of the whole trouble seems to be:

(a) Sergeant Tavagwisa Sibanda was found sleeping with someone's wife (Macala Gebhagebha Sibanda) in Sehe's kraal in a hut in the district of Chief Mtevaidzi, and was hit by Naison Sibanda and Mangena, Mabisa's son. This Sergeant Tavagwisa's clothes were torn and they were sewn at Chiwayi's store. The case at the moment is in the hands of Kraalhead Sehe and Headman Ndani Moyo. This case was about to be discussed and this sergeant was aware of this so he started harassing people in the area by claiming to have arrested people who were attending meetings arranged to discuss the White Paper.

e.g. 2/1/71 the same sergeant attended a meeting at Musiningira School and left before the meeting ended, and waited at Keyara bus station and started intimidating people who had attended the meeting at Musiningira claiming he had arrested such people as Betserai Zhou, Timothy Moyo etc. He had been seen with a long list of names giving details of people who had attended this meeting . . .

At the end of December Chief Mahlebadza announced that there would be a gathering of five chiefs and their people at Humbani on the morning of 5 January to discuss the White Paper. At 10 a.m. on the appointed day Chiefs Mahlebadza, Mtevaidzi, and Chisungu duly gathered at Humbani with their people. Chiefs Mudavanhu and Bangwe did not appear, but their people attended. Reports of the numbers in attendance differed, but all agreed that over 1,000 people were present.

The people were greatly alarmed by the presence of police – C.I.D. from Gwelo and uniformed branch from Belingwe. Sergeant Tavagwisa had already told people that Chief Mtevaidzi had requested that police attend the meeting. People tended to dismiss what Tavagwisa had to say but the presence of the police stirred up some hostility to Chief Mtevaidzi. Perhaps, it was thought, he really had asked for the police to be there. There was also anger because a number of people instrumental in organizing meetings had already been arrested.

As the meeting was about to commence the police arrested Mr Mufaro Hove, a teacher, and Mr Kwirirai Shoko, a student.

Many present were quick to see the significance of this action. The two men had been responsible for the organization of a meeting to discuss the White Paper the previous Sunday, at Musiningira School. There was mounting anger and spokesmen for the crowd demanded that the two men be released before the meeting started as they had only done what everyone present was doing – discussing the White Paper. As the police were putting the two men into the police vehicles the crowd decided to take action. They released Mr Hove but were unable to free Mr Shoko. They then stoned the vehicles and the police fled.

The arrests were an open invitation to trouble. If, as was later alleged, the two men were wanted for questioning about matters completely unrelated to the White Paper then it was the height of folly to arrest them at a gathering of over 1,000 people called to discuss the White Paper. It was equally foolish to attempt the arrests in circumstances where the police were unable to enforce their actions. The most shameful, however understandable, episode was that when the police fled they left government African servants at the mercy of the infuriated people. As the vehicles rushed off Mr

84

Chinamora, Community Adviser, and a government messenger ran after them, crying out for help, pleading not to be left behind. Some people caught them and severely assaulted them, despite the pleas of many others that there be no violence. At length the peace-makers rescued the two men and took them to hospital. People had also turned on Chief Mtevaidzi and as one man lifted the chief in the air, threatening to hurl him to the ground, Mbonisi Moyo, a student from the university, intervened and rescued the chief. Mr Moyo has since been sentenced to two years' hard labour for provoking the violence.

The crowd pulled themselves together and as calmness returned to the gathering it was noted that about a dozen men had run off into the veld. The police informers had identified themselves.

Three hours later police reinforcements arrived. That night Humbani was transformed into a military encampment.

The Rhodesian authorities act on the principle that no-one has the right to receive any news about what happens in African areas unless that news is made available by the Ministry of Information. There were no reports on the incident until I had received reports on the meeting and had made them available to the press. It is possibly because of this that I was eventually arrested.

One of the first arrests made after the meeting was that of my friend the headmaster, Mr Lot Dewa. He was picked up by the police as he was boarding a bus at Keyara bus station. A few hours later the Rev. Isaiah Gumbo, my host at the Mavorovonde meeting, was arrested at his home. The police were picking up people who had spoken publicly about the White Paper.

The violence had occurred on 5 January. I relayed the news on the 6th taking special care to ensure that the Rhodesian press were in possession of the facts. Road-blocks had been set up on the Belingwe roads and wide-scale arrests were taking place.

On the 7th a short report was published in the Rhodesian press stating briefly that violence had erupted at a meeting in the Belingwe area called to discuss the White Paper; that a police vehicle had been stoned and that two Africans had received serious injuries. 'A police spokesman was not able to supply a detailed account . . . but said the police vehicle was slightly damaged.' Even a newspaper as far away from Rhodesia as the *Irish Times* of that date supplied a much fuller account of the meeting than Rhodesians were able to read in their papers.

On 11 January the Rhodesian papers were able to print a fuller story which they had gradually winkled out of the authorities.

The *Chronicle* headlined its report:

BELINGWE INCIDENT – POLICE DENY PROVOKING 'RIOT'

The BSAP [British South Africa Police] has strongly denied provoking a 'riot' among Africans at a meeting to discuss the settlement proposals held in the Belingwe Tribal Trust Land.

The provocation allegations are understood to have been made to the advance party of the Pearce Commission in Salisbury.

The next part of the report was a repeat of initial statements made by the police.

It was earlier reported that police charged one African with incitement to riot, and five with attempted murder, following the meeting at which a Chief's messenger and an African Community Adviser, trying to explain the settlement proposals to the crowd, were stoned and badly injured. The reports said that while the meeting was taking place police arrived to question a man on a matter 'unrelated to the subject of the meeting', but one African present allegedly got up and 'denounced' the police, accusing them of taking away an African 'brother'. According to the report the crowd then stoned the police, and when they withdrew the crowd turned on the Community Adviser and Chief's messenger.

Then the report turned to the material I had relayed.

Allegations about the episode were that police detained an African headmaster who was travelling on a bus to the small rural centre of Belingwe, and had also detained an African minister, the Rev. Isaiah Gumbo. It was also alleged that one C.I.D. car and one ordinary police vehicle went to a meeting attended by 1,500 Africans in the Belingwe Tribal Trust Land and 'provoked' the crowd into stoning, during which a Chief, as well as the Community Adviser and messenger, was injured.

The police spokesman commented: 'We confirm that an African headmaster on a bus was arrested as a result of information received. However, he was subsequently released after investigations. The same applies to the African minister.

'A university student has been arrested and is being held on charges of stoning and incitement to public violence. Investigations continue but the name will not be released until he appears in court.' [The name, Mbonisi Moyo, had already been published in the overseas press and broadcast over the B.B.C.]

'We confirm that two police vehicles were stoned. One was a C.I.D. vehicle and the other a uniformed branch vehicle.

'We strongly refute any allegation that police provoked the incident. The police presence was, in fact, due to another matter not related to the meeting. The crowd was not 1,500 strong. Some 500 to 600 persons were present.

'We confirm that an African messenger and an African Community Adviser were badly assaulted,' said the police spokesman, who added that a Chief was not injured. He said that eleven people including a university student were arrested and are being held on charges of attempted murder, stoning and assault.

'Police investigations continue and an early court date is hoped for,' he said.

The day I heard the news of the meeting and the first arrests my immediate concern was how to effect the release of my friends from Belingwe jail. I had known Lot Dewa, the headmaster, since I was a child. Mbonisi Moyo, the university student (who had signed the 'apologize' letter to my father) and the Rev. Isaiah Gumbo were new friends. I had not the slightest doubt that they would not have been implicated in the violence. On many occasions I had heard them warning people of the necessity to keep the peace, as disturbances would play straight into the hands of the authorities. Others had been arrested, but as I did not know the names of all the people involved it was difficult to help. I was concerned for the people who had not been involved in the violence, and therefore I concentrated on helping them.

At midday on the 6th I telephoned a number of journalists. Then, satisfied that others knew of the occurrences, I telephoned the member in charge, Belingwe police, Mr Mike Stephens, whom I had met the previous Thursday when he had ordered me to leave the Mataruse meeting.

When I got on to him he sounded quite jovial and friendly, and we enquired politely about each other's health. Then I said that I had learned he had certain friends of mine in his jail, that I had a list of their names and that I would be grateful if he would verify my information.

There was a long silence. Then he asked me to read the list of names. I did so.

Another long silence ensued. 'Well,' he eventually said, 'I can't say anything about that list. I mean, you're not their legal adviser, are you? And you aren't a relative of theirs, are you?' He sounded as pleased with himself, in an unmalicious way, as he had when he had observed the previous Thursday that the fact that I was born in an African area didn't make me an African.

I agreed with him. 'I'm not a relative and I'm not a lawyer. But I just wanted to make sure I had my facts straight before I inform the press and the Pearce Commission that you have arrested these men.'

All joviality fled. He started stammering, whether from rage, fright or irritation I don't know. He said that he was not responsible for what was happening and that if I wanted information I should ring the officer commanding the Province, Assistant Commissioner Wright in Gwelo. Furthermore, he said, Superintendent Dodds from Gwelo was in Belingwe and in charge of operations. He was out to lunch, but if I cared to 'hold fire' until 2 p.m. he would be back from lunch and might speak to me.

He was exceedingly unhappy and asked where I was telephoning from and for a description of the area, giving the impression that the police would be with me shortly. I believed him and hustled my informants, who were still with me, out of the house and on their way. Then I put through a call to the offices of the Pearce Commission, thinking that the wide-scale haphazard arrests that were now taking place could not be classed as normal political activity in the Pearce sense, although in the Rhodesian sense what was happening was all too normal.

When I first contacted the Rhodesian press they were naturally alarmed about the story and somewhat disbelieving. They rang back that night and said they would like me to know (as though this invalidated the story) that police had said that anyone arrested had been arrested on charges *arising from* the violence that had taken place, and that the violence had not broken out as a result of arrests. In later days that police statement was hastily withdrawn with no explanations. My informants – men from the Belingwe area whom the D.C. thought too unintelligent to understand the White Paper – had given me so much incontrovertible fact and detail that the initial police statements just couldn't stand up.

Those were terrible days for many people in Belingwe. The days are still terrible. On the morning of 6 January the Rev. Masuva Moyo, a Lutheran pastor at a Swedish mission, was woken at 5 a.m. by violent knocking on his door. When he opened it he was faced by armed police in military kit who demanded certain information. A little girl in a far-away kraal was beaten by members of this same police support unit, when she told them that she didn't know where her father was.

The police support unit – a crack unit trained to deal with 'terrorists' – swept the Belingwe tribal trust land. Hundreds of men were taken away. Again the police, whether they knew it or not, were provoking trouble. Two days after the sweep started people arrived at my home at dawn to say that the women in their areas had been intent on marching to the police station in Belingwe and demanding to be arrested too. But their remaining men had persuaded them to stay at home.

'Who will reap the crops? Who will keep the cattle out of the lands? If we lose the crops we will starve and no-one will be able to do anything. It is your duty to see that the crops are saved.'

The women, reluctantly, had agreed to stay at home 'for the time being'.

My friends who had been released from jail came to see me and to thank me for telephoning Stephens. They told me of a tough, shaven-headed African C.I.D. officer who had interrogated them at Belingwe jail.

'God is dead,' he told the Rev. Gumbo and his fellows. 'Didn't you know? Satan has conquered.' They listened to him in silence. When they were released twenty-four hours later and Superintendent Dodds had apologized for their imprisonment which had been based on 'unreliable information' they went back to the African C.I.D.

'God is not dead,' they told him. 'Satan has been conquered.'

'You are quite right,' he said quietly.

'Oh well,' said the Lutheran Rev. Gumbo forgivingly. 'He was a Catholic, you know.'

Kwirirai Shoko, a poor young student who has been dogged with bad luck since he escaped from Rhodesia to Botswana the previous year, wanting to study abroad, and who had been returned to Rhodesia (under the eyes of the British High Commission in Botswana), was still being held in Belingwe jail. I heard reports about how he had been struck across the face by a white police officer in the charge office. When I heard further reports of how he was being taken away from the prison into the veld by African C.I.D. and was being beaten out of the earshot of other prisoners, we contacted a lawyer in Bulawayo and asked him to look after Kwirirai.

He rang back a day later. 'I have been told that Kwirirai Shoko has been taken to Gwelo jail and is being held there under the Emergency Powers Regulations. There is nothing I can do for him.'

On 8 January our papers headlined the news that there was to be

NO SECOND CHANCE FOR SETTLEMENT – SIR ALEC

There would be no second chance for a settlement if the present proposals were rejected in Rhodesia, the British Foreign and Commonwealth Secretary said . . . if the proposals were thrown out that will be the end of it. There will be no possibility of trying again.

THE RIGHT TO SAY NO

That day, a Saturday, I had been asked to cover a mass meeting in Fort Victoria. The report of the meeting was subsequently published in the London *Times*. Rhodesian papers had been informed of the meeting but they didn't bother to send any reporters.

Over 2,000 people were present. The scene was, in itself, an illustration of today's Rhodesia. Beautiful girls in maxis and minis mingled with grave-faced peasants in rags and tatters. The only whites present, apart from myself, were the police but they were tactful and good-humoured and remained in the background.

The speeches made were prophetic of the statements that were to be made to the Pearce Commission.

'People give us names. One of the worst names you have been called is "irresponsible". Here I say you are responsible. Is it irresponsible to stand for the truth? We know that Smith's 1969 constitution is illegal. We have rejected it. But Sir Alec has endorsed it and has asked us, you and me, to accept it. Can we accept a constitution which forbids our leaders to vote or stand for election for five years after they have been released from detention?'

Mr Samuel Munodawafa, an old man employed by the local Cold Storage Commission, was one of the main speakers. He is an ex-detainee and is obviously deeply loved as well as respected. He referred to the fact that one of the deputy chairmen of the Pearce Commission had just resigned his position.

'We see that Sir Frederick Pedler has resigned from the commission and is not coming. He was unaware that he had business interests in Rhodesia. He did not know all along that he had interests in Rhodesia. But he has just discovered this.'

The crowd moved under the shade of the trees and laughed. Those who had no shade and no sun-shades held little branches of green leaves over their heads, and the leaves swayed gently in the laughter.

'Now the question comes,' Mr Munodawafa continued. 'How many British people have interests in Rhodesia? And how many are unaware that they have business interests in Rhodesia? Why do these people who are unaware of their business interests want sanctions lifted? They say it is because of their pity for us but this is not true. We are prepared to suffer.'

At the end of the meeting he referred to the headlines in the paper that day.

'Do not be afraid that Sir Alec says this is the last chance. This is only intimidation from the highest source. We know the truth and the truth will continue . . .'

Mr Munodawafa was absolutely correct. When the Pearce Commission reported a 'No' verdict Sir Alec, far from repeating his 'there will be no possibility of trying again', said that the door would be kept open. He said the proposals were still on the table and he urged the Africans to think again and accept them. His original statement that there was no second chance for a settlement was after all, as Mr Munodawafa said, 'only intimidation from the highest source', a fruitless attempt to pressure Africans into saying 'Yes', thereby relieving Her Majesty's Government of their responsibility for us.

On Wednesday morning, 12 January, my brother-in-law who had been in Shabani the night before informed us that there had been serious riots in Shabani. One person had been shot dead by the police and others had been wounded in the gun-fire. Buildings in the African mine townships had been set on fire and there was extensive damage.

We were horrified. As we employ a number of young men and women at a store and butchery which we rent in one of the African townships, my father rushed into Shabani to see that they were safe. While neighbouring buildings had been burned and damaged the place we rent was unharmed. The doors were locked but the employees were safely inside. Thousands of mine-workers were on strike and many of them were standing quietly round the houses in the vicinity. The employees let my father in and he sat down with them while they told him what had been happening. The rioting had clearly led from a mine-dispute which was being incredibly ineptly handled by the management of Turner and Newall who own the asbestos mines.

While my father listened to an account of the horrors of the preceding night there was an increasing noise outside the store. Not knowing what to expect he went and opened the doors. His unbelieving eyes rested on a group of fifteen or more strikers surrounding his car. They had a bucket of water and while half a dozen men washed his car with their hands, others were singing and dancing around it. Moved beyond words, but filled with the fear that the police might return, mistake the singing crowd which was fast growing for more trouble, and open fire again, he got into the car and drove off.

It is difficult to explain this event and I suppose most whites would not accept any explanation which pays tribute to the overwhelming longing, tolerance and good will of so many Africans. In the midst of a strike which was having very serious consequences, a few yards from the spot where a man had been shot dead the night before, African mine-workers were singing for my father and washing his car with their bare hands.

91

My father belongs to this area and to the people. He has lived here for thirty-eight years and tens of thousands of scholars have passed through the schools associated with the work of my parents. In earlier years there were no government clinics and hospitals, and many hundreds of the people in this area were delivered and looked after by my father. In 1946 he left the missionary field and went into politics in an attempt to break down the colour bar. When, in 1958, he was ousted from the premiership of Rhodesia the reason was that he had attempted to broaden the franchise so that more Africans could qualify for the vote. I suppose that on that morning in Shabani the people were so shocked by the woundings and killing and violence of the night before, so fearful of what would happen now, that they were overjoyed to see a man who had once had power and who was on the side of the people. I suppose that by so greeting him they were not only expressing their love and friendship but were in a way asking for help.

One of my father's greatest fears has been that at some time he might be the focal point of an outbreak of black-white violence. I remember many years ago when he had been to the United Nations as a petitioner, white parliamentarians were talking of hanging him upside down at the airport on his return. I was at the university in Salisbury and immediately many Africans started phoning me, asking to know when he was arriving so that they could go to the airport and protect him. He slipped back into the country by road to avoid just such a situation where whites and blacks might clash over him. Now the position was just as dangerous for all concerned.

As he drove home through the white centre of Shabani township Africans on the streets recognized his car and waved and cheered. Whites turned to see the reason for the cheering and when they saw Todd perhaps it can be understood why they may have reached the conclusion that it was he who had been the cause of the violence of the night before. (Rhodesian Front logic has it that 'behind every agitating black is a white, usually a Communist, with brains.') When the whites heard the story of the car-washing episode they were appalled and as they told and re-told the story so it grew. First Africans had washed his car with their hands; then Africans had taken off their shirts and used them to wash the car. The last version we have heard was that Africans had held up black mine police, stripped them and used their uniforms to wash the car.

That afternoon we received the first threat. A young white man rang my father. I listened in to the call on an extension phone.
'I want to speak to Todd.'
'Speaking. What can I do for you?'

'You couldn't do anything for me,' the young, rather uncertain voice said. 'You haven't the brains of a kaffir. You couldn't help anyone.'
'I see. Then why are you ringing me?'
'Because we're coming to get you. We're coming to get you now.'

During the afternoon we received three different calls from pressmen. The rumour was abroad that Garfield Todd had been arrested.

Towards evening an African who lives in a house in the area where the violence had flared in Shabani visited us. He was able to give me a detailed report which, as usual, differed seriously from government statements that were later issued. He told me of the shooting, the wounding and the one fatality. He had helped give first-aid to some of the wounded.

He insisted that the police had not been in danger themselves and that it had not been necessary for them to open fire.

A government statement was broadcast that night.

One African was killed and nine were wounded last night when police opened fire on rioting mobs . . . In three days of violence an administrative building was burnt down, vehicles were stoned and innocent African bystanders assaulted . . . The incident was one of several in Rhodesia since 19 December which had necessitated police intervention . . .

A recognizable pattern had emerged . . . in which situations were being engineered to spark off political and national emotionalism . . .

This is being generated in tribal areas and African townships by a carefully planned programme . . .

Violence erupted in Shabani on Tuesday after twelve African employees . . . were dismissed for refusing to obey instructions. An incoming shift of eighty Africans refused to work because their fellow-workers had been dismissed. Mine officials who visited the scene had their cars stoned and elements of the shift stoned houses in an adjacent compound . . .

On 5 January a meeting of 500 to 600 people called in Belingwe Tribal Trust Land . . . broke up in disorder. Several chiefs had called the meeting at the request of the African National Council*
. . . Known agitators who were present used intimidatory tactics to break the meeting up . . . several people were now being held on serious charges arising from severe injuries received by two government-employed Africans and two elderly chiefs . . .

Well, well, I thought. So now they're trying to implicate the A.N.C. in violent activity and the count has gone up from definitely no chiefs

* The A.N.C. was formed to oppose the settlement proposals (see p. 187).

being involved (the first police statement) to two elderly chiefs being seriously injured.

I had written a statement on the Shabani violence based on the report I had just been given and went to the phone to put through a call to Salisbury.

The Shabani telephone exchange, through which our calls are transmitted, is operated by an African from 5 p.m. to 8 a.m. That evening I was surprised to hear a heavy South African voice on the line. 'You've got a new accent,' I said.

'Yes,' the telephonist agreed. 'There's a shift of us down from Gwelo to run the exchange tonight.'

'Why?'

'We've come to help you in your troubles,' he said. His voice was confidential and friendly, and invited my thanks which were not forthcoming. I placed my call to Salisbury and gave him my number to ring back when the call came through. I waited a very long time for the call and eventually rang Shabani to find out what was happening.

This time his voice was as icy as a thick South African accent would permit.

'The lines are very busy,' he said. 'We are unable to transmit any calls either from or to you tonight.'

'So,' I thought. 'I'm not to be allowed to tell anyone what has been happening in Shabani. This time they're going to make sure that only the government side of the picture gets published.'

I thought that the side of the story I had was very important – it was, in fact, totally verified by a statement put out some days later by Mr Howard Bloomfield, president of the Associated Mineworkers of Rhodesia. As he said the mine management's failure to investigate discontent, its dismissal of anonymous letters demanding more pay, its refusal to discuss the situation could only prolong the position of stale-mate.

There was no alternative, if I wanted to get what information I had into the hands of other journalists. I packed an over-night bag and then drove through the dark, rainy, ominous night to Bulawayo, over 100 miles away. I booked into a hotel at about 10.30 and once I was safely in my room placed calls to various journalists in Salisbury. I got through to them with no delays at all. Then, worried about my parents, I placed a call home. I didn't really think that the young man who had phoned earlier with his news that 'they' were going to come and 'get' my father should be taken too seriously, but by now the bar in Shabani would have closed and I wanted to make sure that all was well at home.

The hotel operator rang me back. 'No reply from that number,' he said.

'But I've just come from there,' I said, 'and I *know* there are people waiting for a call.'

'Well,' he said in a resigned voice. 'I'll try again and ring you back.'

My phone tinkled a few minutes later. 'Absolutely no reply.'

By this time I was worried and angry. I could guess what was happening and asked him to put me through to the Shabani exchange so that I could speak to the operator myself. Instead he put me on to the Bulawayo exchange.

'What's the matter Mam?' another South African voice asked. I repeated that I had just come from the place in Shabani that I was ringing, that I knew there were people waiting for a call from me and that I didn't believe there was no answer.

'But Mam,' he said, 'the kaffir's off-duty in Shabani tonight. There's white men on duty there tonight. *They* wouldn't make a mistake.'

'They obviously have,' I said. 'Would you put me through to them please?' As he was raising Shabani so he attempted an inconsequential chatting-up scene. 'You by yourself Mam? Lonely Mam? If that kaffir was on duty tonight, know what I'd do for you Mam? I'd send him on his bicycle with your message . . .'

'Thanks very much,' I said in an unfriendly voice and was delighted to hear one of his fellow-operators say laconically in the background: 'Why don't you send one of those whites in their car?' At that point Shabani answered.

'*Sorry* to bother you again Shabani . . .' Bulawayo started.

'No bother,' Shabani said amicably. 'It gets boring doing nothing . . .' ('So,' I thought, 'they're too busy to put through any calls, are they?')

'But,' continued Bulawayo, 'this lady says she knows there are people at 01-222 waiting for her call.'

'No there aren't,' said Shabani.

'There *are*!' I said forcibly. Shabani gulped. He hadn't known I was on the line. Then he recovered with admirable swiftness.

'Well, I'll ring them again and you can see for yourself. Ohhh,' he breathed, pretending to dial the numbers 'whunn, tew, tew, tew . . .'

'Oh one two is the number which identifies the party line,' I said. 'You don't dial it. And you don't dial two two either, you ring it – two shorts and two longs. Maybe that's why you haven't raised the number tonight.'

All the glaciers of dislike re-assembled in his voice. He had obviously realized who I was. 'There is NO reply MADAM. GOOD NIGHT!'

There was nothing I could do. The next day my parents confirmed that the telephone had not rung all night.

Life was becoming rather frightening. My father and I had reached a new peak of unpopularity with many of our fellow-whites and the Rhodesian authorities. Their anger was perhaps understandable. All loyal 'Rhodesians' were expected to say YES to the proposals. We were saying NO with the Africans. As Africans were the enemy, so were we. Moreover, my father had accepted an invitation to speak at an A.N.C. meeting in Bulawayo the previous Monday.

The following day the *Chronicle* had published a photograph of hundreds of smiling people running to the meeting. There was, naturally, a conspicuous absence of white faces. The headlines were: 'Todd Urges Dialogue Between Black and White – U.K. Would Ratify Agreement Reached In Rhodesia.' Hundreds of people were present at the meeting and the report read:

> Mr Todd said he agreed with Sir Alec Douglas-Home that the present Conservative government would not give Rhodesia a second chance of settlement talks if the people rejected the present chance.
>
> 'That does not worry me at all,' he said, 'because the next conversation should be between white and black . . .
>
> 'The only document we could accept is one agreed between the present administration and representatives of the African people and then ratified by Her Majesty's Government' . . . The proposals 'should be even more unacceptable to whites than they are to Africans. They make no provision for uniting people on a basis of equal opportunity for all, and so they leave the white population in a privileged and dangerous position . . . If Africans say YES then absolute power will be given to white people to rule over 5 million African people. I believe that such power will corrupt us absolutely.
>
> 'That is why I must say NO.'

CHAPTER EIGHT

Prison

Tuesday evening, 18 January 1972

THE sun dipped over the radiant horizon and pools of water lay on the road like patches of heaven. My car windows were down and I was savouring the rainy season which covered the land with soft, shimmering grasses, filled the rivers, polished the old, dry leaves on the trees. The sunnhemp, a dark rolling crop, flickered under its first golden torches of flower and cattle stood fat and lazy along the road. As I swung the car round a corner, I glanced in the rear-view mirror to see how far my father was behind me on the slow, bumpy track which winds four miles off the main road to our house and then slammed on the brakes, simultaneously pulling the car off the road.

The car facing me must have braked and pulled off the road at exactly the same time. It was full of people and in the instant I became aware of it I registered the set faces of its occupants and saw that there was a woman in the back seat.

'Police!' I thought. 'A woman, too. So it has to do with me.'

My father pulled up behind me. The driver of the car by my side got out and looked into the cab of my vehicle as he walked past towards my father. A second car and a Land-Rover edged round the corner and stopped behind the first car. I saw a fourth vehicle glinting in the distance.

'Mr Todd?' asked the man on the road. I watched in the rear-view mirror. My father grinned, pushing his hat back on his head. 'Yes,' he said. 'What can I do for you?'

The man, grim-faced and city-suited, seemed taken aback.

'We would like to talk to you and your daughter.'

'Fine,' said my father. 'We're just going into our house. Would you care to follow?'

The man climbed back into his car and started turning in concert with his fellow-vehicles. I started my car and set off again, leading the way home. The old blue Peugeot truck I was driving responded magnificently to my alarm and galloped over the well-known road, leaving the party far behind. I reached the house a full minute ahead of the others and rushed on to the stoep where my mother and my father's sister, Edith, were having a drink.

'Police!' I said. 'Masses of them. Just behind me.'

'Good life!' said Edie. 'What *is* this country coming to?'

We listened to the vehicles arriving and understood by all the different sounds that they were finding it difficult to park themselves on the little hill on which our house rests. But then there was quietness and we heard a tramp of feet. My father came round the corner, leading what seemed to be a host of people.

I don't know what we were expecting. At most, I suppose, we thought they had come to question us on our opposition to the settlement proposals, and perhaps to search for material on the proposals. When, a few minutes later, we realized that they had come to take my father and myself to prison the situation became horribly unreal. Superintendent Tomlinson, the cocky city-suited gentleman in charge, served detention orders on us which were signed by D. W. Lardner-Burke, Minister of Law and Order and of Justice. We didn't protest, but accepted them quietly.

The others were identical except that one stipulated that my father was to be held in Gatooma jail whereas the other stated that my place of detention was to be Marandellas jail.

You are hereby notified that it appears to me that it is expedient in the interests of public safety or public order to make an Order against you in terms of sub-section (1) of regulation 16 of the Emergency Powers (Maintenance of Law and Order) Regulations, 1970.

2. The making of this Order is based on a belief that you are likely to commit, or to incite the commission of, acts in Rhodesia which would endanger the public safety, or disturb or interfere with the maintenance of public order.

3. Now, THEREFORE, in terms of subsection (1) of section 16 of the Emergency Powers (Maintenance of Law and Order) Regulations, 1970, I do hereby order that you shall be detained by being kept in the place described in the Schedule to this Order until the revocation or expiry of the Declaration of a Public Emergency in Rhodesia or until this Order is revoked or varied . . .

After the orders were served the police started searching the house. The party consisted of Superintendent Tomlinson who, I thought, looked rather like a moustacheless Charlie Chaplin playing a distinctly humourless role; Detective Inspector Nigel Seaward, a tall, fair, bloodless-looking young man; Patrol Officer David Hawkes, short, fat and troubled by some doubtful food he had eaten en route to us; Section Officer Keyser who, when many weeks later I commented that he looked rather like Mr McNamara of the World Bank, took it as a compliment; a quiet, pleasant man from Gwelo, Superintendent Bradshaw; a policeman from Belingwe, Taverner, who had come (with two African police) to show the way to our house. He hadn't done so well as when we met the police they were on their way back to the main road, convinced that no one could live at the end of the track they were on. The woman was Miss Helen Pronk. She was about twenty-five, slim and atttactive, with long brown hair, and she initially spoke to me as, I discovered later, she speaks to Africans. Brittle and hostile. Going through my cupboards she discovered an old copy of *Outpost*, the magazine for the B.S.A. police force. It greatly excited her.

'Why have you got this? What purpose have you got it for? How did you get hold of it?' I sighed, and my mother explained rather curtly that my brother-in-law, a former policeman, had lent it to me. Miss Pronk was disappointed and put it back in the cupboard without further comment. Her great finds of the evening were a letter and enclosures to the Pearce Commission, and the visitors' book in our guestroom.

While Miss Pronk went through my room Keyser and Seaward searched my parents' room, sifting through my mother's clothes and the accumulations of forty happy years of marriage. They asked if there were further papers, obviously dissatisfied with the contents of the house. Looking at each other wryly we informed the police that our offices were at Bannockburn, eight miles away, where there were indeed further papers. What they didn't realize at the time, but soon discovered to their horror, is that our papers at Bannockburn fill a whole house. The house is a library containing hundreds of box files, piles of newspapers, cartons of photographs and unclassified papers all going back to the early 1930s. Included in these papers are records of my father's premiership, confidential minutes of cabinet meetings and government decisions. They are the only full record of their kind of 1953–8. When we mentioned that the Rhodesian archives were working on these papers one of the police said it was a pity they hadn't known, as they could have provided a man to help with the cataloguing.

Before we left the house to start the search of Bannockburn I asked Superintendent Tomlinson if I could have a bath. He looked at me with distaste and supposed I could, provided Miss Pronk was in the bathroom with me. I then supposed that I wouldn't in those circumstances. My mother came to the rescue and without even looking at Tomlinson told Miss Pronk and me that we should go to the guestroom where Miss Pronk could sit in the bedroom while I left the bathroom door open. We set off, Miss Pronk becoming more and more reasonable. By the time we reached the guestroom she said I could shut the bathroom door. When I reached Marandellas Prison at dawn the next day I was very glad to have bathed and washed my hair.

Then we set off for Bannockburn in a police car, my father sitting in the front with Superintendent Tomlinson and Miss Pronk keeping an eye on me in the back. Bannockburn is on our ranch and is our headquarters. We have a store, a butchery and the ranch office there and my father runs a daily clinic from the old, dilapidated house which is the library and my office. But Bannockburn in itself is primarily a small, white railway settlement. As we reached it Tomlinson commented on a house which was festooned with coloured lights and asked what it was.

'The Railway Club,' my father explained. He paused for a few seconds, laughed and added: 'Tomorrow they'll probably have more lights up.'

'Why?'

'Well, when they hear you've arrested me.'

Superintendent Tomlinson shared in the joke and laughed heartily. 'They don't like you much then,' he said. He was thawing gradually. When we got back home he called me 'Miss T.' which, in the circumstances, almost had a ring of friendship about it. He also had something friendly to say to my father.

'Mr Todd, I've been in the force for . . . years. You don't have to worry that I'll introduce incriminating material amongst your papers.' My father replied that the possibility had never crossed his mind. Five weeks later, when we were released from prison, the thought still appalled him. And yet this was exactly what seemed to have happened to the Dean of Johannesburg, whose tribulations we had been following with a close and personal interest. For some inexplicable reason, newly arrested on the flimsy basis of 'a belief' of Mr Lardner-Burke's, without any possibility of being charged or tried in open court, we still expected the Rhodesian police to be incorruptible. However much one might fight a political system, it is painful to have to admit that the very structure of one's country is rotten to the core. Superintendent Tomlinson unwittingly admitted it himself that night.

We had been arrested just before 6 p.m. When we returned home from Bannockburn it was close on 9 p.m. My mother had arranged food for us all and the police ate on the stoep while my parents, Edith and I drank some soup in the lounge. A few days later a friend of ours from Shabani came to see my mother. She is a honey-haired South African who is almost totally incapable of concealing her true feelings. She asked if we had eaten before we left home, and my mother told her that everyone had. She stared at her in shocked disbelief. 'Do you mean to say that the police came to take your husband and your daughter and you gave them food? You . . . you . . . you . . . CHRISTIAN!'

I knew that night would be far worse for my mother than it was for us. I slipped past the police on the stoep, and locked myself into her bedroom. Then I scribbled a note to her, attempting to get a few words of love and comfort on paper. I pushed it under the sheet on her side of the bed, smoothed the blankets down and walked back past the police who looked at me with suspicion, but did not attempt to find out what I had been doing. Then it was time to go. My mother came to the car. 'I am very proud of you both,' she said, holding me close. There was nothing adequate I could say. My mother, who has always longed that we could lead a peaceful, normal life, was being left with the burdens of the ranch, the weight of our imprisonment. I don't like thinking what that night must have been like for her. The memory I took with me was of her standing in the headlights of the police cars, strong and brave, waving us goodbye as though she were quite confident we would be back the next day.

The car we were taken away in was an Austin Westminster. 'How ironic,' I thought, squeezed up in the back between Miss Pronk and Mr Hawkes. 'The Westminster model.' My father sat in the front, his feet uncomfortably perched on a typewriter. The boot was full of papers from Bannockburn and somewhere there were two suitcases of clothing for us. So we sped through the night, en route to Gatooma Prison, 200 miles north where my father would be jailed. I would then be taken on to Marandellas, over 300 miles away from home.

I suppose, looking back, that my father and I unconsciously regarded both ourselves and the police as victims of the political situation. Certainly, as the miles flipped by, the police became more friendly and relaxed. Miss Pronk kept offering welcome peppermints and now and again displayed flashes of undiluted coquetry when she addressed my father. Mr Hawkes was determinedly self-contained. He had had the misfortune to eat a meat-pie at Spike's café in Shabani, fifteen miles from my home, when the police were on their way to arrest us, and was now feeling very ill.

Spike's café is run by a couple of uhuru-hoppers – people who have fled from 'freedom'. Mr and Mrs Spike are immigrants from Zambia and treat every African customer with the purest form of dislike imaginable. They are polite to whites, even when their name happens to be Todd, but they loudly proclaim their allegiance to the present Rhodesian state with numbers of copper plaques of Mr Smith which decorate their walls. A few years ago when I was abroad my father wrote to me and said that the sanctions policy against Rhodesia was now openly effective. A plaque of Mr Ian Smith in Spike's now carried a price tag which read: 'Reduced to 7/6d.'

Two days before our arrest a friend of ours and his son were breakfasting in Spike's. The Ritsons are English, north-country gentlemen and as frank as businessmen can afford to be in Rhodesia's present circumstances. Their food had arrived and they were starting to eat when a Shabani-ite walked in and said to Mrs Spike:

'Todd's been arrested.'

'About time too,' said Mrs Spike, a very short, pudgy lady. 'He's done enough harm.'

Alan Ritson looked over the table at his son Jefferson and winked. 'So,' he said. 'Todd's been arrested, has he? And when did that happen?'

'Eight o'clock this morning,' said the informant complacently.

'Funny,' said Alan. 'Garfield Todd rang me at nine to say that one of my cattle off the trucks at Bannockburn was lame.'

There was, momentarily, a dead silence, then Mrs Spike rallied: 'Amazing,' she said pointedly, 'who some people will associate with.'

Jefferson kicked his father under the table.

'Wouldn't make a good looking bull-dog, would she?' he observed.

Alan choked. 'Come on, Jefferson,' he said. 'Let's get out of here.'

I remembered the incident with pleasure when, some miles after Gatooma, Mr Hawkes was violently sick. If policemen were ill after visiting Spike's it would be all too probable that the Spikes would have to be hopping off somewhere else before long.

Eventually we reached Gatooma Prison. We got out of the car and my father and I said goodbye. The police would not allow me to go into the prison with him. The jail was a squalid block of buildings set in a wired-off desert. An African warder stood with a gun at the gate.

'We'll just take you in and finger-print you, Mr Todd,' said Nigel Seaward who had been driving us.

'Finger-print me?' said my father incredulously. 'I have done nothing criminal. I'm not charged with any offence.'

Seaward drew himself into a rigid icicle. 'Those are my orders!'

'Well,' said my father, 'if this is so, I would like to place on record that I will give you my finger-prints under protest.'

Hawkes, Seaward, my father and the prison Superintendent, Mr Edwards, set off together. Miss Pronk remained behind with me, and asked me to get back into the car. I remained outside for a few seconds, knowing I would never forget what I was seeing.

The prison lay still and soulless under harsh electric lights. The guard swung open the gates and locked them again behind the four men. I watched my father walking over to the prison block, visible through the high fence of barbed wire. He was tired and stooping and his white hair shone under the lights. When, exactly five weeks later, the Special Branch and I called to pick him up again his hair was dead and lustreless, he was ill and had aged alarmingly. The prison doors slammed behind him. Then I heard him laughing somewhere inside. My throat ached and when Miss Pronk called to me I couldn't answer. I wondered which of the tiny barred black eyes set in the buildings would be his cell. The guard started marching up and down, his gun over his shoulder. I couldn't hear the men inside any longer and climbed back into the car.

'And what does your father do?' I asked Miss Pronk when I had recovered control of myself.

'That's a funny question,' she said. 'Why do you ask?'

'Oh. I was just wondering what you would feel like if it was him being imprisoned in Gatooma jail.'

She reacted almost angrily. 'I'm not callous, you know. I didn't want to come on this exercise. But my boss said I must.'

'Who is your boss?'

'Inspector Seaward.'

I didn't for one moment believe that she hadn't wanted to come. It had been an interesting excursion which she had started to feel fleetingly uncomfortable about only after she had met us. Now she started talking to me incessantly. I supposed she was trying to keep my mind off what was happening and felt somewhat appreciative. Now I wonder whether she wasn't trying to keep her own mind off what was happening.

'I don't suppose you remember me?'

'Have we met before?'

'I was at your National Affairs meeting. Sitting near the front, on the right.'

I looked at her reflectively in the dim light inside the car, and had a vague recollection of having seen her. 'Of course,' I said, 'I was told that the Special Branch were at that meeting. But if I had seen you I don't think I would have realized that you were Special Branch.'

She obviously thought I was being extraordinarily tactless. 'But I don't go to those meetings because I'm Special Branch. I go because I'm *interested*.'

'Did you enjoy the meeting?'

She paused, and then said she had found it 'very interesting'.

'I was so surprised to see who was there – a lot of my old teachers were there, you know.'

I thought back to the meeting. It had been quite an experience for me as it had been the first public meeting I had ever addressed in Rhodesia. August 1971. The hall had been full of people, predominantly white, and before the meeting started I was quite literally terrified. The following morning the *Rhodesia Herald* had headlines on the front page: 'Rhodesia Hijacked Says Judy Todd' under which there was a full report of what I felt about Smith's declaration of independence, which I referred to as the hijacking of Rhodesia, and the racist policies of the Smith regime. It was the first report I had seen published in the Rhodesian press which, throughout, referred to Smith's government as the 'illegal regime' and I had thought then that there might have been trouble. But it was important, so far as I was concerned, to say exactly what I had been saying outside Rhodesia and I had done so. The audience, to my surprised delight, had been polite and generous with their applause. No action had been taken against me. But there had already been calls in the press by various individuals to have me 'dealt with', and Ian Smith, in response to one of these calls, had said that he was confident that the police were capable of doing their duty. Well, here I now was, I thought, sitting in a police car.

Miss Pronk had started chattering about her family who are immigrants from Holland. 'And Rhodesia's such a marvellous country that our relatives are all following us out.'

'Holland,' I said. 'You must know a lot about the Nazis then.'

She was silent. I remembered that she was younger than I and that I had never known anything about the Nazis myself on a personal basis. 'Or at least you must have *heard* a lot about them?'

She started talking about her forthcoming marriage.

'Tell me, Miss Pronk,' I said. 'Have you ever heard of someone called Niemoller?'

'No,' she said, with a considerable lack of interest.

'Well,' I said, 'he was imprisoned by the Nazis and he said something once that I can't help thinking of tonight. I forget how he put it, but it was something about his saying nothing when the Nazis first started picking up the Jews. Then, when they started picking up the Catholics he said nothing. Then, when they came for him, there wasn't anyone left to say anything for him.'

She was silent and I wondered if she remembered how I had ended the National Affairs speech. I had been referring to all the people held without trial in our country. 'And if we don't care about them how can we expect others to care for us when tomorrow the police may be told to come for you, or for me?'

The prison gates swung open again and Mr Hawkes and Mr Seaward rejoined us. Miss Pronk took over the driving and the other two slept in the back. Although the clouds burst over us and we travelled through a constant barrage of rain she drove swiftly and competently to Salisbury, accepting cigarettes and her own peppermints from me. I considered that it was as much in my own interest as anyone else's to keep her awake and alert. Our captors had had a long day, leaving Salisbury early that morning, arresting us in the evening, and then having to drive the long miles back to Salisbury and on to Marandellas with me.

We pulled into a Salisbury garage just before 4 a.m. The police were thirsty and wanted Cokes. They offered me one, but I declined. It was then, when Miss Pronk was asking the African attendant for Cokes, that I realized she had initially addressed me in the tone she now used. 'You haven't any straws? What sort of a garage is this?'

A small group of Africans stood near the car, hunched over a copy of the *Rhodesia Herald* which was just appearing on the streets. I heard one of them saying 'Garfield Todd . . .' and another responding 'Ahhh!'

I leant out of the window.

'Please,' I said urgently, 'could you show me that page?' The Africans looked at me suspiciously. We must have looked like a group of young people back from a party. The police were all in plain clothes. Seaward and Hawkes started muttering in the back. '*Please*,' I said to the Africans. Doubtful and unwilling they held the front page up to the window for me to see. There was a frightening photograph of soldiers in gas-masks, controlling a riot in Gwelo. They looked like invaders from outer space. Alongside was a picture of Mr Lardner-Burke, a rose in his button-hole, a policeman crouching over a gun behind him. The Minister of Law and Order and Justice was inspecting the situation in his constituency of Gwelo, smiling broadly. On the opposite side of the page to him, on the same level, was a headline: 'Todd and Judy Held.' Hawkes muttered louder in the back. I turned to him.

'You don't have to worry. Very few people recognize me.' Then I turned back to the Africans. 'Thank you very much.' They lowered their eyes, suspicious and resentful, and gathered the newspaper back into their exclusive possession. It was at that moment that I began to feel so intolerably lonely. Those Africans had presumed I was with friends. I was with police who were taking me to prison. But now the police, despite themselves, had become friendly and were embarrassed that I should be talking to Africans.

We went to the police station where we filled up with petrol. I caught a glimpse of a beautiful little African policewoman in an Afro-wig and smart, miniscule clothing. A policeman informed my escorts that another white male had been arrested that night on what is known as Salisbury's Vice Mile. I began to like Nigel Seaward more when he groaned and said 'Not again!' The Vice Squad have been using this woman to trap many white men. We do not, in Rhodesia, have the formalized cruelty of the 'Immorality Act' which exists in South Africa, outlawing sexual relations between those of differing races. We have other laws which have the same effect, and this ravishing little snare and delusion is used by her fellow-police to capture white men who do not know how to maintain their racial superiority when it comes to prostitutes.

Seaward took over the driving and we drove on through the night calling each other Dave, Helen, Nigel and Judy, lighting each other cigarettes and passing peppermints around. As dawn placed a cold, bleary finger-print on the horizon we pulled into Marandellas jail, which is set in bleak plantations of fir trees, far off the main road.

The morning was grey and cold and I thought there could never have been such an unwilling sunrise. We raised the prison staff from their beds and eventually assembled in the Superintendent's office – my three escorts, myself, the superintendent Mr Darney and his wife, Gay. Mrs Darney looked as tired and miserable as I felt. The Darneys had been transferred to Marandellas the day before from some other far-flung prison and had spent most of the night waiting up for us. They had only just got to bed when we arrived and they had to get up again.

Soon we were joined by Mr Darney's deputy, Mr Proud, a tall, quiet, grey-headed man in a dressing-gown. The prison staff were as wary of me as the police had initially been and were obviously surprised to find that the police were now on first-name terms with me. Seaward asked for the finger-printing material. I pointed out that the police already had my finger-prints which had been taken at the end of 1964. 'They were taken when the government was legal and you weren't assisting in an illegal arrest. If I *have* to give them to you again then, like my father, I do so under protest.'

They took my prints, rolling each finger in turn over the ink and on to the paper. Mr Proud then showed me a tiny washroom where I tried to wash the ink off in freezing water. Then Mrs Darney brought us hot, sweet tea and we drank together.

Eventually the police rose and prepared to leave. As they reached the door Nigel Seaward turned to me and standing thin, blond and formal against the dark morning he said:

'I would like to thank you, Judy, for being so co-operative.'

That one sentence undid any vestiges of self-control I had left and I turned away from the people, struggling against tears. There is something very humiliating about not being able to maintain a rigid control of oneself in such circumstances. My eyes smarted and I could feel my mouth drooping far beyond immediate recall. When the Darneys asked what I needed to take to my cell from the suitcase I couldn't speak. But in a few seconds I had pulled myself together and took a couple of books from my possessions which would all have to be checked before I received them. 'Come on then, love,' said Mr Darney, and the three of us set off for the cells.

Morning was by now in full possession of the immediate world and the huge tangerine sun ballooned swiftly over the horizon behind rows of dark fir trees. We stepped across brilliant puddles of water to the first barbed-wire stockade.

'GATE!' Mr Darney shouted and an African warder ran over with a key. The key was fastened on a long chain to his belt and when the gate was unlocked he stood attached to it until it was locked behind us again. We reached the second high shield of barbed wire, the second gate.

'GATE!' Mr Darney shouted. Another warder rushed over and got hopelessly mixed up between saluting Darney and unlocking the gate. He was in charge of the third gate leading through the third barricade of barbed wire and we waited while he unlocked himself from the one gate and locked himself to the next while we passed through.

It all looked very grim to me. On the way to Marandellas I had asked Helen Pronk why I wasn't being taken to Gwelo where I thought most white female prisoners were kept. She was shocked. 'But that's a *criminal* prison,' she said. So I supposed that I wasn't regarded as a criminal and that Marandellas must be a gentler place than Gwelo. When I saw the prison I dreaded to think what Gwelo must be like.

We reached a block of cells to which Mr Darney had the keys. There were two huge padlocks on the steel door and he unlocked them, slid the steel bars back, then held the heavy door open while I walked into my new home.

The door opened on to a little concrete courtyard which formed an apron for three cells and an open washroom. The middle cell, No. 13, was mine. The other two were kept locked.

We walked into my small cell. There was a primitive bed, a rickety table, a chair, a basin and jug and an enamel chamber pot. There were two narrow, high grilled windows, air-vents really, one of which faced into the courtyard and the other of which was above my bed and looked out (I discovered later by standing on the bed) across the other prison blocks. Then the Darneys went out, leaving my cell door unlocked and locking me into the self-contained block.

I sat on my bed listening.

Bang! The outside door shut. Bang! The first padlock was locked fast. Bang! The second padlock slammed into place.

Footsteps.

'GATE!' I heard the first and second gates being unlocked and locked again. Footsteps squelched across the wet, sandy soil.

'GATE!' The third gate was unlocked, locked again.

And then I found myself alone.

I sat on the edge of the bed, quite numb. Gradually recollections of the past night drifted across my mind and remembering the sight of my father, stooped and white under the glaring lights, being locked into Gatooma prison, and my mother in the lights of the police cars, I found it very difficult not to cry. So, to stop thinking, I walked out of my cell and looked at the tiny grey courtyard. I stood and listened outside the other two cells and when I was sure there wasn't anyone inside I looked through the warders' peepholes. The cells were identical to mine, but quite empty. Red, polished concrete floors. Dull red walls. But cell No. 12 had a huge iron ring set into the centre of the floor, absolutely awful in the thought of prisoners being chained to it. I often looked at that ring, hoping it wasn't ever used. But it was so shiny. One day I asked Mr Darney what it was for. 'Lunatics,' he said.

Then I went to inspect the washroom. There was a cold-water shower and a lavatory, open to the courtyard save for a small wall which cursorily screened the lavatory. The lavatory consisted of a high concrete block, embedded into which was a circular enamel bowl. The bowl had at one time been edged with a downward sloping rim of enamel, but this had been chipped away until the bowl was raw and jagged. It was a flush lavatory and when the chain was pulled the water descended with such force into the bowl that a large percentage of it sprayed straight back, reinforced, on to the concrete block. The block was always wet, and water trickled down the walls from the cistern. I was thankful I didn't have to share the facilities with other prisoners.

I wandered round and round the tiny courtyard, then sat down and looked upwards through the steel mesh which shut the sky away. I remembered Wilde's phrase 'that little tent of blue which prisoners call the sky' and thought the concept of a tent was too gentle to describe this network of tiny ironed blue patches so far above. Then a great milky cloud floated over and hung frothing above me. I lay back and watched it. It looked free, beautiful and suddenly very sleepy.

My bed was initially most uncomfortable. There were sheets, rigid with filthy stains, two odorous blankets and a pillow in a pillow case. I crawled fully-clothed between the blankets and went to sleep.

Not long afterwards I woke, hot, itchy and uncomfortable and lay half awake, listening to harsh, unhappy sounds.

'GATE!'

'GATE!'

Locks, keys, jangling steel.

I opened my eyes.

Prison!

'Nonsense,' I thought, and shut my eyes again.

Padlocks unlocking. One. Two. Tramp, tramp, tramp of boots on concrete.

'PRISON!' my mind shouted.

My door pushed open. The cell was dark and I blinked at the silhouettes of three uniformed men against the fierce sunlight which splashed in from the courtyard.

Prison.

I sat up and swung my legs on to the floor. Mr Darney came in with a tray of food. Mr Proud stood behind him. I wondered who the third man was and discovered later that he was a visiting policeman from Marandellas who had come to have a look at me, just for fun.

Prison.

They left and I went back to sleep again. When I was once again aroused Mrs Darney was at the door with another man in khaki uniform.

A prison chaplain.

Then the minutes flowed slowly, so slowly into hours, the hours through nights into days and soon enough I got round to believing that I was indeed in prison.

CHAPTER NINE

The Only Way Left

KIM EDGE is a husky-voiced, dark-eyed little niece of mine. Her parents, Cynthia and Derrick, work on the ranch with our father. Kim turned five shortly before we were taken to jail and the day after our imprisonment she embarked on the great adventure of graduating from nursery school to 'big' school. Her parents decided not to say anything about the imprisonments as they hoped Kim would assume that we were in London, Salisbury or anywhere else but jail.

Ten days after our imprisonment my mother went across to the Edges, who live about five miles from us, driving the diesel Peugeot my father normally drives. Kimmie was in the bath and she looked up eagerly at my sister.

'There's grandad!' she said.

'No, Kimmie,' said Cyndie. 'I think it's grandma.'

Kimmie studied the water for a few quiet seconds. Then she looked up into Cyndie's face. 'Where's prison?' she asked.

It is difficult to imagine what Kimmie may have gone through in her first days at school, bottling up the knowledge her parents didn't realize she possessed. She is reserved and wise and in many ways an adult. But, having been a pupil at Shabani School myself, I can guess what it was like. We do know that on one occasion a group of older children came up to her and said: 'They've *locked* your grandad up. Next they're going to *string* him up.' It's probable that they didn't know what the phrase 'string him up' meant and that it was borrowed for the occasion from their parents. Kim was greatly relieved to discover that we weren't, as she put it, 'in cages like animals' which she had obviously associated with being strung up.

When we came home she stood and looked at us consideringly, her head tilted to one side, her hands comforting each other. She was anxious and quiet for a long time.

That evening I was bathing her and she was lying on her tummy, her chin cupped in her hands and her tiny body floating in the warm,

110

deep water. Without warning, almost as though she were talking to herself she said: 'I wonder if it's very dark in prison.'

I was filled with an instant, deep longing that I could handle the subject adequately and that between us we might lay dead a few bad memories. I took a deep breath. 'Kimmie, I'll tell you all about it if you want.'

There was a flurry of water and Kim sat up, her arms folded around her knees, watching me intently.

'It isn't dark. In prison there are tiny bedrooms called cells, and in the morning they unlock your cell so you can go out into the sunshine. Then, at night, when they lock you back into your cell they leave the light on for a bit so you can read.'

'Why?' she asked. 'Why did they lock you up?'

'Well,' I said helplessly, 'I suppose they locked me up so that I couldn't run away.'

Kim looked at me disbelievingly for a moment then she gurgled with laughter, lay back and turned over and over in the water, a sleek, shining, amused little girl. The subject was closed. I had told her all she wanted to know. Prison was quite obviously nothing more than a glorious game.

The conditions were not bad at Marandellas. My days fell into an orderly pattern and as I was the only female at that jail, let alone being the only white, I had special treatment. The superintendent's wife looked after me and as it was easier to feed me from their table rather than prepare special meals, I was given excellent food. The Darneys were, on the whole, thoughtful and pleasant. On the third day Mrs Darney arranged for two buckets of hot water to be brought to me each morning, and provided a small tin bath. She had her own household to look after and a small daughter to prepare for school each morning, so while the other prisoners rose with the sun I stayed in bed until eight when my cell was unlocked and tea and hot water were brought to my block. Then I breakfasted, bathed and washed the clothing I had been wearing the day before, taking as long as possible over the process. At about nine I turned to my typewriter which I was, for a time, allowed to have. Sometimes Mrs Darney took me for a walk in the prison area. She was pretty and sensitive and lent me some books and magazines. The worst time was at night when I was padlocked into the small cell. I don't suffer from claustrophobia but it was then that I started wondering whether, in civilized countries, the authorities bothered about the possibility of claustrophobia amongst prisoners and, if so, what they could do about it.

The strangest matters concerned me while I was in prison. For a

111

few weeks I was allowed a radio and one day I heard a choir singing 'I vow to thee my country . . .' At school I had loved that hymn. Now, reminded of the words, I found them chilling.

> *I vow to thee my country, all earthly things above,*
> *Entire and whole and perfect, the service of my love;*
> *The love that asks no question, the love that stands the test,*
> *That lays upon the altar the dearest and the best;*
> *The love that never falters, the love that pays the price,*
> *The love that makes undaunted the final sacrifice.*

But awake or asleep – my nights were full of dreams and nightmares – I was preoccupied with what I could learn of the Pearce Commission and the response to it from the country.

The morning the police had brought me to prison we had bought copies of the *Rhodesia Herald* in Salisbury. I was allowed to take the copy to my cell and that first afternoon, 19 January, I read and re-read the paper, alternately appalled and delighted.

The headlines were shocking. 'One Dead. Two Wounded. 42 Arrests In Gwelo.'

'Throughout the days of violence,' it was reported, 'demonstrators have made their views known with chants of "No, No, No" and with scrawled placards rejecting the terms. A huge crowd that gathered at Monomotapa Township yesterday morning intended marching to the [white] city [centre] to see the [Pearce] commissioners, Mr John Blunden and Mr Mark Patey, but they were stopped by police and police reservists. An Air Force Dakota fitted with loudhailer equipment was used to explain to the crowd that the commission was not sitting . . .'

Inside the paper were the first reports of African response at Pearce Commission meetings. 'ROWDY CROWDS, MASS "NOES". BRITISH BEGIN TESTING.' Noes were being registered in the first parts of the country visited by the commissioners. But those Europeans who were seen appeared to be saying Yes.

At Umtali 'a placard with "Sorry, Mr Smith. It's a big No", echoed the sentiments of an excitable crowd . . .'

'At the Mutasa T.T.L. meeting a large crowd sat quietly on a hill and heard Mr Rawlins explaining the simplified terms, and then their own councillors addressing them. The people then decided that rather than see the commissioners personally, they would give their opinion as a group.

'A drawn-out "No" was followed by excited dancing, clapping and cheering. Mr Rawlins thanked them for making their opinions very clear.'

At another meeting a commissioner, Mr John Harrison, expressed my own fears when he was reported as saying: 'How can sixteen men speak to five million? We will be lucky to see five thousand. It is a question of scratching the right part of the surface.'

I had brought some money to prison and this was kept by Mr Darney for my use. I was told that I could buy newspapers and on my second day in prison repeatedly asked Mrs Darney, the few times I saw her, for one. It was eventually pushed through the warder's peephole and I heard it thud on to the concrete. When I retrieved it I saw that the first four pages had been torn out and that items had been cut from the remaining pages. I read what there was left of the paper, then lay on my bed and thought very carefully for a long time. I was in prison without, not surprisingly, being charged with any crime. The Pearce Commission had started testing opinion. Normal political activities had been promised. And yet at this vital, exciting time of our history I was not going to be allowed to know what was happening outside my own solitary confinement, let alone participate. By the time Mrs Darney came in with my afternoon cup of tea I had written a letter to her husband which I gave her. The letter stated very clearly and briefly that I would not be eating anything at all until I was allowed to see uncensored newspapers, including a new copy of the mutilated paper I had just received.

That night Mr Darney accompanied his wife when she brought my dinner. They looked at my untouched tea and then Darney said he had telephoned 'the powers that be' and that I would be allowed to receive uncensored copies of the *Rhodesia Herald*. He did not have another copy of that day's paper, but would get me one the following morning. I thanked him and ate my dinner.

This was the first indication I had that the prison authorities were almost as completely uninformed as I was about the conditions detainees should, according to Rhodesian 'law', be held under. There is no doubt that had I not protested immediately and decisively, in the only way open to me I could think of, I would never have received uncensored papers while I was in jail. My father, in prison, received a copy of the *Sunday Times* from which every item of Rhodesian news had been cut except excerpts on the front page from my diary which had somehow escaped the authorities' attention. The fact that people would know from the diary that we had only been concerned with the most normal of political activities cheered him greatly.

On 20 January, the *Rhodesia Herald* reported the first protests against our imprisonments from the House of Commons, New Zealand and the World Council of Churches. The *Herald* itself said:

The Rhodesian Government must have expected that the detentions would be thus seized on in attempts to wreck the settlement and put the blame on Salisbury. Therefore we assume it did not act lightly . . . To us it seems that if the acceptability test as now being conducted is wrecked, it ought to be crystal clear that the reason is African violence and African defiance of the Commission's procedures – not the consequential actions, even if they can be shown to be misguided, of the Rhodesian Government.

There was no suggestion that we should be charged with a crime and brought to court. Far from attempting to defend the right of free speech and normal political activity while the commission was in the country, the *Herald* in effect defended the detentions and the actions of the Rhodesian regime and made no attempt to suggest how anyone in our position could prove the actions of the regime 'misguided'. And anyway, the regime was going to do its utmost to show that it was not misguided. After the storm of protests about the detentions hit home in Salisbury, the *Rand Daily Mail* (Johannesburg) headlined a report on 17 February: 'CAMPAIGN IN MAKING TO SMEAR TODD?'

'The Rhodesian Government,' the report read, 'is believed to be preparing a smear campaign against Mr Garfield Todd, the former Rhodesian Prime Minister, who is being detained without trial in Gatooma jail.'

'The Foreign Affairs Ministry is preparing a document on Mr Todd for publication overseas. The document will quote incidents in Mr Todd's life and statements he made over 20 years ago . . .'

Public money was being spent by a government ministry to defame a man they dared not bring to court in their own country for lack of evidence of any crime.

A few days after my imprisonment Mrs Darney told me that the following morning two members of the Pearce Commission would be coming to see me. 'Lord Pearce himself and Sir Glyn Jones.'

I turned to my typewriter in a mixture of joy and despair. The 40,000 words of my 'so-called diary', as the Director of Prisons, Mr Frank Patch, has referred to it, have been confiscated by the prison authorities. But I remember imploring myself on paper to set out the case against the proposals as cogently as possible; to remember all the names of people I knew to be detained or restricted so that the commission would know of them and visit them; to do what I could for all of us. I hardly slept that night, going over and over in my mind all the things that must be said.

Not surprisingly, after I had seen the commission members, I discovered that I had left practically everything unsaid. The morning of the visit Mrs Darney brought me a mirror so that I could see what I looked like. (Conditions improved dramatically after the visit of the Pearce Commission.) I had already tried to make myself as presentable as possible, inspecting myself in the dull chrome handle of my radio which I had recently been allowed. The mirror was of no comfort whatsoever as there was nothing I could do to improve my rather crumpled appearance. But I was grateful to have it. Soon I was called and led into the superintendent's office to meet the commissioners.

Lord Pearce was not there. But as I recognized the man standing opposite me, so he put out his hand and, smiling, introduced himself, 'Harlech.'

Then I shook hands with Sir Glyn Jones. Mr Darney was in the office and just when I was starting to worry about whether he would have to supervise the interview, Sir Glyn made it very clear that Darney could leave. Turning away from Mr Darney he gestured to the grand superintendent's chair behind the desk and said: 'I think you should chair this meeting, Judy.' At that moment a silver tray of tea and sandwiches was brought in and put on the desk. 'You be mother, Judy,' Mr Darney said with a rather heavy handed, probably embarrassed familiarity, and left. We sat down, Sir Glyn on my left and Lord Harlech on my right. I poured the tea and found to my horror that I was shaking so badly I could hardly hold the cups. I wasn't nervous, but all my internal griefs and fears seemed to have transferred themselves visibly to my hands.

Sir Glyn was brisk and dry and informed me almost immediately that he had been to see my father. I was very grateful. He described my father's cell and said that he, Sir Glyn, had inhabited many a worse place when he had been on tour in his colonial service days. I restrained the impulse to say: 'But at any time you could have got up and walked out.' Lord Harlech leant quietly across the table with blue, sympathetic eyes. At this time I was hoping that the commission would be forced by recent events to abandon their test of acceptability, believing that this would mean the abandonment of any proposed settlement with 'Rhodesia' which, in reality, meant the Rhodesian Front. Lord Harlech disagreed. He was sure, he said, that the Pearce Commission should continue its task because he believed that its eventual report would be of the utmost value to any British government. For instance, he said, the British Government would then know that any settlement arrived at without participation by Africans would be unacceptable to Africans.

He spoke of our detentions and I asked what reasons had been given to Lord Pearce for them. None, he said. Sir Glyn then remarked that the detentions made him feel very uncomfortable about the detentions he had authorized when he had been a governor in his Colonial Office days. I thought of all the people who, when it was announced that Sir Glyn was to be part of the commission, had said: 'Well, *he's* all right. You don't have to doubt *his* impartiality and integrity,' but somehow I didn't think that any consolations from me were necessary.

Then Lord Harlech hinted that the commission had protested as strongly as possible against the detentions and that the only protest left to them would be to pack up and go home. He thought that line of action would be unwise. I silently disagreed with him at the time but, in retrospect, I know that he was correct.

Sir Glyn said that the commissioners would be going once more to see my father, but that none of them would be able to come back and see me. They had only managed to get permission to visit me on this occasion by stating that they wished to hear my views on the proposals for a settlement. Then he asked for some advice. They were going to find it difficult to test African urban opinion, he said. Had I any suggestions on how this could be done? I thought swiftly but came up with only two immediate ideas.

The first was in relation to the hostels, great unhappy blocks of dormitories which exist for men living without their families in the African townships which serve the white cities. I supposed that not all the occupants could be seen, and suggested that the commission ask for a specific number of delegates from each block to see them. Then I thought it might be possible for the commission to request the use of churches in the townships for public meetings. Lord Harlech intimated that the authorities might not consider the churches a neutral meeting ground, and laughed. He laughed too when we spoke of a broadcast that Mr Ian Smith had recently made in which he had said that if the proposals were rejected this would mean that Africans preferred living under the 1969, Rhodesian Front, republican constitution. In fact we all laughed – as did most of the country, I should imagine, when they heard Mr Smith's broadcast the previous Friday night, 21 January.

> ... *we have consistently made it clear to the British that while we agreed to their request to hold such a test* [of the acceptability of the proposals], *in no way were we prepared to relinquish our responsibility for maintaining law and order. This they accepted. We warned the British of our concern over the release of detainees and, indeed, warned the Pearce Commission of the trouble which would occur under certain conditions.*

As is now abundantly clear to all, our predictions were correct. Government has already taken firm action to deal with the problem, and this will be repeated whenever the need arises.

In case of doubt, let me warn that anyone trying to undermine law and order will come off second best, and will have to accept the consequences . . . Those responsible for all this barbaric destruction have, ironically, played right into our hands. What greater proof could anyone have of their lack of maturity, lack of civilization, their inability to make any constructive contribution?

. . . It is my belief that the majority of our Africans disagree with the hooligan element which we have witnessed recently. I hope they will come forward in a quiet and dignified manner and present the commission with their sincerely held views. Indeed, I hope our European population will do likewise, and not let their views go by default.

Once again, let me reaffirm Government's support for the proposals, and in so doing commend them to all Rhodesians. Having said that, let me make it clear, particularly to our African people, what the consequences would be should the proposals be rejected.

As you are all aware, we accepted these proposals as part of a package deal, in which we made certain concessions in our present Constitution, in return for recognition of our independence and the removal of sanctions.

There can be no doubt in anybody's mind that we in the Rhodesian Front prefer our present Constitution with its very high standards. If, therefore, the proposals are rejected, I and my party will be perfectly happy for the present Constitution to remain, and if the Africans reject this offer, if their answer to the Pearce Commission is 'No' then this is a clear indication of their preference for our present 1969 Constitution.

If they do this sincerely and honestly, of their own free will, then this will prove to be a most pleasant surprise – indeed, a great day in our history. It is this which would be our 'best first prize', to which I referred in my New Year message.

But let me reiterate: In order to arrive at this conclusion, the Africans must say 'No'.

In spite of what I have just said, let us hope that the answer is 'Yes'.

It is our carefully considered opinion that we can make the concessions contained in these proposals, and at the same time maintain those standards necessary to ensure that our Government is retained in civilized hands. We have made this offer in complete sincerity, and we stand by it – in this I believe I speak on behalf of the vast

117

majority of Europeans in Rhodesia. Let me repeat to the African people that it is our intention to fulfil this agreement – if it is accepted – in both the letter and the spirit.

. . . Let me say to the broad mass of our decent African people, that it would be tragic if history recorded that they were so bemused, so susceptible to intimidation, that they rejected an offer which is obviously so much to their advantage. An offer to advance the position of the African in every way – politically, socially, economically.

If the present generation of Africans are so stupid as to reject this offer of advancement for their people, they will bear the curses of their children for ever. However, I do not believe that we should be too pessimistic.

Despite the categorical assurances by both Sir Alec Douglas-Home and myself, that there will be no further negotiations, some people are still misleading the Africans, by saying that if they reject these terms, better ones will be offered.

Such advice is not only mischievous, but is clearly aimed at deceiving African opinion.

Then I spoke to the commissioners about the broadcasting facilities made available to them and said that when the first broadcasts had been made all the people I was in contact with were very excited by the Pearce Commission's call-sign, and the initial messages which had obviously been prepared and taped in London. But now their call-sign had been cut down and some of their broadcasts were being made by Rhodesia Broadcasting Service personnel. In particular, I said, it was unfortunate that such people as Leslie Sullivan, a very popular broadcaster amongst the whites, was being used. His early morning jokes often had a racial flavour. ('What do you call a terrorist financed by Rowntrees Trust? A Chocolate Soldier. Ha ha ha ha.') What would Africans think, hearing him broadcasting for the Pearce Commission?

Lord Harlech made a note and said he would look into it, explaining that the call-sign had been abbreviated as there simply wasn't enough time to get across the messages of where the commission could be seen and when.

They soon left and drove off in their Mercedes with the Union Jack flying in front of them. I had never been more glad to see the Union Jack than when I was being escorted past their car into the office. Despite the combined and perhaps unwitting efforts of successive British governments, the Union Jack is still an emblem of wavering hope for many people in Rhodesia.

Mr Darney was very proud of being visited by Sir Glyn and Lord Harlech. He asked them to sign his special visitors' book and was disappointed when they declined to add a comment after their signatures. When I next saw him I asked what he had thought of the commissioners. He pondered for a moment and then said: 'I wanted to show them the quickest way to the nearest barber.'

Every week a magistrate visits Marandellas Prison to see if the prisoners have any complaints. How they get to see him I never discovered, and during my three weeks at Chikurubi Prison I never saw a magistrate. Perhaps I was lucky enough to see the Marandellas magistrate for the simple reason that he came at a set time every week which coincided with my mother's weekly permitted visit. The visits took place in Mr Darney's office where he could censor our conversation and interrupt us each time he thought we were broaching a forbidden subject, such as the news my mother had for me that the Prime Minister of New Zealand was protesting about our continued detentions.

When the magistrate, a nice looking young man called Mr Lake, stepped round the superintendent's door on the first occasion, he seemed extremely harassed and gave the impression that he just might, if hard-pressed, find ten seconds to spare for me out of his worrying life. 'Any complaints?' he asked.

'Yes,' I said, with great sincerity. 'I don't like being illegally imprisoned without charge or trial.'

He threw me a quick, exasperated look. '*Apart* from that!' he said.

On the last occasion I saw him he was carrying, with some embarrassment, a bowl of carnations, ferns and chrysanthemums. They were from mutual friends whom I hadn't seen since 1964. I nearly wept. Of all the friends I had had at Rhodesian schools and at the Rhodesian University, they were the only two to make contact with me. They must have explored all the possible avenues of contact and discovered that I wasn't allowed to receive letters or telegrams. Because the flowers were brought by the magistrate I was allowed to have them in my cell. I will never forget what they looked like.

Our imprisonments would not have been as bad as they were if we had known we were to be jailed for only five weeks. But as far as we knew it could have been for five months, five years, or for ever. Some detainees in Rhodesia have been held in jails for eight years. One has been held for thirteen years – no charge, no trial. There is no doubt that we would still be in prison had it not been for the protests of a few governments and hundreds of individuals throughout the world. On countless occasions over the past few years I have despaired of the possibility of any individual being able to do anything to alter any situation. I no longer despair. Our release from jail was due to the effort of individuals who exerted pressure on the New Zealand and British governments, and on the Smith regime, plus the coverage given to the situation by journalists from all over the world. When we were released we received many letters from politicians, journalists, bishops, students, ordinary people – very special people indeed – from all over the world.

'Perhaps you might like to know about me,' one wrote. 'I have a cat and a dog and I live over a small shop in a back street of London. But it is not only because I am lonely that I care about you. I have written to Mr Smith, demanding your release. I did not tell him that I have only a cat and a dog and one room. I tried to give him the impression that I was as important as anyone else and that he must listen to me and set you free. I have always cared about justice, and even though I am now old and have never achieved anything, I still care. I still try.'

One of my greatest sources of delight in the lonely days at Marandellas was a fellow-prisoner in a neighbouring block. Every evening when the convicts – 'bandits', they are termed by the prison staff – returned from working on the prison farm, this prisoner would start singing in his full, rich, sad voice. His song never varied.

> *'I'm leeeeea-ving,*
> *On a jet plane.*
> *Don't know*
> *When I'll be back again . . .'*

Sometimes I whistled back, but the warders and their prisoners never attempted to communicate. On the occasions I was taken out of my block and walked past the prisoners who crouched outside the superintendent's office, they all lowered their eyes. The warders would never look at me. Only one, when he had the chance, would murmur 'Good morning Madam', as both Mrs Darney and I walked past. Then, if she was ahead of me and couldn't see, he would flash me a swift, secret smile.

In the evenings and early mornings I stood on my bed and watched the other prisoners. The grill in my window consisted of steel mesh, glass, steel mesh the other side and beyond that another barbed wire fence which separated my block from the others. I was obviously in the Marandellas equivalent of maximum security. I wondered who the last prisoner in my cell had been when I discovered his half-smoked, obviously precious cigarette hidden in the grill. It was a mixture of grass (of the field) and tobacco, rolled in newspaper.

He obviously hadn't had the chance of finishing it.

Every morning at sunrise the prisoners assembled in rows of sitting men while their work was ordered for the next day. They were housed in airy dormitories, long, barred but openable windows on each side of the buildings, and when they were not working they lay under trees in the long green grass. After they were locked in at 5 p.m. the evenings throbbed with their singing. There was such harmony, such pathos, such grandeur in the singing.

They could not see me watching them and sometimes I felt that I had no right to be doing so. But I was lonely, and watching other people was next best to being with them. One shining evening a young man who looked rather like Mohammed Ali stood opposite my cell shaking out the thick mat and two blankets of which their bedding consisted. ('Every prisoner in Rhodesia has a bed,' Ian Smith has informed David Frost in public. The interview was not screened in Rhodesia, or watching prison authorities might have found cause to doubt the veracity of their leader.) Suddenly a fellow-prisoner darted up to him with a letter. He looked round to make sure no warders were watching, dropped the blankets and then slowly and delightedly consumed the letter. I could see his face clearly. He was smiling and reading the words with his lips. When he was finished he glanced anxiously round again, stuffed the letter into his prison shorts and once more shook his blankets – with such rapidity that the three movements blended into one. I had some idea then of what letters from Amnesty International must mean to so many hundreds of prisoners, if they are allowed to receive them.

I spent the days writing and reading. I know now that I was allowed a typewriter and paper so that what I wrote could eventually be seen by the authorities – ever eager and so far disappointed in their quest for material to use against us. What I wrote may have been of interest to them, but was obviously of no pleasure since they have confiscated it. And all through this time I was driven by the thought: 'What can I do?'

I pondered this problem on paper, looking at it from both my point of view and that of the authorities. Eventually I reached the conclusion that the Rhodesian Front regime would wish me to be a quiet, tractable prisoner whom they could release in their own good time. The Pearce Commission had seen me and had assured me that they had done what they could for the new detainees, Josiah and Ruth Chinamano,* my father, myself, and two other men. The *Rhodesia Herald* had reported that Mr Philip Mansfield, head of the

* The Chinamanos, prominent African leaders, were detained with Mr Nkomo in 1964, released in 1969 and redetained in January 1972.

Rhodesia Department in the Foreign and Commonwealth Office had been sent to Rhodesia by Sir Alec Douglas-Home after the imprisonments. If he had attempted to do anything for us, he had obviously failed.

So, after days and nights of thought I reached the conclusion that if we were to be released from prison, it would depend more than anything else on ourselves. I could not contact my father, seek his approval or involve him in any planned action of mine, so any action would have to be carried out on an individual basis. I could not implicate any other person in what I planned to do.

The only action I could think of which would be possible was that of going on a hunger-strike. For days I worked on a letter to the authorities, planning how it might be possible to smuggle a copy out to friends so that they would know what was happening. Against great odds I managed to do this, and my hunger-strike started two and a half weeks after we were imprisoned.

The letter was addressed to the prison superintendent, Mr Darney.

Dear Mr Darney,

Would you please inform those responsible for my illegal detention that I am going on a hunger-strike from Saturday, February 5th. This hunger-strike will continue until I am released from prison. I am no longer able to tolerate without protest the vindictive reaction of the Smith regime to those of us who reject the settlement proposals.

The letter went on to recall that immunity had been promised to any witnesses presenting evidence to the Pearce Commission.

This immunity has been negated by the imprisonments that have taken place while the Pearce Commission is yet with us. It has been further negated by the fact that the police have seized from me, and other people, letters and petitions to the Pearce Commission.

In seizing these documents the Special Branch blatantly demonstrated their contempt for the Commission and their indifference to the assurances in the White Paper. Their action also showed that it is not possible for the Pearce Commission to safeguard the confidentiality of evidence prepared for them . . .

The Commission assures us that we have as much right to say NO as we have to say YES. The statements of Sir Alec Douglas-Home and the actions of the Rhodesian authorities do not confirm these assurances.

The Rhodesian authorities may believe they can force us to accept the settlement proposals by shooting, beating, imprisoning or threatening those who may wish to say 'No'. They are wrong.

The letter concluded by saying that in these circumstances I would remain on hunger-strike until I was released from prison 'whatever physical action may be taken against me', I added optimistically.

'This, sadly, is the only way left to register my non-recognition of the illegal, racist Smith regime, my rejection of the racist settlement proposals, my reaffirmation that I consider myself and my fellow-citizens the responsibility of Her Majesty's Government.'

On Friday night when Mrs Darney came in to collect my dinner tray, the letter to her husband was amongst the dishes. I didn't speak to her about it. At that moment I felt, more than anything else, embarrassed, although I was also frightened about what might happen to me. Unless one is a very disciplined person, which I am not, even a short time of solitary confinement tends to make one doubtful about the wisdom of one's actions. That night I fervently hoped my copy of the letter to Mr Darney would reach my friends because now the die was cast. Mr Darney would have my letter in his possession and I was honour-bound to go ahead, whether anyone outside the prison knew or not. I did not know, until after the hunger-strike was ended, that my message had been safely received.

I lay that night in a fever of doubt, humiliation and helplessness. When my luminous watch registered 11.30 I got up in the darkness and felt amongst my possessions. Feeling unutterably bloated and miserable I assiduously ate two apples and some biltong. That took me through to midnight when I stopped eating. Eventually I slept.

I woke at dawn and thought how likely it was that even my friends would think I was being stupid and dramatic. They certainly would have, had they seen my diary. For a week it had agonized about the possibility that even if it had been known outside that I was on hunger-strike the Rhodesian and British authorities might not be in the least concerned, and I might die.

In a sudden rush of memory and nostalgia I wanted to be able to greet once more all the friends I had ever had. I wanted to do crazy, impossible things like freeing my friends and their friends from the detention camps and prison cells of Rhodesia, and talking to the Monday Club. I wanted to walk with Ian Smith through the Belingwe area, and say to him: 'Look. This is how things really are.' I didn't even want to consider the thought of dying, but it was a possibility that had to be faced before I started refusing to eat.

I drifted back to sleep and then woke with the usual, deafening sounds of padlocks being unfastened.

Mrs Darney brought in a big breakfast. This was significant. I had, some time before, managed to convince her that I wanted only a cup of tea or coffee in the morning. She greeted me as though everything was normal, but put the tray on the table without looking at me. I realized that she was either as embarrassed as I was, or angry.

'Mrs Darney,' I said. 'Did you read my letter?'

'Yes.'

'I do want you to know that it's nothing personal . . .'

She came in and out that day delivering trays of food and collecting them again. We exchanged very few words, but those were as normal as possible. I was sorry that she found it so difficult to look at me, but I realize now that I probably did great harm to the Darneys in the eyes of the Director of Prisons, Mr Patch. She knew then, which I did not, that if anyone was damaged in the process of this hunger-strike it might be me, but it would certainly also be the Darneys. The authorities were furious that I had managed to smuggle a letter out of prison.

On Sunday Mrs Darney brought me roast pork, apple sauce, fresh vegetables and steamy, delicious roast potatoes. I know they were delicious because there was a tiny one, lurking under the gravy, that I thought wouldn't be missed, so I ate it. As a second course there was lemon-meringue pie shrouded with thick cream. I put the tray outside my door which I then closed. I was beginning to feel very hungry.

That night Mr Darney and the wife of a new prison officer Mr Isles brought my dinner to me.

Mrs Isles came into my cell behind Mr Darney and said not a word. Mr Darney was red-faced and gruff. 'So you haven't eaten anything again today?'

'No, Mr Darney. But it's nothing to do with the prison staff here. Did you pass my letter on to the authorities?'

'Yes. They've got it.' He picked up the tray and went out. As they left I said goodnight.

'Goodnight love,' said Mr Darney and Mrs Isles in a surprised, antagonistic little voice echoed the 'goodnight'. She must have thought that if the boss could say goodnight then she must, however much she regretted having to do so.

The following morning, Monday, Mr and Mrs Isles brought me breakfast. It was a thoughtful breakfast in that they had wrapped the two boiled eggs in foil paper to keep them warm which I thought was a very kind thing to do when they knew their prisoner would not eat.

Mr Isles looked quite reasonable, but Mrs Isles was a different matter. She was an example of the typical, stylized, young, white, attractive Rhodesian woman, to which, of course, there are many exceptions. She stood with her arm round her husband in the court-yard while they gave me time to refuse to eat the food. Then she sent him away and supervised the prisoners who brought in two pails of hot water for me.

After I had heard the outside door clanging shut behind everyone I went out into the courtyard and found, to my surprise, that Mrs Isles was still standing there. 'What are you waiting for?' I enquired.

With the ease of a switch being flicked on the wall she transformed herself from standing lovingly with her husband to dealing with a loathsome prisoner. 'For you to have your bath!' she snapped.

'Oh. Well Mrs Darney usually leaves me when the water is brought in . . .'

'She might! I don't!'

I bathed as rapidly as possible while she stood sullenly in the yard. It was a relief to see her go.

Later that morning Mrs Darney came back and took me for a walk. She didn't mention the hunger-strike but, as we neared the superintendent's office she said hastily and clumsily: 'Are you deter-mined to keep on in this way?'

'Can you think of anything else I can do?'

She didn't reply, and walked me into her husband's office. I realized then that she had been asked to take me for the walk and had only managed to raise the subject she was meant to be dealing with at the very end. So she stood with me before Mr Darney and obliquely reported failure.

'I see,' said Mr Darney, looking most uncomfortable. 'Well.'

He dispatched Mr Proud and Mr Isles to accompany me back to my cell with Mrs Darney. They removed my typewriter, paper, the precious 40,000 words I had written since my imprisonment, the limited correspondence I had been allowed to have and most of my books. They searched for any food and took all newspapers and my radio. I was to be allowed no communications of any kind until the hunger-strike was ended, and my mother had been informed that she could no longer visit me.

That night, Monday, was the worst time I went through. I was fortunate in that they had left my cigarettes but I was smoking little by that time, and told myself that I wouldn't have minded had they taken the cigarettes too. But I was glad they hadn't.

I lay awake most of that night. My body sent electric impulses through every limb, begging for food. I reminded myself that the percentage of people in our world who could get food when they were hungry was not great. The thought didn't comfort my body. It was a bad, long night.

The following morning Mrs Darney brought coffee, toast, bacon and egg. 'No one,' she said rather strangely, 'will think the worse of you if you start eating.'

When she left I carried the tray through to the washroom, as far away from me as I could get it. I was feeling very hungry indeed. Then I dressed, filled my body with water and lay in the sunshine which fell through the tiny bars of mesh onto the yard. My body had stopped throbbing and I was feeling warm and much better when the gates, the padlocks, the steel doors started clanging open again. Mrs Darney.

'You are wanted at the office?'

'By whom?'

'You'll see when you get there.' I looked down at myself, my tattered shorts and shirt. 'Should I change?'

That was her last gesture of friendship. 'If you want,' she said, and allowed me to do so.

We went to the office.

'What are they here for?' I asked myself in an internal panic. 'Force feeding? What does force feeding mean?' There were three new prison staff in the office, two female and one male.

I was so scared that I sank, uninvited, into the chair opposite Mr Darney's desk. I couldn't stand, but tried to disguise the fact.

'Judy,' said Mr Darney. 'They have come to take you away. You are leaving.' He looked at me over his desk, but I couldn't manage a comment. 'I don't know where you are going.'

'Liar!' I thought, and felt even more terrified. The new prison officers moved closer to the desk and swam in my eyes.

The man was called Mr Hazlehurst. He was a thick-set man in khaki uniform and a peaked cap. One of the wardresses was a pretty, short-haired girl who, when the opportunity presented itself, started talking about Colorado and the mountains. She was a Rhodesian I discovered but had travelled and hadn't yet recovered from the experience. Then I looked at the other wardress and while I record my apprehensions I must also state that in the short time I was with her she didn't vindicate them. She was large, tall and muscular and she had a scar on her cheek.

'Oh no!' I thought, 'what are they going to do with me?'

'I suppose I had better pack,' I said to Mr Darney, doing my best to appear nonchalant.

'It's being done for you,' he said. Now I understand why the last prisoner in my cell had come to leave his cigarette behind. I sat in the office and everyone present chatted to each other and tried to ignore me. I came to the conclusion that if Mr Hazlehurst wasn't an idiot he certainly had an unfortunately idiotic presence. Practically every statement Mr Darney made was greeted with a large, nicotine-stained chuckle. I knew by now that Mr Darney was originally Welsh, and that his wife had been born in Liverpool. Perhaps, if they hadn't come to Rhodesia, they wouldn't have become racists. But one of the last remarks I heard Mr Darney making was in relation to an African warder who walked past the office on his way off duty.

'That's one of your smart monkeys for you,' Mr Darney told Hazlehurst. 'Sometimes he wears spectacles. Sometimes he doesn't. And I've told him – MAKE UP YOUR MIND! He drives me crazy!' I was tempted to observe that when Mr Darney read anything he wore spectacles, but otherwise he didn't. But I refrained. Mr Hazlehurst was drowning the office with his appreciative laughter at the expense of the man walking past.

My belongings were brought in with the exception of my diary which was already in the possession of the Director of Prisons. The Darneys didn't respond when I thanked them for their various kindnesses, expressing the polite but not very fervent hope that we might meet again but in normal circumstances. It was clear that they did not want to appear to be friendly in the presence of other whites. And anyway they probably didn't have many friendly feelings left.

I was so apprehensive on that journey from Marandellas, not knowing where I was being taken, or for what, and I attempted to conceal my fear by concentrating my being in every passing tree I could isolate, every cloud on the horizon ahead.

Just before we reached Salisbury we turned off along a subsidiary road. 'Salisbury Prison,' I thought and remembered released friends in England telling me of the condemned men who sing hymns in the Salisbury death-cells. But I was taken to Chikurubi Prison Farm, on the outskirts of Salisbury, where the three warders left me. I was glad to see that trio go.

Miss Joan Wright, the officer in charge, female section, checked me into the prison. My watch was taken from me as were all my other belongings. Later that afternoon I was permitted to collect a few clothes and books. I never suspected that I would not be allowed writing materials again, hunger-strike or no hunger-strike, but by some miraculous chance I happened to smuggle a biro pen into my cell in my clothing.

Then Miss Wright's deputy, Miss Wells, took me down to the clinic which is run at Chikurubi by a white nursing sister. At Miss Wright's request I was offered aspirin. I'm not sure why but anyway I declined the offer. Then I was weighed and noticed that I had lost over a stone since my imprisonment. The authorities were unaware of this as I hadn't initially been weighed. The sister took down some particulars on a medical form, Miss Wells watching her. Then without looking up she asked how I felt.

'Fine.'

'Are you eating regularly?'

I was startled.

'Didn't you know? I'm on a hunger-strike.'

'Why?'

'Because I have been imprisoned without charge. Because I am not being brought to court. Because I am not guilty of any crime.' The words, on paper, look rather dramatic. The scene itself was very quiet.

'Only your conscience can tell you whether you're innocent,' the sister said.

'It does,' I assured her, and then I was taken to my new cell.

As yet no-one had told me what their names were. It was Judy this and Judy that and just Yes or No from me. On the way to the cells I asked Miss Wells what her name was. She reacted so sharply that I jumped.

'Matron Wells to you,' she barked, looking just as fierce as the Alsatian dogs with which she and Miss Wright were always surrounded.

That afternoon a series of African wardresses took turns to guard me. They were not allowed to talk to me, but I enjoyed their presence.

'What is your sentence?' one of them eventually murmured.

'No sentence,' I murmured back, 'I'm a detainee.'

The magazine she was reading slipped out of her hands and as she was recovering it she asked softly:

'Are you for us?'

'Yes,' I said, rather tentatively. I guessed that by 'us' she meant Africans in general, but wasn't sure.

'What's your name?'

'Judy Todd.'

'Judy! Are you Judy?'

'Yes.'

She looked intently at her magazine. 'Now I know why we are not allowed to speak to you,' she said. 'We can only listen to you when you ask us for something.'

Later that day Miss Wright came and shooed the wardresses away. I had refused lunch which looked eminently refusable anyway, and Miss Wright asked what I thought the poor white prisoner who had to cook it would feel like. I considered the question. 'Indifferent,' I replied.

No morning and afternoon cups of tea were offered to me as they had been at Marandellas. I was not the only white female around any more and I had to fit in with the established pattern of meals. In the early morning there was a cup of tea, followed later by a slice of bread, sometimes with jam, and sometimes a cold, soft-boiled egg. Lunch was the only real meal of the day and consisted of a plate of meat and vegetables and a cup of tea. Then the last food of the day was a cup of tea and two slices of bread sometimes with jam. It was really quite easy to refuse the food. My shrinking stomach was learning to content itself with water.

At 5 p.m. I was locked into my cell for the night. The reason I didn't sleep very well that night was not basically hunger but the dread which bubbled physically and ceaselessly just below my ribs.

Why have they brought me here? What are they going to do to me?

CHAPTER TEN

Force Feeding

I OPENED my eyes as once again a key grated harshly in the lock. The lights flared on, the door swung open and Miss Wright walked in. 'Uppies time!' she called.

I lay still, momentarily stunned by the greeting which was, to me, unique. Then I managed a conservative and unimaginative 'good-morning' and crawled out of bed as Miss Wright informed me that it was nearly six o'clock and that I should have been up and dressed and had my cell tidied before the door was unlocked. I wondered aloud how I would be able to wake in time each morning as my watch had been taken away from me and the cell was still dark. Miss Wright was remote but not unpleasant. She said that in future she would get the wardresses on night duty to waken me, then left. The wardresses on night duty had, in fact, been waking me thoughout the night, and they continued doing so until the hunger-strike was over. They had orders to keep checking on me and one of them, a young not very bright girl, would often keep the light on until I was properly awake and prepared to help her pass a few minutes by chatting about how dark the night was, how many mosquitoes there were, how soon the morning would come and other related subjects.

I dressed and made my bed. Then I looked round the cell and wondered what there could possibly be to tidy. I was wearing jeans and a shirt and the two dresses I had with me were hooked on one of the bars which stood guard on the windows. Chikurubi is a very modern prison and only the punishment cells are barred. The few books in my cell stood in a humble pile by the bed which was the only piece of furniture apart from a grubby steel locker, and a small bag containing toiletries and underclothes sat tidily by itself in a corner. The cell could have done with a sweeping but there was no broom. The only thing I fervently wished it was possible to clean out were the mosquitoes. Literally hundreds of them covered the ceiling in a delicate, grey cloud. During the night they had caused me so much misery that eventually I took the pillow-case off my pillow and put it over my head. A few days later I was given a mosquito net – after the force feeding. Conditions improved when I was once more 'co-operating', as they put it.

My door was now unlocked so I went outside and surveyed my new quarters.

Chikurubi is infinitely preferable to Marandellas Prison. So it should be, according to Rhodesian philosophy, as Marandellas Prison is for male Africans whereas my new quarters were specifically designed for female whites.

My cell was brand new and painted turquoise. Whoever had planned the colour scheme had displayed an enthusiasm which compensated for a lack of harmony. The steel door was mustard yellow and the door frame an orange-pink. There were a number of cells in the block but of course, as I had to be isolated, these remained empty. The block formed three sides of a rectangle, the fourth side being a wall with a gate through which you could see. Next to my cell was the washroom with a full-size bath, hot and cold water, a shower and a modern flush lavatory. On the other side of me was the maximum punishment cell which was just another cell without windows but instead a tiny grilled air-vent and a heavy wooden door with a generous supply of bars and padlocks on the warders' side. It wasn't anything like as grim as cell No. 12 at Marandellas. Best of all was the beginnings of a small garden within the rectangle. Five little trees had been planted and the earth was lush with long silky weeds. The sky stretched unfettered above the block and I could see the tops of gum-trees in the distance and fresh white clouds breathing softly in the sky.

The side of the rectangle facing my cell was a kitchen block which formed a common arm with another rectangle of cells on the other side. Here the white female prisoners took it in turn to cook for their fellow-white and 'coloured' (mixed-race) prisoners. During the day they could see me through the kitchen windows but we tried not to look at each other. What they had been told about me I hate to imagine but they had certainly got the message loud and clear that they were not to have contact with me. Now and again sitting outside reading I would feel someone's eyes on me and looking up would see some white woman's eyes falling. But one day one of them smiled at me.

My breakfast came at eight, two hours after my cell was unlocked, and consisted of tea and a bowl of porridge. I was extremely hungry and thought longingly of all the choice bits and pieces of food I had left on my plate in various London restaurants. When the African wardresses came later to collect the utensils they were shocked to see that I hadn't eaten.

'Are you unhappy?' one of them asked. Once again I explained that I was on a hunger-strike, and why. She was appalled. 'But you are our friend. What if you get sick? What if they let you die?' Thus started the hardest pressure of all to resist. Some of the wardresses were downright disapproving. Others seemed genuinely upset. 'Look, I have carried your food in my own hands. Won't you eat it for me?' Only one was of help. 'They (meaning the whites) are getting very worried,' she told me and there was a rich satisfaction in her voice.

Miss Wright and Miss Wells became progressively more pleasant. I am sure they were concerned about the welfare of those in their charge, but, like every arm of the Rhodesian civil service, their prison service was now corrupted with political pressure and riddled with political influence. They were both slight, short-haired women in their early forties. Miss Wright was the gentler of the two and although Miss Wells was initially harsh in the way she spoke to me, and perpetually scowling, she soon started smiling, although she rationed her smiles carefully. She had beautiful blue eyes which were normally cloaked by her scowl, but when she smiled they lit up and transformed her face. I went out of my way to try to make her smile because the effect was so startling and so attractive. One morning she came into my cell and, unconsciously wringing her hands and scowling just as fiercely as she could, she made a short, very muddled speech. In essence she said that if I only learnt to keep my mouth shut and stopped making people feel angry with me, then I wouldn't bring all this suffering on myself. I was deeply moved, but could feel that if I said anything appreciative, I would increase her embarrassment. She looked as though she might bite me if I did. So I listened in silence, and will not forget the anguished frowning muddle of her dawning comprehension that all was not well in the state of Rhodesia today.

On Wednesday afternoon, the fifth day without food, the sister came to my cell with a gaunt, elderly man dressed in a safari-suit – an attractive matching combination of light-weight shirt and shorts or trousers which white men and some Africans wear in Rhodesia. They are known, by Africans, as the Rhodesian Front uniform.

The man introduced himself as Dr Baker Jones. I hope and believe that during most of that period I managed to keep a tight rein on all my internal fears, and that they did not show in my face. But when I heard his name I relapsed into the same kind of inward panic I had felt when I was being taken from Marandellas to a destination unknown.

In November 1970, an inquest was held on a detainee and prominent African leader, Leopold Takawira, who had died in prison. It was found that his death was due to undiagnosed diabetes. The doctor responsible for him was Dr Baker Jones.

I had kept the press clippings of that inquest and while little was reported, what was published was horrifying. Baker Jones had said amongst other things that he supposed that Takawira had substituted urine samples from other prisoners for his own as, Baker Jones alleged, Africans did not like giving substances from their bodies into the hands of an enemy. He further said that many detainees pretended to be sick so that they could be sent to hospital, where, he alleged, they were able to pass uncensored messages to each other. Fellow-detainees of Mr Takawira's were called to give evidence. Their names were not published because in Rhodesia, as in South Africa, detainees are relegated to the limbo of non-persons and the press is not allowed to publish their names. One detainee who was, in fact, Mr Robert Mugabe, made it quite clear that there would have been no inquest had he not insisted, through his own solicitors, that an inquest be held. It was a very frightening case and it revealed that there was no trust or liking between the prison doctor and the detainees. At one point the lawyer representing the prison service asked the magistrate to warn Dr Baker Jones before he said anything more – the inference being that Baker Jones was laying himself open to criminal charges.

Dr Baker Jones and the sister asked me to lie on my bed. He examined me and took my blood pressure. Throughout this time we kept up a desultory conversation and once again I registered with amusement that he was surprised by the fact that I was very different from what he supposed me to be. He became more and more friendly. When he tapped my knees for reflexes he said, 'You're as bad as I am.'

'Is that very bad?' I asked.

'Oh, I'm just an old alcoholic,' he replied. Each time I saw him his breath was heavy with whisky. I felt sorry for him and wondered how the Takawira case had affected him. But what filled my mind was how Mr Takawira had been affected.

On Thursday afternoon he came back with the sister, a buxom, hard-mouthed lady. They went through the ritual of weighing me and testing my blood pressure (which they had done that morning) and then Dr Baker Jones announced that I was in a critical condition and that he could not let me die.

I was very surprised. This was the sixth day without food and I felt in good health, and far better than I had during the first few days. But I have no medical knowledge and there was no-one I could turn to for advice or help. I didn't want to die, but I certainly didn't feel that my condition was critical. Dr Baker Jones sat on the edge of my bed while the sister moved restlessly in the background. He looked unhappy and distraught. That morning, when the sister was out of ear-shot he had said as he was leaving: 'I wish there was something I could do to help you.' Then he embarked on another conversation. I think he was priming himself for what lay ahead. He said that the countries to the north of us were in a terrible condition, and that when my father had been Prime Minister of Rhodesia he had been nothing more than a dictator. I have heard this line of conversation so often before that I couldn't suppress a grin. I didn't attempt to argue. He got off the bed and walked round the cell. I lay in silence and the sister, after agreeing that my father had been a dictator, started fussing with what equipment she had with her. Baker Jones came back and sat on the bed again.

'Will you eat?'

'No.'

'Then we will have no alternative but to force feed you.'

There was a long silence.

'Will you resist?'

I tried once more to explain why I was on a hunger-strike, and said that I wasn't trying to inconvenience the people who had me in their care.

'Do you really think Mr Lardner-Burke knows you're in prison?' asked the sister.

'I know he does,' I replied. 'He signed my detention order.'

She snorted. 'I can tell you,' she said, 'that Mr Lardner-Burke is as much responsible for you being here as Mr McLean (Minister of Health) is for the rats in Harari Hospital.'

Dr Baker Jones seemed encouraged by this line of conversation. He stood up and looked at me with a new unfriendliness. I stopped talking to them. It seemed quite hopeless so I just lay on the bed and waited for what was to happen, battling to keep my composure.

And that was another lost battle.

The cell filled with people. From the very moment the doctor had walked in to see me, about twenty minutes before, these people must have been standing outside.

There was the sister, whose name I never dared ask for, Dr Baker Jones and behind him Miss Wright and Miss Wells, crisp and smart in their uniforms. A medical orderly, aptly named Mr Large, joined the company. He looked the most human of the lot. In the background the burly figure of Mr van der Merwe, superintendent of both male and female sections of Chikurubi Prison, stood framed in the doorway. He was talking to someone outside, who, I think, was his deputy, Mr Kray.

They put a blanket over me and asked once more if I would resist. I said I would not as my battle was with the Smith regime, not them personally, and I was sorry that they were involved at all. Then in a last appeal, I asked them if they had heard of the Nuremburg trials where it was ruled that it was not always an adequate defence simply to do one's duty. Dr Baker Jones looked uncomfortable and irritated. The sister was uncomprehending and irritated. The others couldn't hear me.

Mr Large, who smiled at me now and then, stood at the head of the bed on my left. The sister, the doctor, Miss Wright and Miss Wells were on my right. The sister, I observed, looked more cheerful than I had yet seen her.

Mr Large applied a gag to keep my mouth open. Then the sister started screwing a long tube down my throat. I suppose I simultaneously started crying. The tube hurt badly and no-one had explained that it had to be forced right down into the depths of my body. I understand it all now, of course, and know that the tube has to be forced down past a muscle which closes off the stomach. But then I had no idea of what they were doing. I was choking, crying, pouring with sweat and, I was quite sure, drowning. I simply could not breathe.

'Breathe through your nose! Breathe through your nose!' the sister kept ordering, although she must have realized that my nose was blocked.

The doctor stood behind the sister with an ewer and started pouring a thick, white mixture down the tube through a funnel. The funnel blocked. I was quite sure that by now I was indeed, as Dr Baker Jones had earlier asserted, in a critical condition. The cell, blazing with electricity, was turning black.

I pulled my hands out from beneath the blanket and, as what they had got into me came up, I yanked the tube out of my stomach. I was prepared to be force fed. I was not prepared to be asphyxiated. I lay in the mixture, choking, coughing, gasping for breath. The same procedure was repeated so many times that, losing consciousness, so I lost count.

Eventually Dr Baker Jones said that he knew I was not vomiting deliberately and that they were going to inject me, to relax my muscles. There was a general lighting up of cigarettes and some of them left the cell while the sister injected me. The doctor's hands were shaking.

In what seemed to be a very short time they all trooped back and tried again, and again. One of the most humiliating parts of the exercise was a mental struggle I was fighting. As I was attempting to cooperate Mr Large had little to do. One of his hands lay empty and relaxed on the bed beside me and it was all I could do not to hold it. I didn't.

At some point Mr Large said that it was 4.45 p.m. and that he was meant to be off duty at four. They packed up their equipment and prepared to leave, saying they would be back the next day. At that point it flickered across my mind that Dr Baker Jones had been lying. If I was in a critical condition they would not be leaving me with nothing inside me. Moreover they now knew I would not resist and if I was seriously ill, as he had said, they could feed me intravenously.

Dr Baker Jones's estimation of my present condition was such that before he left he ordered the prison personnel to ensure that nothing was left in my cell with which I could commit suicide, and then the medical party went away.

Miss Wells and Miss Wright had gallantly cleared up most of the mess from the floor and I staggered through to the washroom, my body a knot of helplessness, reflex vomiting. I collapsed on the floor while the washroom swung around me in darkening circles. Then Miss Wright came in and helped me off the floor, half-carrying me back to the cell. She helped me undress and get into bed. Then, as it was 5 p.m. she went out, locked the door and left me in a bed soaked with vomit until six o'clock the next morning.

That morning, Friday, 11 January, she came in with an African prisoner and ordered her to scrub the floor. 'Normally I wouldn't allow this,' she said, 'but you're too weak to do it yourself.'

At about 10 a.m. the sister came in and injected me. I lay on the bed for what seemed about an hour, but I was soon semi-conscious and couldn't attempt to measure time as I had no watch. Then the sister came back with Miss Wright and together they pushed the tube down and poured the mixture in. The doctor was not present. (He has since died and I am thankful that I did not proceed with a proposed case alleging assault, as he would have died half-way through. I would have hoped, or believed, that his death had nothing to do with the case, but I would never have been certain. Poor Dr Baker Jones. He was just as much a prisoner of the Smith regime as I was.)

The force feeding was this time successful, and Miss Wright sat with me for some time after that, ensuring that I kept the food down. She was very busy and the sister had proposed getting other people to stay with me, but I think Miss Wright was sad for me and she

136

sat quietly and gently by my side for some time. When I felt a bit better I asked her what her philosophy was – she had said something which introduced the subject – and I remember her saying that what she cared for above everything else was absolute honesty.

I don't know what I was injected with, but I slept heavily after Miss Wright left. The sister had said they would be back at 3 p.m. to force feed me again, and that they would continue doing so until I started eating voluntarily.

At about 2 p.m. food was brought to me. I ate what I could.

The hunger-strike is not an episode I can recall with any pride. When it was all over I was dejected and demoralized. For weeks afterwards I suffered from profoundly depressing, choking night-mares, and would wake up each day feeling exhausted and sad. One of the ways I made Miss Wells smile was to tell her as though it were a joke, which it wasn't, that every night I had nightmares about being in prison and that it was no relief to wake up.

Both Miss Wright and Miss Wells had told me that no-one outside the prison knew I was on hunger-strike and that no-one ever would know. So why not give up? When I did I was allowed my radio again as a reward. Up till that time I had thought that my smuggled message had not reached the outside world.

When I received my radio I soon discovered that the prison staff had been lying. On the Saturday I regained the radio I learnt from Radio Pakistan that I was entering the eighth day of my hunger-strike. Some other station informed me the next morning that I was bravely enduring the ninth day. I buried my head under the pillow on my bed and groaned. I was so ashamed of myself. Perhaps if I had known that people outside the prison knew about the hunger-strike I would have been able to continue with it. But I'm not at all sure. Refusing food is one thing. Force feeding another.

When I was released from prison I felt better, in retrospect, about the hunger-strike but this was only because of other people. First and most importantly I saw a paragraph in the Crucifer column of the *New Statesman* in which Dr Donald Gould was reported as saying that force feeding was comparable with torture. The reactions of a person being force fed were described and corresponded exactly with what I had been through. But Dr Gould used a phrase which clarified a feeling I hadn't been able to isolate, let alone describe – the feeling that 'the core is threatened'. I had been greatly puzzled about why this experience had upset me so greatly. Now I understood why, and with understanding came relief.

Secondly, a flood of letters had poured in from around the world, comforting me and assuring me that 'you have not failed'. When

I was allowed to see my mother again our conversation was, as usual, censored, and I was not able to tell her exactly what had happened. She said that many overseas journalists were in contact with her and wanted to know what had happened. What should she tell them?

'Tell them I failed,' I said truthfully.

I still cherish all those letters which assured me that I had not, for one reason or another, failed, and I wish I had been allowed to receive them in prison. They would have helped me a great deal.

Then there had been some interesting and unusual reactions from the local press. I was not aware of this until after my release from prison. As soon as the hunger-strike was ended all 'privileges' were returned to me, and I was allowed to see the daily newspaper. But the newspapers which in any way referred to me were conveniently 'lost', or had been 'borrowed by someone else' before they reached me.

On Thursday, 10 February, Mr Ian Smith was asked at an hour-long televised news conference whether or not I was on hunger-strike. He said he did not know.

That afternoon I was force fed for the first time. Our Ministry of Information would no doubt say that it was an amazing coincidence.

On Friday, 11 February, Mr Ian Smith was interviewed for London Weekend Television by Mr David Frost. Mr Frost left a copy of the video tape to be screened on Rhodesian television – free of charge. At the personal request of Mr Smith the tape was not screened.

At the time of the interview no-one outside the Rhodesian authorities knew that I had been force fed, and Mr Frost touched on the hunger-strike on a couple of occasions.

Frost: Why is Mrs Todd able to visit Mr Garfield Todd and not Miss Judith Todd?

Smith: I am unaware that that is the position.

Frost: That is the position. She can't get permission – it has been in the Press of the world, again all over the world, that Mrs Grace Todd can't get permission to visit her daughter but she can get permission to visit her husband.

Smith: Well, I am sorry to have to tell you that I did not know that.

Frost: Is Miss Judith Todd, as you were asked yesterday, is she on a hunger-strike?

Smith: Not that I'm aware of.

Frost: Not that you're aware of?

Smith: Not that I'm aware of. She may be. I don't . . . er . . . I don't get a daily report of these people.

Frost: You were asked about it yesterday at the press conference.

138

I guess you have probably checked up since, have you, because you said you didn't know at that time?

Smith: No. What I did check up on was the state of health of Mr Todd because I would be sorry to think that a person's health is suffering, especially an elderly person, but if Miss Todd does not wish to eat the food given to her this doesn't worry me a great deal, you know.

Frost: After a week or two of that situation though, what would you do? Force feed her or let her die?

Smith: It hasn't entered my mind. I've got so many other things to think about in my job that if this proved to be a problem no doubt it would be brought to my attention. Then I would have a look at the problem.

Frost: But it hasn't been brought to your attention at all?

Smith: No.

Frost: How do these things get brought to the attention of everyone round the world except you?

Smith: Well, I suppose there are a lot of people who have nothing better to do but read the newspapers of the world . . .

At the beginning of the interview Mr Smith knew nothing about the hunger-strike. At the end of the interview he gave himself away.

Frost: But the fascinating thing is . . . the fascinating thing to me anyway in the course of this conversation, Mr Smith, has been how whenever anything, however globally significant, came up that was inconvenient, you automatically, you always say: 'I'm not aware of that' or 'I haven't had that brought to my attention.' But when it's a story of a burning hut to intimidate an African you know about that. You don't know whether Judith Todd's on hunger-strike or not, and a million more things. Is that your shell – that whenever an inconvenient fact comes up you claim not to know about it?

Smith: No. I would say to you that if a person's house is burnt down this is something serious and I'm very concerned with it. But because somebody is not willing to accept the food put before her *because she is deliberately doing this for some political motive*, I honestly would say to you that this is of very little consequence . . .

Up until the time of my hunger strike the Rhodesian newspapers had, to their partial credit, refused to obey the regulations which make it a criminal offence to publish the names of detainees. My

father is, after all, the only former Prime Minister of Rhodesia alive.
I say partial credit, because while the newspapers printed the names
of the white detainees, they did not print the names of the Chinamanos.

On Sunday, 13 February, the *Sunday Mail*, which has the largest
circulation of all Rhodesian newspapers, printed a brave, front-page
editorial entitled 'THE LAW IS A ASS . . .' It read:

Everyone knows that the law is 'a ass – a idiot'. The Rhodesian
ass brayed in deafening fashion last week.

It was a question of the Emergency Powers Regulations, a
section of which forbids publication of anything at all about
people who have been detained or restricted.

Up to last Monday virtually all Rhodesian newspapers ignored
this particular regulation, in the knowledge that if they obeyed it
they would be making bigger asses of themselves than of the law.

To its credit, the Government graciously accepted the situation.
But then things changed. There was a story afoot about a certain
detainee which, if published, would most gravely embarrass the
Government.

At once the word went out, in the form of a gentle reminder
about the Emergency Powers Regulations. The hint, naturally,
was taken. Alas for the law, the Prime Minister himself was an
accessory to the breaking of it. In his hour-long televised news
conference, the regulation was broken again and again. [Mr Smith
had referred to the Chinamanos, my father and myself, by name,
as being responsible for violence.]

The question arose: when is a law not a law? The answer, it
appears, is 'when it suits the Government'.

That is why the Rhodesian story of the week – which just about
everyone outside Rhodesia will be reading this morning – does
not appear in the *Sunday Mail* today. It has been made pretty
clear to the *Sunday Mail* that to publish the whole of the tricky
story that barely raised its ugly head last Monday – and which has
since become a very ugly story indeed – would be to invite
retribution. Readers may imagine this is just another dreary
squabble between Government and Press. It is not.

It is a matter which gravely affects the proposed settlement.
The story concerned is already known in London, and is causing
embarrassment there. The longer the unhappy situation of the
detainee continues – indeed the longer all the recent detainees
remain in captivity – the more difficult it becomes for anyone to
accept that one of the conditions of the settlement is being met:
normal political activity during the test of acceptability.

By its continuing and inexplicable failure to bring the detainees to court, the Government is imperilling the settlement – whether wilfully or otherwise is anyone's guess.

There has been much talk and evidence of intimidatory tactics being employed by one side or the other in this settlement affair. The Emergency Regulations are legalized intimidation.

The Emergency Regulations are legalized intimidation.
Yet these emergency regulations, in essence, remained untouched and untouchable in the proposed settlement document, signed by the British Foreign and Commonwealth Secretary.

It was probably coincidental, but the day after they learned of my hunger strike the Pearce Commission issued a statement in which they said that 'in the absence of any satisfactory explanation from the Rhodesian Government about those detained under ministerial orders, and the failure either to prefer charges against them or to release them, the commission must infer that the purpose of their detention is to inhibit the free expression of opinion.'

CHAPTER ELEVEN

Companions of Honour

AT a press conference on Thursday, 10 February, Mr Smith stated that the Chinamanos, my father and I were amongst those responsible for 'burning, intimidation, violence, rioting and looting'.

The *Rhodesia Herald* which reported Mr Smith did not reach me so I did not know of these accusations until my mother next visited me. After she left I pondered what Mr Smith had said and felt relieved that he had made these accusations. I thought they were so serious that charges must be laid against us and I welcomed the possibility that we might be brought before an open court, however little respect I have for the courts of Rhodesia. Our judges, under the Chief Justice Sir Hugh Beadle P.C., have allowed themselves to be bullied into a position where they cannot stand effectively for justice as they are now second in honour and in power to the political executive whose concern is not for justice, but for 'law and order'. If a minister rules that it is 'in the national interest', courts must be cleared, names of accused persons and witnesses suppressed, and coverage of the trial, if permitted, must be censored.

The Minister of Law and Order may decide to by-pass the courts altogether. Not only have people been held in prisons or detention camps for eight years or more but hundreds of people are restricted to certain areas throughout the country. People from Bulawayo may be restricted to within a certain radius of Salisbury and vice versa. One man, Mr Enos Choga, was a taxi-driver in Salisbury and so he was restricted to a twelve-mile radius of Gwelo where he couldn't operate as a taxi-driver. His family had broken up while he was in the detention that preceded his restriction. The authorities were not in the least interested in his plight and when he appealed to one section for help they would pass him on to the police, who would pass him on to someone else. The Rhodesian authorities lack any vestige of compassion. Another man, Mr Daniel Madzimbamuto, has been detained for thirteen years without trial. Questioned in the David Frost interview, Mr Ian Smith said he was unaware of the details of the case.

Mr Smith was probably depending upon finding evidence in our papers with which to charge us. Thousands of documents had been seized from us by the Special Branch but many weeks later they were all meekly returned. As Mr Ian Colvin of the *Daily Telegraph* reported with his customary dispassion – 'searches of the Todd home were, however, disappointing in so far as evidence of clandestine activities fell short of expectations.' The police never even bothered to question us.

At his 10 February press conference Mr Smith said that 'within a few days he would present a dossier to the Pearce Commission on cases of intimidation as well as the activities of Mr Garfield Todd, the former Prime Minister, Miss Judy Todd, Mr Josiah Chinamano and Mrs Ruth Chinamano who had been organizing the NO campaign of the National Council' (*Daily Telegraph* 11 February). When the dossier was published our names were conspicuous by their absence.

After some thought I told Miss Wright that I would like to see a particular lawyer. Miss Wright told me that she had already been making enquiries to see if my case could go to the Review Tribunal, a government appointed 'board of justice' which examines the cases of detainees in secret. She asked me why I wanted to see a lawyer. I said that I wanted to explore the possibility of suing Mr Smith for libel and defamation, as this was the only way I could think of getting our cases aired. She looked at me incredulously and left the cell.

A short time later she returned. 'Do you mean to say that you want to see a lawyer about suing the *Prime Minister*?'

'Yes,' I said, surprised at her reaction. 'I thought I had made that quite clear.'

She laughed. She was obviously both shocked and highly entertained. 'Do you really think I could allow a lawyer into my prison to discuss with you the possibility of suing *the Prime Minister*?'

'Yes, of course I do.'

'It's quite impossible,' she said, and left.

But my lawyer was allowed to come and discuss the possibility of appearing before the Review Tribunal. He is a friend of mine but had not acted as my legal adviser before. I particularly wished to see him as some months earlier I had discussed with him the predicament of people brought before Rhodesian courts whose legal standing they did not recognize. Decisions handed down by judges appointed since U.D.I. are not recognized outside Rhodesia and it appeared that the courts themselves were now an integral and willing part of the illegal administration. At the time he had said that he

143

knew how to deal with this problem. Although I was most unwilling to appear before the Review Tribunal, I asked to see him. In the event both my father and I refused to appear before it.

The Review Tribunal consists of three white men. The chairman, Mr H. E. Davies, is a judge of the high court. The tribunal sits in camera. If a detainee appears before it and later reveals what has happened, what has been said, even what he himself said, he is liable to a fine of up to R$1,000 or two years' imprisonment or both. The detainee is not informed in advance what the allegations against him are. Indeed, while the tribunal sits, the detainee may be excluded from the proceedings.

The detainee is allowed to have legal representation at the hearing and a short while before proceedings commence he is given a document prepared by the Special Branch. This details the case against the detainee. The copy he is given is usually heavily censored and sentences, paragraphs or even pages may be fully blacked out. The copies given to the three members of the tribunal are not censored. If the detainee is given a censored copy this is because it is held not to be 'in the national interest' for him to know what he is accused of, what information has been used against him, what the sources of the information are.

If the detainee appears before the tribunal he is placed on oath. His accusers are the Special Branch and the 'trial' is nothing more than the interrogation of the detainee, on oath, by the Special Branch in the presence of the tribunal.

At the close of the proceedings the chairman, instead of pronouncing a verdict, presents a report to the Minister of Law and Order and Justice, Mr Desmond Lardner-Burke. If it should so happen that the tribunal recommends the release of a detainee and the Minister disagrees, the case goes for final decision to Rhodesia's President, Mr Clifford Dupont, who reaches his decision on the advice of his Minister of Law and Order and Justice, Mr Desmond Lardner-Burke.

In a general report of the Review Tribunal, published in February 1971 and signed by the three members of the tribunal it is stated:

In every case the Tribunal has before it the memorandum referred to in Section (3) (b) of the Regulations [the Tribunal is appointed in terms of the Emergency Powers (Maintenance of Law and Order) Regulations], documents supporting the allegations made in the memorandum, and a current report on the particular detainee's conduct whilst in detention. In addition, general evidence pertaining to the security position in Rhodesia was placed before the Tribunal. To the extent that it was possible to do so, without prejudice to security, each detainee who appeared before the Tribunal was fully informed of the allegations made against him . . . *Detention is not to be regarded as a punishment for what a detainee has done in the past, but as an administrative expedient designed to prevent him from doing anything in the future which would imperil the safety and order of the State* . . .

The tribunal sat in February to consider the cases of the Chinamanos, my father and myself. We learnt from the B.B.C. that the tribunal had recommended the continued detention of all four. The Rhodesian press reported that the tribunal had recommended the continued detention of four detainees but, of course, our names were not published.

We ourselves have never been informed that our cases were brought before the tribunal or that our continued detention had been recommended. If we were not able to see newspapers or listen to the B.B.C. we would not have known that the tribunal was even aware of our detention.

On 4 March the *Rhodesia Herald* commented: 'this finding will be of interest outside this country as well, but whereas most Rhodesians will accept it as justification of the Government's action, it could well draw a different reaction from outside.

'It is likely to be answered with the question: if the evidence put before the judge is conclusive, when will the detainees be tried in court? In the countries whose opinions matter to us, nothing less will suffice.'

The editor did not understand the function of the tribunal. The 'conclusive' evidence leading to a continuation of detention did not have to prove guilt of any criminal action but had only to convince a man, whose position as a High Court Judge should have placed him above political intrigue, that in the estimation of the Minister of Law and Order it was 'expedient' for political reasons to continue the detention orders.

Initially Mr Smith had said it was likely that criminal charges would be laid against us 'after current investigations have been completed'. They were not. At a press conference he said his dossier on intimidation would cover the actions of the four detainees. We were not mentioned.

By ensuring that the tribunal recommended our continued detentions, for reasons unknown and undivulged, Mr Smith was able to clasp a few rags and tatters of propriety over his naked inability to find us responsible for any improper activity.

At 6 a.m. on Tuesday, 22 February, Miss Wright came to my cell and asked me to pack. I asked why, rather wearily, as I supposed I was going to be moved to another jail.

'The Special Branch are coming at eight to take you away.'

'Where to?'

'I think you are probably going home.'

I was quite overcome and, in retrospect I am quite ashamed of my reaction and the surge of joy, disbelief and sorrow that flooded over me. When she came in I was standing on the opposite side of the cell. After she said I was going home the next awareness I had of myself was standing with her in the doorway, tears smarting in my eyes. She was laughing and smiling and was herself considerably moved. She shook my hand and said 'I wish you the very best, all the very best,' then went away.

My cell door now unlocked, I went through to the washroom and shut myself in the lavatory. I sat on the floor and cried and cried. The only other time I had wept was when I was being force fed, and at that time I was desperately struggling against tears. Often at night I had thought it would probably be a good thing to cry and try, that way, to relieve some of the tension, misery and sleeplessness. But I had not been able to. Now, weeping silently on the floor of the lavatory, I recognized the fact that I had successfully shut away for so long. I had now been in prison for five weeks, and had, unconsciously, been steeling myself for an unending imprisonment. Daniel Madzimbamuto has been held for thirteen years without trial. Many of my friends have been held since April 1964.

I gathered my belongings together, cleaned the cell, swept the washroom and weeded the little garden for the last time. I drank the cold tea and ate the slice of heavy bread. Then I sat, waiting, waiting. The hours between six and eight were the longest hours of my imprisonment.

At eight o'clock an African wardress who had been the most reserved and seemingly the most in sympathy with the prison authorities came to see that everything was in order. She helped me carry my belongings away from the cell. 'I am very happy today,' she said. 'My prayers have been answered. Do you know why I am happy?'

'No.'

'I have been praying for you,' she said. 'But don't tell anyone.'

We walked through the gates up to Miss Wright's office which is outside the prison compound. The Special Branch escort was waiting for me outside the office.

'Hullo, Judy.'

'Hullo, Nigel. Hullo, Helen.' What a crazy state Rhodesia was in,

146

I thought, as I was conducted into the office. Africans were praying for me and the Special Branch was greeting me as a friend. So much for Mr Smith accusing me of being responsible for violence, intimidation, looting and burning. Those around me, be they Special Branch or prison staff, gave no impression that they thought of me as being anything but a person in slightly awkward circumstances whom they were happy to greet or farewell.

Once we were in Miss Wright's office Detective Inspector Nigel Seaward served me with another detention order. I was not free. The order specified that I was now to be detained within an 800-metre radius of my home.

We set off from the prison to collect my father from Gatooma jail on the way home. Inspector Seaward drove, with Miss Pronk next to him. I sat in the back seat. Miss Pronk offered me a peppermint and embarked on the next installment of news about her forthcoming marriage.

We drove through the centre of Salisbury in the same Austin Westminster in which I had originally been driven to jail. I folded my hand longingly round the door-handle next to me. Oh, to be able to open the door, walk out on the street, visit my friends. Oh, to be able to go to the Jameson Hotel and the Ambassador and be greeted by the waiters with all their usual questions: 'Where have you been? Why haven't we seen you for so long?' We passed the old block of offices, Chaplin Buildings, where, as a little girl, I had visited the then Prime Minister, my father. Oh, to be able to knock at the door and gain admittance again. (I didn't think of who might be opening the door these days.)

We drove swiftly through the city, through the outskirts, past Cold Comfort Farm. I remembered the police take-over of the farm, the deportation of Mr Clutton-Brock for the simple reason that he had demonstrated non-racism in practice. I remembered how occupying members of the police force had become so friendly with those who lived on Cold Comfort that new police had had to be drafted in.

The sky was creamy with rich, promising clouds and the fields along the way were crowded with luxuriant crops. I knew this road so well, but now I saw it and the surrounding countryside with new eyes. I had never before been aware of how much I loved that part of our country. Perhaps this was because I didn't know when I would be able to see it again. We were to be detained indefinitely. Others of my friends who had been placed in detention loved the land as much as I did, if not more, and some had died in detention, never seeing the beautiful country again.

Eventually we reached Gatooma jail. Once more I found myself struggling for every atom of strength in me to appear calm as the door of the prison swung open and my father walked out. He was smiling and, superficially, was as gay as ever. I hoped that, like me, he had not been allowed a mirror in jail. His hair was dead and snow-white. He was stooped and thin and his skin was grey. He was very ill.

Miss Pronk took over the driving. I was asked to sit in front and my father and Nigel Seaward sat in the back. It was difficult to converse in the circumstances. My father had not been in the company of these two Special Branch people as much as I had been, and he was less at ease than I had become. In an attempt, which was unsuccessful, to be humorous I asked my father about his mail and recalled how derogatory letters had initially been willingly handed over to me while friendly letters were held back. I had been surprised to receive a letter with a Marandellas post-office stamp as I hadn't thought I had any friends in Marandellas. When I read the letter I saw I was right. It was from a young man who said that he was very glad I had been imprisoned and hoped that, as well as being imprisoned, I would be well thrashed. Like me, he said, he was twenty-eight, and after my imprisonment he would welcome the opportunity of taking me out and discussing the future of Rhodesia. Nigel Seaward shook his head and looked horrified.

At Gwelo, 200 miles from Salisbury and 80 miles from my home, we were dropped at the police station where further orders were served on us. The orders, in part, read:

WHEREAS, you . . . are lawfully detained in terms of an order issued under the hand of the Minister of Law and Order in terms of section 16 of the Emergency Powers (Maintenance of Law and Order) Regulations, 1970 . . .

AND WHEREAS, by paragraph (a) of subsection (1) of section 39 of the said regulations it is provided that a protecting authority may, by an order, prohibit either absolutely or subject to such conditions as he may fix, any detained person from communicating by word of mouth, in writing or otherwise, with or receiving any such communication from, any person who is outside the place of detention;

AND WHEREAS it is further provided by subsection (2) of section 39 of the said regulations that a protecting authority may take such measures as he considers necessary to ensure that no person other than a person ordinarily resident in a place of detention is present therein without the permission of the protecting authority;

AND WHEREAS I consider it necessary to make such an order;

NOW, THEREFORE, I do by this order prohibit you . . . from communicating by word of mouth, in writing or otherwise, with or receiving any such communication from, any person who is outside the place of detention referred to . . . and for the purpose of giving effect to this prohibition further direct . . . that no person other than members of your family, your present bona fide employees employed at Hokonui Ranch and such legal and medical practitioners as may reasonably be required by any person ordinarily resident at the place of detention . . . may be present in the said place of detention without the permission in writing of the undersigned . . .

D. W. Wright

PROTECTING AUTHORITY FOR MIDLANDS PROVINCE IN TERMS OF SECTION 3 OF THE EMERGENCY POWERS (MAINTENANCE OF LAW AND ORDER) REGULATIONS. 1970.

Others may consider, as I do, that the creation of detainees who automatically become non-persons, their names forbidden to be mentioned publicly, their hopes governed by the Review Tribunal which secretly deliberates information on them which they do not know of, is indefensible.

DETENTION WAS UPHELD AND PROVIDED FOR IN THE BRITISH DOCUMENT, 'PROPOSALS FOR A SETTLEMENT'.

The document ratified the continued existence of the review tribunal. 'The recommendations of the Tribunal will be binding . . .' the proposals stated.

Sir Alec Douglas-Home has, before, during and after the test of acceptability, made much play of the fact that Rhodesia would, under the proposals for a settlement, have had a 'justiciable' declaration of rights. He said that this would be a great improvement on the declaration of rights instituted under the 1969 constitution which was not justiciable.

Sir Alec has failed to point out that the justiciable declaration of rights provided for in the settlement proposals does not affect any law passed to date in Rhodesia. People may continue to be jailed and detained indefinitely without trial. Parties may continue to remain banned, and new bannings may take place. Rhodesia may continue to be governed under a perpetual state of emergency. Police may still arrest people without charge or warrant. No provision is made for the release of African leaders held for years without charge or open trial, except that it is provided for that they will once again have their cases reviewed by the Review Tribunal, and that a British observer will be present. Not surprisingly, that British observer is given no power to intervene or to disagree with the findings.

Sir Alec's 'justiciable declaration of rights' as laid down in the settlement proposals is just about the most cynical and dishonourable document that could have been devised.

The very first section, Section 1, states that 'no person shall be deprived of his life intentionally, save . . .'

It then lays down that if a person is deprived of his life 'a person shall not be regarded as having been deprived of his life in contravention of this paragraph if he dies as the result of the use of force to such extent as is reasonably justifiable in the circumstances of the case:

(a) for the defence of any person from violence or for the defence of property;
(b) in order to effect a lawful arrest or to prevent the escape of a person lawfully detained;
(c) for the purpose of suppressing a riot, insurrection or mutiny or of dispersing an unlawful gathering;
(d) in order to prevent the commission by that person of a criminal offence;
or if he dies as the result of a lawful act of war.

This is all bad enough. The ultimate cynicism lies in the fact that it is then stated that if a person dies under circumstances that would have been considered 'lawful' (by whom?) before this justiciable declaration of rights was enacted, that person shall not be held to have forfeited his life in contravention of the declaration of rights.

According to this justiciable declaration of rights, to translate it on to a personal level, Mr Mike Stephens could have shot me dead when he found me attending the meeting at Mataruse Council if he thought that, by so doing, he would be dispersing an unlawful gathering.

If I had resisted arrest on 18 January, I could have been shot dead 'in order to effect a lawful arrest'.

If I had become so miserable about being held without trial or charge in prison, and had therefore attempted to escape, I could have been shot dead with impunity by my killer, 'in order to . . . prevent the escape of a person lawfully detained'.

If, on the other hand, I had been a white property owner, determined at all costs to protect my property (be it a huge area of unused land surrounded by thousands of land-starved Africans) and had shot dead any encroachers, this, under the proposed declaration of rights, would have been permissible. The British, in this document, agreed with the Rhodesian authorities that property is more valuable than life.

When I was last in London I went, with an anti-apartheid delegation, to see Lord Lothian, then Under-Secretary of State for Foreign and Commonwealth Affairs. He has since in effect been replaced by Lady Tweedsmuir.

Lord Lothian is kind, courteous, gentle and well-meaning. I am certain that he would not knowingly or willingly betray any person, or any people.

The final details of the proposed settlement were not at that stage known by the public. As they had not yet been published – if indeed they had as yet been formulated – I urged him to consider the fact that anyone declared a detainee in Rhodesia automatically lost his civil rights for five years after his detention had come to an end.

While the Review Tribunal urges its belief that detention is not to be regarded as a punishment, but as an administrative expedient, detention is in fact a long-lasting punishment. Detainees may be held indefinitely as were my father and I, in solitary confinement. (Mr Ian Colvin of the *Daily Telegraph* reported that the Rhodesian authorities had corrected the wrong impression that we were being held in solitary confinement. We were, he repeated, just 'segregated' from other prisoners.) While convicted prisoners may, on their release, resume normal lives, detainees may not take part in any political activity in the sense of voting, or standing for election, for the next five years. My father, for example, after having been restricted from 1965–6, had been in the possession of the right to exercise what civil rights there are in Rhodesia for only three months before he was once again detained.

Lord Lothian appeared startled by the information that detainees were not truly free until five years after release from detention. He turned to the Foreign and Commonwealth official present, Mr Mason, who is deputy to Mr Philip Mansfield on the Rhodesia Desk.

'I must say I wasn't aware of that,' said Lord Lothian. 'Will you take note of that?'

'We are aware of the fact,' said Mr Mason, 'and we are at present working on it.'

I am not aware of how much work was done, but when the settlement proposals were published it was clear that the British Government not only countenanced the continued detention of people but had also allowed for the continued denial of their civil rights until five years after their release from detention had elapsed.

When the Chinamanos, my father and I had been imprisoned,

Sir Alec Douglas-Home expressed his regret to the House of Commons and, during a later debate, said that he must not be held to condone the detentions.

While we appreciate his regrets, and while he may claim no responsibility, the settlement proposals which bore his honourable initials provided for the detention, continued detention, or re-detention of the Chinamanos, my father, myself, and all the other hundreds of present and future detainees. Today detentions are effected by the Smith regime, but with a Rhodesian Government legalized by Britain and armed with the authoritarian powers allowed by Sir Alec under the settlement proposals, would the British Government in fact, if not in theory, be free of blame and responsibility? Under the 'honourable and just' proposals worked out by Lord Goodman, Sir Peter Rawlinson, Mr Miles Hudson, Mr Philip Mansfield, Sir Denis Greenhill and others, opponents of the Smith regime had little promise of any justice.

The proposals would in the end have achieved little more than providing relief for Her Majesty's Government. The Foreign and Commonwealth Secretary would no longer, had there been a settlement, have had to go through the continuing embarrassment of publicly washing his hands over Rhodesia.

CHAPTER TWELVE

Smith versus Pearce

ON 23 May 1972 the findings of the Pearce Commission were made public. At 4.30 p.m. Rhodesian time on a grey, cold day, the B.B.C. and the R.B.C. simultaneously announced that the commission had found that the proposals for a settlement were not acceptable to the people of Rhodesia as a whole. It was announced on the R.B.C. that the Prime Minister, Mr Ian Smith, would be making a statement on radio and television later that afternoon. We tuned in to listen to Mr Smith at the appointed time.

This is the Rhodesia Broadcasting Corporation.

> SO RIGHT WHEN YOU'RE THIRSTY –
> FANTA ORANGE.

Here is the Prime Minister.

Mr Smith was understandably furious.

... it is necessary for me to say a few words to you this evening, in order firstly to ensure that we get this episode in its true perspective, and, secondly, to counter the mischievous and distorted speculation which we can expect during the next few days.

The report of the Pearce Commission shows that the overwhelming majority of Europeans, Asians and Coloureds in Rhodesia supported the settlement. So did a considerable number of Africans who realized the benefits which would flow from the agreement. Regrettably, however, Lord Pearce and his colleagues formed the opinion that a majority of Africans were opposed to the settlement and from this they have concluded that the people of Rhodesia as a whole do not accept the proposals.

The report is a comprehensive document, covering 200 pages, and it takes time to study it carefully and thoroughly. I would not have credited that any report could contain so many misinterpretations and misconstructions of the true position ...

Four thousand subsidized copies of the Pearce Report had been flown in from Britain and these sold out within a few hours. One bookshop in Salisbury had sold out, on order, its allotted ration of 500 copies before they had even arrived. Special editions of the newspapers summarizing the report were on the streets that night. The following day photographs of happy Africans and gloomy whites illustrated the way the news had been received.

It took some days for a report to reach us. As I read it memories of the days before the test of acceptability came flooding back. In some ways it all seemed so long ago, so recent in others.

My recollections of the mood of the people I had seen before the commission arrived were vivid. I knew that there would be rejoicing throughout the country that night, but that it would be muted. Rhodesia's armed forces were on stand-by. The Africans, against great odds, had scored a significant victory, and once again the Rhodesian authorities were misjudging their likely reactions. Had the Pearce Commission reported that the settlement proposals were acceptable there might have been the necessity for an armed alert throughout the country. But most of the people that night were happy, not angry and there was no need for a show of force.

From the very beginning there had been profound interest amongst Africans in the proposed visit of Lord Pearce and his team. The promise that 'In the period before and during the test of acceptability normal political activities will be permitted to the satisfaction of the Commission . . .' had been received with enthusiasm and hope, although the unspoken acceptance of the fact that normal political activities would cease with the accomplishment of the test of acceptability did not pass unnoticed. But before long, interest, hope and enthusiasm were threatened by a rising tide of despair, fear and frustration.

It had been generally thought the proviso that normal political activities would be permitted *to the satisfaction of the commission* meant that the commission would, in some way, be able to safeguard these activities and that there would be commissioners in the field immediately to ensure that they *were* satisfied that normal political activity was being permitted. But the safeguarding of normal political activity soon proved to be beyond the resources of the commission. So the frustration which eventually led to violence began to build up.

The African National Council was prohibited from holding meetings in the Tribal Trust Lands. The Rhodesian authorities agreed that 'District Commissioners had refused to allow the African National Council to hold meetings in the tribal trust lands. They argued

154

that meetings were not normal political activity in these areas' (Pearce Report, Par. 143). The District Commissioners started informing the people in their areas that only those who had made appointments with the District Commissioner would be allowed to see the commission. Many of the District Commissioners leant heavily on the chiefs, using both threats and blandishments. 'If you accept the settlement proposals all will be well. If you don't . . .' It appeared that the chiefs were being brought more and more closely under the District Commissioners' control.

Then the Chiefs' Council was summoned to Salisbury where it deliberated in secret, as usual. After the meeting a statement was issued by the Prime Minister's office – before the arrival of the Pearce Commission – stating that the chiefs unanimously favoured the settlement proposals.

In the earlier weeks Africans could find no place to which they could address letters for the Pearce Commission and a deep, spreading fear started finding tentative expression in the following rumours which spread rapidly throughout the country. The people were not going to be allowed to see the commission. The commission had been rigged, and would listen only to the chiefs and the District Commissioners. The people would not be allowed to assemble in groups and invite the commissioners to hear them. The commission would only see small groups of people who had been screened by the District Commissioners. If people were assembled in small groups and seen under supervision of the police and other government authorities they would be too afraid to express their real feelings. They needed the comfort and the partial safety of numbers.

Spokesmen and leaders began to disappear and by 27 January over 1,000 arrests had been made, although the great majority of these arrests were made after the outbreak of violence. Nonetheless many people disappeared before they had any opportunity of seeing the commission and were released, uncharged, after the commissioners had left their area.

But perhaps the greatest fear in each district was that people from other areas would not have the courage to say what they felt. This was another expression of the yearning for the safety which numbers would give. So the tension increased daily – not because the Pearce Commission was coming, but because it was feared that it would not be possible to see and speak with the commissioners.

When the Pearce Report was published it was clearly revealed that the people had been absolutely correct in fearing the worst. Had the Rhodesian Government had their own way the exercise would have been so tightly controlled that the only possible result would have been a report that the proposals were acceptable to the people of Rhodesia as a whole.

Before the exercise had even started the Rhodesian authorities had offered to send Senator Morris, a former Chief Native Commissioner and former Secretary for Native Affairs to London, to 'advise' the commission on how to go about the test of acceptability. The commission politely deferred the offer. 'We felt it to be of supreme importance that our report should command respect in Britain and elsewhere,' reported Lord Pearce. 'It was therefore vital that we should do all that we could to establish our credibility as a commission . . . We had also to be seen taking our own line about where and how to test opinion.'

Then the Rhodesian authorities presented the commission with an itinerary in which it was proposed that fifty district headquarters be visited within twelve to twenty-two days, so that the entire test of acceptability would take no more than a month. In the event the commission stayed in Rhodesia for about two months and did not limit their itinerary to visiting fifty district headquarters.

Nothing daunted, the Rhodesian authorities then suggested that as the commission would need interpreters they should employ Rhodesia government interpreters as, Lord Pearce quotes, 'interpreters employed by the government would be regarded as not politically aligned and would therefore command greater confidence among Africans than would persons drawn from the churches, schools or the University which were the only other source of supply.' There would have been much hollow laughter throughout Rhodesia if that offer had been generally known. Poor Mr Chinamora, community adviser in the Belingwe area and interpreter for the District Commissioner, Mr Bissett, had been beaten up at Humbani because, amongst other things, people were already so deeply angry that at chiefs' meetings where he had read the White Paper, he had translated 'normal political activities will be permitted' as 'no more political activities will be permitted'. The commission obviously had studied the offer but 'to diminish the risk of criticism of bias on the part of the interpreters we decided to limit our field of selection to persons who were no longer in government service or who were interpreting in magistrates' or higher courts and whose professionalism would tend to exclude bias. We excluded those known to be politically aligned. We also invited churches and the University to suggest names for consideration.'

Then the Rhodesian authorities started raising the spectre of 'security reasons' which dominates all undemocratic activity in this country. For example, Mr Ian Smith had said early on during the test of acceptability, that the Chinamanos, my father and I would not be taken to court immediately 'for security reasons'. For security reasons, the government said, they wanted all meetings conducted by the commission in tribal trust areas to be held within district courts or council halls. District courts and council halls are physical symbols of government in the Tribal Trust Lands. The authorities, moreover, asked the commission to accept the hospitality of the District Commissioners and to stay in their guest-houses. 'The Rhodesian authorities,' the report states, 'were opposed to the use of missions for meetings or night stops on the ground that as so many churches had declared their opposition to the proposals we should endanger our impartial standing if we were too much in their company. After discussion, we decided that our commissioners would stay at hotels except where there were none within reasonable reach, and that the majority of our sessions would be held in council halls or courts but that we should also use some missions and other centres where to do so would improve our coverage of a particular area.'

The next effort made by the Rhodesian authorities to prejudice the investigation by the commission fulfilled all the worst fears of the people in the Tribal Trust Lands. Had the people known that their suspicions were indeed fact, there would almost certainly have been violence throughout the rural areas.

'Rhodesian officials considered that the proposals had already been adequately explained through the distribution of their explanatory material and our own version of them, and the meetings held by the District Commissioners with tribal leaders. They did not therefore consider it necessary for the Commission to try and meet large numbers of ordinary Africans. They argued that the Africans in the Tribal Trust Lands traditionally made their views known through their tribal leaders; so consultation with these leaders and other representative groups would give the most accurate indication of the views of the rural areas. Accordingly, the Rhodesians wished Commissioners to attend at a limited range of meeting places and to meet in small groups only those who had made appointments. They suggested that these could best be made through the District Commissioners and that no person other than those for whom appointments had been made should be allowed to be present at the meetings with our Commissioners.'

That is paragraph 156 of the Pearce Report. Paragraph 157 is vindication of the integrity of the commission and a rebuke to those who, like me, had initially thought that the commission might bow down to the will of the Smith regime.

'We favoured a more open approach. We believed that our Commissioners should meet as many Africans from all walks of life as they could in the time. It would be impractical to do this through an appointment system and some Africans might hesitate to approach the District Commissioners for this purpose. We thought that subject to security considerations our Commissioners should go to the people and visit as many and as wide a range of centres as they could; and that they should be prepared to explain the proposals to groups of whatever size were assembled and answer their questions . . .'

The Rhodesian authorities then asked that the minimum of publicity be given to forthcoming meetings. 'We believed,' wrote Lord Pearce, 'that details should be published well in advance through the press and radio so that anyone interested would know where our Commissioners would be and could arrange to go to meet them. The Rhodesians considered that this would give too much opportunity to those opposed to the proposals to organize opposition and intimidate our audiences. They therefore wished to do no more than make a general announcement that our Commissioner would be in a certain district over a certain period, leaving it to people to ascertain by local enquiry where meetings would actually be held. Moreover they did not want to do this more than a day or two before our Commissioners were expected in the district. We thought it would be wrong to accept this limitation on publicity and the Rhodesian authorities initially conceded this point. They came back to it later and we then agreed in certain cases to local publicity only. We found, in practice, that news got around just as well this way.'

But the Smith regime did win, temporarily, the overwhelming concession from the Pearce Commission that, for security reasons, meetings in rural areas should be neither public nor open. For security reasons, it was insisted, the Pearce Commission should meet people in small groups and indoors. The Pearce Commission agreed.

'We accepted that, unless agreement was reached locally for some alternative arrangements, our Commissioners should only meet people in small groups and indoors.' But then the people themselves frustrated that victory of the Rhodesian authorities. 'Circumstances in fact dictated otherwise. As soon as our Commissioners started their journeys it became clear that the large numbers of people gathered at the place appointed for the day's hearings expected some form of explanation from our Commissioners and that this could only be done through talking to people in large, usually open-air meetings.'

I often wonder if Sir Alec Douglas-Home and the British government have ever begun to realize what so many hundreds of people had to go through to ensure that the Pearce Commission knew what they felt. People walked for hours, through day and night, to reach the Pearce Commission. Some would have cycled and the lucky ones found motorized transport. I wonder if the courage of the people is appreciated. In the meetings I attended there was always the fear of the police, of the District Commissioner, of the Smith regime. The fear was real and the suffering has been great. When I was arrested I was treated well and, on the whole, courteously. I was given time to pack and say my farewells. I wasn't taken from a poverty-stricken village where many people might have depended upon me for their food. I didn't leave a wife, a husband or children behind. I knew that I wouldn't be beaten up or just disappear for ever. I was white and people knew of me, and those two factors were immensely important. But I have so many friends in the area who have lost their jobs, who are still in prison, who have been assaulted. One of my friends whom I most admire was being sought for by the police long before the Commission arrived, because he had been organizing meetings to explain the terms. His wife was a teacher – she lost her job – and he has four small children. The last time I saw him his wife had been arrested the night before. When he got home he saw the police Land-Rovers waiting for him, dodged them and set off to tell me what was happening in his village. He hoped that neighbours would be caring for his children, 'but they are themselves so poor'. After he had given me his news he stood up and bade me farewell. 'I'm going back home. I think the police will have left, but I know they'll find me sometime. I don't think I'll be seeing you again but I'm hoping to see Lord Pearce before they take me to jail.' He chuckled, as a thought struck him. 'The police will be very angry. I'm not there and they'll have been sitting there waiting for me and looking at the "NO" written on my door.'

A neighbour of ours, Senator Chief Mafala, a poor man materially, who depends completely on the Smith regime for his present uncertain wealth, did what he could to ensure that the commission would receive a 'yes' to the proposals from his people. He arranged that only he and his councillors would see the Commission, no doubt with the guidance of our local District Commissioner, Mr White. But word reached Mafala's people and they came to his village to see the Commission. The chief asked them to go home and said that he was expecting no-one more interesting than the District Commissioner, Mr White. The people pretended to go away, but in fact they hid in the area. When the Commissioners arrived, so did the people, and they all said 'No!' Before the present wave of repression came crush-

ing down after the Pearce report was published, Chief Mafala and
his councillors were attempting to heal their image with the people,
and quiet reports were circulating that in fact both he and his
councillors had themselves said 'No' to the proposals. Whether this
was true or not only the Commissioners could say. But at present
Chief Mafala is back in the Senate in Salisbury busy castigating the
Commission, so he obviously feels that for the time being the people
to placate are those who form the Smith regime. This may not be
creditable and there is no doubt that many of his people are very
angry with him. But the police and the army are on the move and
threats are being made that those 'weak' chiefs who allowed themselves to be 'misled' into saying 'No' may be replaced. So the position
of Chief Mafala and some of his fellows can be understood if not
admired.

Shortly after the Commission left, Mr Lance Bales Smith, Minister
of Internal Affairs, spoke very strongly to the chiefs of Rhodesia.
The newspapers reported his speech fully, alongside a photo of
Mr L. B. Smith. The picture gave the impression of a well-built man
in his fifties or early sixties whose hairline is just receding over the
top of his head. His lower lip is full and soft, his upper lip as stiff
and straight as it should be. He wore a very determined expression –
it was, after all, an official Ministry of Information photograph – but
his eyes, under low-flung bushy eyebrows, looked a little startled.
All in all he looked tough, wary and very uncertain.

'You must put your house in order,' he told the chiefs. 'You must
remove those who are weak and fail to govern justly . . . You must
regain and hold the confidence of your people and, when intruders
threaten your territory, deal with them.'

He went on to tell the chiefs that during the presence of the Pearce
Commission there had been a serious breakdown in discipline and
that in some areas chiefs and their senior followers had capitulated
to the 'intimidation of a few people acting under instructions of
other people alien to the tribe and motivated by personal gain'. In
case the chiefs didn't recognize who these people were he described
them in graphic detail.

'They are the weevils in your grain, the ticks on your cattle sucking
out the blood, the bugs in your bed that will not let you rest.
Search them out and deal with them. The law stands behind you
to help.'

He went on to say that he was aware that intimidators who were
prosecuted received short sentences and were soon back in circulation. Until such time as those intimidators and those who went
along with them could have been shown to suffer severely for their

misdeeds – *preferably in front of the people they had victimized* – they would not be deterred.

'I am doing my best to draw the Government's attention to this problem so that these people may be made aware that not only do their misdeeds not pay, but that they are going to be punished to such a degree that will make them fear to return to their evil practices.'

If Africans could have been absolutely sure that the Pearce Commission would be honest and impartial and would fearlessly report what they had found, there would have been no violence. This is quite clear in retrospect. The way to violence had been paved not only by the repressive, racial policies of the white Rhodesian authorities, but by those who had sought a settlement without consulting African opinion within Rhodesia. Sir Alec Douglas-Home, Lord Goodman and others involved on the British side had, no doubt unwittingly and unintentionally, cast doubt on the objectivity of the Pearce Commission. They did not cast doubt on the Pearce Commission in itself but on any commission which would be sent to Rhodesia in the light of past negotiations. By the time the Pearce Commission arrived in Rhodesia there was so much fear and so much uncertainty amongst so many people, that Lord Pearce himself observed: 'On Monday, 17 January, our Commissioners dispersed to begin their circuits in the Provinces . . . These operations opened against a background of mounting tension.' The African people were by this time certain that they would be stopped from seeing the Commission and that they must, therefore, take upon themselves the responsibility of by-passing officialdom to reach it.

'During January 16,' Lord Pearce reports, 'large numbers of Africans from the townships adjacent to Gwelo assembled on the roads leading to the city centre, apparently with the intention of marching on the High Court where the two Commissioners were erroneously thought to be sitting, to inform them of their rejection of the settlement proposals. The security forces took charge of the situation, but our Commissioners' offer to address the crowd was not taken up by the authorities. Some lives were lost; a number of beerhalls in the townships were later destroyed by fire; and at least one store was looted. In view of the tense situation, the two Commissioners at Gwelo agreed with the authorities to postpone the meeting scheduled for that day.'

What the commissioners may not have realized at the time was that the initial fury in Gwelo had been sparked off by local employers inviting their employees to sign forms which stated that the signatories accepted the settlement proposals. Threats were made that those who did not sign might be sacked. Threats of this kind in a country where unemployment is a major problem were enough to spark off direct action. When the police then sealed off the roads which, people thought, led to the commission, violence was almost inevitable.

The places eventually attacked were associated in one way or another with the authorities. When the security forces started using tear gas the people were immediately advised by the African police to soak cloths in water and wrap them around their faces. No doubt Lord Goodman, when he wrote 'My Case for Settling with Smith' for the *Observer*, believed absolutely what he had been told and what he then used in his argument: '. . . the white man retains control over the black man because of the formidable forces he is able to deploy . . . He maintains a police force largely composed of Africans wholly loyal to the regime and the same is true of the black troops in the Rhodesian Army.'

But Lord Goodman's argument was fallacious, as he would immediately have recognized had he met a fair cross-section of black police, or black soldiers. Black individuals in the police and the army actively, if surreptitiously helped their fellows back during those terrible hours in Gwelo.

On 19 January violence broke out in the Salisbury African township of Harari. Four people were killed. Lord Pearce reported that 'It was difficult to pinpoint the exact cause of the disorder, but there was no question of it being directed against the Commission.'

Had the Commission been able to have observers throughout Rhodesia before and during the test of acceptability to ensure that normal political activity was permitted to the Commission's satisfaction, it would have been recognized immediately that the refusal of permission on a number of occasions to hold meetings in Salisbury's townships, and the strict supervision of the deliberately limited numbers allowed to attend those which were held under police surveillance, would probably eventually lead to a breach of the peace. When Africans in Harare, on the morning of 19 January, saw the newspapers, they would have read of death and destruction in Gwelo, and further arrests of people and they would have seen pictures of police with guns, soldiers in gas-masks. Like the people in Gwelo they would have interpreted it all as a build up to prevent the people of Rhodesia as a whole from expressing their opinions to the Pearce Commission.

Lord Pearce reported that: 'In Fort Victoria, too, our two Commissioners arrived to find the atmosphere tense. They were able to complete their meetings as planned, but their visit was followed by serious disturbances in one of the townships there.'

I am very sad to say that I believe that the violence in Fort Victoria which followed the visit of the Pearce Commissioners may have been provoked by the Commissioners themselves as well as by the authorities. I do not believe that the violence was in any way provoked deliberately.

On 20 January, two days after I was arrested, *The Times* of London carried a report I had written on a mass-meeting in Fort Victoria held twelve days previously. It was a peaceful meeting of over 2,000 people which assembled under the eyes of the police. The main speakers included Mr Samuel Munodawafa who called attention to the resignation of Sir Frederick Pedler from the Pearce Commission, and Mr Siloka Chiringoma, who said, at the meeting: 'We have come to form a National Front to oppose the proposals. We have the chance of showing the whole world that we are people to care about. We do not like violence or any emotion. People must lower down their temperatures and get the issue as we explain it. But one thing that must be clearly understood is that we are going to challenge what is not correct.'

On 19 January, the morning I reached prison and the day before *The Times* carried my report of the Fort Victoria meeting, the *Rhodesia Herald* carried a lengthy report of the first public meeting of the Pearce Commissioners in Fort Victoria. When I read it in my cell I was desperately afraid that the Commissioners, judging by this report, would turn out to be as biased as we had feared they might be. The report read:

A rowdy session at which 'No' cheerleaders had it all their own way developed here yesterday leaving the two Pearce Commissioners for Victoria Province plainly dissatisfied with the validity of testing African opinion at open meetings . . .

Mr Burkinshaw said the Commissioners were left in doubt as to what extent the African had been organized by 'rabble rousers'. He and Mr Dawkins were trying to find a way which would reflect African opinion more accurately.

The Africans refused the Commissioners' invitation to give evidence in private. Spokesmen for the crowd claimed that they would be intimidated, despite Mr Dawkins' saying that there would surely be more danger of intimidation in public sessions.

At another rowdy afternoon session with Africans the Commissioners tried to question the audience on the proposals to see if they were understood, but the questions were parried. Africans merely said they were against the terms – drawing tumultuous applause.

The Africans protested and said they understood the terms completely and that they had not come to be questioned.

Mr Burkinshaw was howled down as he tried to explain how the terms provided for progress to African rule, a commission into racial discrimination, fairer land distribution and greater African representation in Parliament.

Mr Burkinshaw eventually told the Africans, 'I do not know whether there is any point in me carrying on any further, because you are to some extent ridiculing my words. We are not here to argue the terms of this agreement. We are here to tell you what they are and to hear your opinions.

'*If you want the present Constitution to stay as it is, then your answer presumably will be NO to the proposals.*

'*If you want to enjoy any of these improvements for the African people then you will say YES!*'

By saying this, Mr Burkinshaw said, in advance, what Mr Ian Smith was to say later . . . 'if the Africans reject this offer, if their answer to the Pearce Commission is "No" then this is a clear indication of their preference for our present 1969 Constitution.' By saying this Mr Burkinshaw was not adhering to the letter of the simplified version of the White Paper put out by his own Commission, which stated, 'If you do accept, then the present dispute will end and Britain will declare to all the world that your country is now independent. If you do not accept, then things will continue as they are and how this will turn out no-one can easily say.'

The Africans in Fort Victoria, as I knew, were not fools. At the meeting which I had attended the terms were fully explained and the most complex questions were asked and answered. The *Rhodesia Herald* report of the Commissioners' meeting ended:

In the end the Commissioners put it to the crowd: 'We are saying: "Do you want what is in the White Paper or do you want what you have got now?"' [The question was not fair, and in the circumstances the reply was brilliant.]

A crowd spokesman said, 'We want what we want'.

At the end of the day a delegation of four local members of the African National Council gave evidence in open session. Their spokesman, Mr Samuel Munodawafa [The *Herald* spelt various names wrongly so I am here substituting the correct spelling into the report] said he objected to the terms because Africans had not been consulted. He also said the proposals were a means of recognizing U.D.I.

Mr Munodawafa claimed that people were being intimidated into accepting the terms by being told that they would 'remain as they were' if they did not accept them.

To this Mr Dawkins replied: 'I do not accept that there has been intimidation by people saying it is this or nothing . . . That is not intimidation. That is fact.'

Mr Munodawafa claimed that a local A.N.C. organizer, Mr Siloka Chiringoma, had been arrested, and Mr Dawkins said law and order had to be maintained and this was not necessarily a matter for the Commission. Mr Munodawafa replied that he wasn't talking to the Commissioners, but to the press.

As I sat in my cell that morning and read the report I was gravely disturbed. If Mr Munodawafa had said to the commissioners that he wasn't speaking to them after, as I knew, doing all he could to ensure that people in Fort Victoria *could* speak to the Pearce Commission, then he obviously thought that the two commissioners were not worth speaking to. It was that press report, more than anything else, that made me hope while I was imprisoned that the Pearce commission would pack up and go home.

But now I am glad, having read the full Pearce Report, that the Commission fulfilled its duty. Very few of the commissioners seemed to have interpreted the proposals in the same way as did Mr Dawkins (schoolmaster; from 1945–62 served in Sierra Leone mostly as a district commissioner and provincial commissioner apart from the years 1956–60 when seconded as administrator in Montserrat) and Mr Burkinshaw, O.B.E. (a queen's messenger; H.M. overseas civil service 1949–64. The earlier part of his service in Sierra Leone as a district commissioner and the last five years as a district commissioner and deputy provincial commissioner in Nyasaland. Deputy administrator of the Turks and Caicos Islands 1966–8).

On the day I was reading the report of the Fort Victoria meetings in my cell and Africans were being shot and wounded in Harari, the authorities were hopelessly mismanaging matters in Umtali. This led to the tragic and not unintentional (from the point of view of the killers) loss of eight lives. The Pearce Commission had advertised a meeting. The Manicaland Provincial Commissioner cancelled the meeting.

'Our Commissioners,' says the Pearce Report, 'asked that news of this be at once communicated to the people of the area stressing that this was a postponement not a cancellation. It is not clear to what extent this was done although the local radio station certainly carried news of the change. The township authorities were unaware

THE RIGHT TO SAY NO

of the postponement and a crowd of about 1,000 had gathered at the site of the meeting at the time it was due. Apparently they were at first well-behaved when told by the police that there was to be no meeting, but they subsequently broke up into groups, some of which were involved in extensive disorders which, according to official figures, led to the tragic loss of eight lives.'

Once again people had thought they were being prevented from seeing the Commission. Had they been allowed to do so it is possible that, *according to official figures*, eight lives would have been spared.

Once the Pearce Commission managed to assure the people of their impartiality and their willingness and eagerness to assess Rhodesian opinion as fairly as they possibly could, there was no more violence on the part of the public so far as we know. And when all the evidence had been collected and sifted through, the Pearce Commission reached the clear conclusion that: 'We do not accept that there was ever a moment when a majority of Africans, on reflection and with some understanding of the proposals, would have answered Yes.' One of the commissioners who had assessed opinion in Salisbury wrote:

Many of the meetings that I held with small groups of Africans – male and female – were with educated and responsible citizens. These people for the most part argued their case logically, calmly and cogently. Very often they were prepared to admit that there was much in the proposals that they recognized of potential value and assistance to the African population, but always they found their objections outweighed the other factors. Their points were always made forcefully but without bitterness or apparent anger. At both large and small meetings I was impressed with the courtesy and good humour with which I was treated. The restraint of the African audiences even when they were arguing that they had been betrayed or insulted or when they were alleging injustice, discrimination and harassment was commendable and remarkable.

In contrast, as the Rhodesian press reported on 13 May, ten days before the Pearce Report was released, the retiring Secretary for Internal Affairs, Mr Hostes Nicolle, had told British officials that they were 'stark, staring mad' when they told him of their plans for the test of acceptability.

'It was clear to me,' said Mr Nicolle, 'that certain elements well known to us had a significant hand in the preparation of the plan. The plan envisaged that the test would be undertaken on the basis of the complete exclusion of our district administration and police, and through the medium of mass public meetings by show of hands or in private if desired.

'I told these British officials in very plain language that they were stark staring mad, and I forecast to them the implications of this stupid plan.' But, the press reports continued, the British insisted on their plan, and Mr Nicolle told them, whether they liked it or not, the Rhodesian Government would apply the necessary security measures to maintain law and order, including the cancellation of public meetings if the security situation warranted it.

'In the event the operation turned out as had been forecast by us on 7 January, and it became necessary at the outset to accord security priority to the exercise. We forecast the shambles experienced in this operation and we warned the British officials in the clearest terms.'

Mr Nicolle said that this situation could easily have been predicted by anyone with knowledge of the African and the government's machinery, because the plan neutralized the administrative machinery and applied non-traditional methods of consultation.

'In other words, a free-for-all in which rabble-rousing techniques, intimidation and mob irresponsibility could be exploited by elements imbued with chaos ideology.

'As we know, many sociologists support this ideology because they see it as a vehicle through which a political structure can be changed and communistic doctrines fulfilled.'

It is unlikely that when he made this speech Mr Nicolle had seen an advance copy of the Pearce Report for he concluded his speech by paying tribute to Lord Pearce and his commissioners saying that they portrayed the 'true British ideals of diligence, integrity and impartiality'. Before the report was issued the commissioners were held to be British and to portray the best of British virtues.

After the report was published Mr Ian Smith described the commissioners as 'a group of foreigners stumbling around' and Mr Newington, M.P. said they demonstrated the decay of Britain.

CHAPTER THIRTEEN

Post Pearce

If, as honourable members opposite are so fond of saying, we are to have no more Munichs, then it is up to them to see that there is no more weakness.

Sir Alec Douglas-Home, then Lord Dunglass

ON Saturday, 11 March 1972, Lord Pearce left Salisbury and returned to London. Almost a month later the *Sunday Mail* reported that Mr Ian Smith was touring Rhodesian Front branches 'selling the settlement proposals'.

'With utter amazement I read in your paper that Mr Smith is now going round the various R.F. branches explaining the settlement terms,' wrote a correspondent in the *Chronicle* on 14 April. 'Surely this is four months too late. Perhaps he plans to give explanations to the Africans too.'

Far from giving any public explanations to anyone about anything Mr Smith held his meetings behind closed doors and the press was not permitted to attend. It was clear that the Smith regime believed that the only group of people in the country who merited receiving information and participating in discussion was the Rhodesian Front party.

This was taken to its extreme when the first parliament to assemble since the previous November, opened and closed on 30 March after a sitting of an hour and half.

'Government in its wisdom considers that at this stage, for the benefit of law and order in Rhodesia, it is not advisable to hold a debate,' announced the Leader of the House, Mr Desmond Lardner-Burke. From 1 April 1971 to 31 March 1972 the Rhodesian Parliament sat for a total of forty-two days. Rhodesia is ruled by Regulations under the continued state of emergency and there is no need for parliament except to vote funds.

Behind the storm of reaction and counter-reaction to the visit of the Pearce Commission and the publication of the Pearce Report, white Rhodesia settled down rather less comfortably than usual to the prospect of continued isolation from the world community and continuing sanctions.

Rhodesia is quite clearly in a desperate state economically. There is an acute shortage of rolling stock on the railways and emergency measures have had to be taken to transport fertiliser by road for the next growing season while the railways attempt to move what they can of the past year's crops. Foreign currency has been diverted from industry to keep the white inhabitants supplied with luxury goods and happy. The fact that foreign cars are available in Rhodesia has tended to mislead outside observers who have sometimes stated that the availability of Mercedes, etc. is indicative of the wealth and economic stability of Rhodesia. This is not so.

Post-Pearce the shortage of foreign currency became so acute that even the white man in the street became aware of some discomfort. Whisky and wines were in short supply and, at the beginning of April, the Ministry of Commerce and Industry appealed to the public to limit their buying of toilet rolls strictly to the amount they immediately required.

The *Sunday Mail*, in a front page story on 9 April, reported that housewives were angry about the shortage of toilet rolls. 'What are my family supposed to do?' asked a shopper as she piled eight rolls into her supermarket trolley yesterday. 'We all have runny noses.'

The film *Catch 22* was banned. One of the many objections lodged against it by the censorship board was that a queue outside a brothel was 'over-long'. Mr J. C. Andersen, for the board, also objected to a hospital scene in the film. 'What would Florence Nightingale have thought of . . . a bandaged patient with a urinal tube sprouting from his groin?' he asked.

The censorship board was not alone in its concern for Rhodesian morality. On 20 April the *Rhodesia Herald* printed a letter from Mrs Paddy Spilhaus, National Council of Women of Rhodesia (who incidentally heads the government-sponsored birth control programme for African women).

'Members of our Council wish to protest very strongly about the daily pictures of nude young women that appear in your paper.

'Many members have heard lurid comments from African men about this and they feel in a mixed society such as ours this is asking for trouble eventually.

'Several members said they felt embarrassed about letting their servants read the papers.'

On 5 May the *Rhodesia Herald* printed a reply from Mr Ernest Mpofu of Que Que under the heading 'Do nudes not attract Europeans?'

Mr Mpofu asked if European men were so passive or too civilized or both 'to be attracted . . . Or is it that Mrs Spilhaus cares less about men of her own colour looking at nude girls?

'Mr Editor, these nude pictures should continue appearing in your paper until Mrs Spilhaus and her friends learn to be positive in their criticisms.'

There was a footnote from the editor. 'The President, National Council of Women [perhaps forgetting who had started the correspondence] comments that her organization is a non-political, multiracial association . . . and does not wish to take part in a controversy on the lines suggested.' Hardly anyone tumbled to the fact that the *Rhodesia Herald* has never printed a picture of a naked woman.

On 5 May it was reported that the chairman of the Matabeleland division of the Rhodesian Front, Dr Piet Barnard, would ask several cabinet ministers what methods their ministries use to screen visiting pop groups 'likely to have a bias towards the permissive society' who might 'encourage young Rhodesians to abandon decent self-control', and on 30 May headlines stretched across the centre page of the *Chronicle*.

PROBE SOUGHT INTO 'TOO MANY BLACKS' IN TV SHOWS

The Board of Rhodesia Television Ltd. is to be asked to investigate complaints from some viewers about the increasing number of films and programmes in which black actors are shown in prominent roles . . . The MP for Hillside, Mr Fawcett Phillips, said one of the problems of television was that in all imported films the emphasis was either 'blatant sex, leaving little to the imagination, or a colour theme where Negroes were depicted as heroes and the whites as villains . . .'

While members of the Rhodesian Front expressed their concern generally about deteriorating standards in morality, none was more anxious or specific than Mr P. Martindale of Salisbury who wrote in the *Rhodesia Herald* (17 April) that the university and its 'degenerate students' were 'representative of what is symptomatic throughout the country as a whole. That is, a complete breakdown of all moral principles . . .'

He suggested that the 'treatment' of such 'un-Christian immorality' should be taken to its logical conclusion. 'That is, a Government-established surgery which could, for example, scar and disfigure any exposed parts of the female body above, say, the knees. This would at least restore some form of "morality" to the university and country . . .'

The continuing discussion on morality led naturally into the fields of religion and politics. Mr Mark Partridge, Minister of Local Government and Housing, urged ministers of religion to stick to their calling which was, he said, to preach the Ten Commandments and refrain from dabbling in politics. Members of Parliament heartily assented including the Rev. Cronje, a Dutch Reformed Church predicant who sits on the Rhodesian Front benches in Parliament.

But the prevailing white belief that politics and religion are divorced subjects which should, therefore, be strictly compartmentalized was (or should have been) shaken when on 22 March the Minister of Law and Order and Justice, Mr Desmond Lardner-Burke stepped into the pulpit of the Anglican cathedral in Salisbury to deliver a sermon on: 'What is a Christian?'

Christ had never preached that everyone was equal, Mr Lardner-Burke stated. Nor did he preach that everyone was entitled to equal divisions in all spheres of life.

'As I understand it, when He said "In my Father's house are many mansions – I go to prepare a place for you", he indicated that there could never be equality and that each person should be dealt with according to his abilities and his achievements.

'If there was to be equality, why should there be different mansions in his Father's house? Surely there would have been one mansion where everyone was entitled to go?'

Mr Lardner-Burke then attacked religious people 'who become involved in politics'.

'How many times have we heard from professed Christians that the present Government is not acting within Christian principles? I deny this. Why are these statements made? Presumably because those professing those thoughts do not care if there is chaos in the country.

'Surely we must have laws for the protection of all the people in the country and if these laws are broken, punishment must be meted out to the wrongdoer.

'If by removing a person from circulation we entitle other persons to live in peace, then surely it is the Christian duty of the Government to remove such a person.'

Bishop Abel Muzorewa, chairman of the African National Council which had campaigned successfully for the rejection of the settlement proposals and who is under constant attack by the Rhodesian authorities, replied to Mr Partridge and Mr Lardner-Burke, comparing their view that religion and politics should be kept separate with the belief that the earth is flat.

'What Mr Partridge and Mr Lardner-Burke want to do is to divide the priests of this land,' he said. 'On the one side are the sheep who bleated their "Yes" to the proposals, and are therefore not considered to take any part in politics. On the other side they have placed the goats. These are the daredevils who said "No" to the proposals and consequently have been dubbed "politicking priests".'

Quoting from the New English Bible, Isaiah 10, the bishop said: 'Shame on you. You who make unjust laws and publish burdensome decrees, depriving the poor of justice, robbing the weakest of my people of their rights, despoiling the widow and plundering the orphan.'

'I suppose,' said Bishop Muzorewa, 'if Jesus were to come to Rhodesia and spell out what it means to love God and neighbours, he would be called a "political priest" by our preacher politicians.'

There was a flicker of interest in the reported possibility that the Australian Government might close down the Rhodesian information centre in Sydney. In the event the Australian Government did little more than admit that there had been 'technical' infringements of the sanctions regulations, but that the office could remain open. During the discussion it was revealed that a Mr Harry Parry had been attempting to run a Rhodesian information office in Auckland, New Zealand, financed from Rhodesia through the Sydney office. Mr Parry's information office closed down but there was at least one tribute paid to him in Rhodesia. On 14 April the *Rhodesia Herald* printed a letter from Mrs Wendy Turner, Greendale, Salisbury, under the heading *Rhodesia 'underground' helped them return.*

It was most interesting to read (8 April) a poignant note that Harry Parry has closed his Rhodesian Information Office in Auckland, N.Z.

It was poignant because we lived there last year and met this dear old retired JP, who is nearly ninety, during our frantic efforts to re-immigrate, with our three Rhodesian children, to this country.

We had no success with direct correspondence with Salisbury, and were introduced through the 'underground' in N.Z. to the Friends of Rhodesia, of which Mr Parry was the head.

I was rushed off secretly to his home where, in a decaying old barn in the backyard, we ploughed through stacks of ancient immigration forms and magazines – so outdated that we recognized them from our first entry to this country in 1958. Everything was covered in dust and cobwebs. Mr Parry himself has failing eyesight and recently lost a leg in an accident.

We filled in the old forms, since Harry had gone to so much trouble (he even cabled Salisbury for us), and finally were given the OK to come in as 'tourists' provisionally. Well, we're happy to be back, and have our residence permits now . . . but I wonder how many Harry Parrys there are in remote spots all over the world, trying to do their bit for us against such odds?

I'll always remember the old-fashioned varnished sign-board, lettered in gold leaf, nailed over his barn door where no one could see it – Rhodesian Information Office. It was the most cloak-and-dagger experience I've ever had.

On 7 April the *Rhodesia Herald* printed a report on 'How The Rioters Came To Die'.

. . . In a statement produced at the inquiry into the deaths of Majonga (juvenile) and Mandezha, police said that three warning shots had been fired into the air before they had fired into a crowd of about 200 who were throwing stones at them . . .

The police statement said that after shots were fired directly into the crowd they dispersed. As the police drove off again they saw Mandezha's body.

When police returned to the scene they found Majonga, who was unconscious, and he was taken to hospital where he later died.

The magistrate found that Majonga's death was due to a gunshot wound to the brain. In the case of Mandezha he found that death was due to inhalation of blood after gunshot wounds. Police said they had used automatic pistols.

At the inquiry into the death of Joseph, a police statement said that at the intersection of Beatrice and Manchester Roads they were accosted by between 200 and 300 Africans throwing stones. When they got out of their Land-Rover the Africans started to throw stones at them.

One policeman fired a shot-gun at an African who stood out among the rest. He fell to the ground.

Moments later the policeman saw the African rising. He fired at him again and the man fell again. He said the African, later identified as Joseph, was alive when they reached him, but died soon afterwards. The magistrate found that death was due to haemorrhage after gunshot wounds.

At the inquest into the death of Robbison, a police statement said that as they drove down Cripps Road they came across a burning car tipped on its side. Nearby was a large crowd of

Africans. They investigated and the Africans started to throw stones at them.

Two policemen raised shot-guns but the crowd refused to disperse. Both then fired into the crowd which broke up. After the crowd had gone they found Robbison curled round a pole. He was alive at the time. The magistrate found that death was due to haemorrhage after gunshot wounds.

At the inquest into the death of Nherere the court was not told how he came to be shot.

A police statement said that a policeman spotted Nherere coming towards the Mbare Hostels. His shirt was bloodstained and he appeared to be wounded.

He arrested Nherere and took him to Southerton police station. A police officer there sent him to hospital where he later died.

The magistrate found that death was due to peritonitis following multiple ruptures by gunshot wounds.

When the Rhodesian Parliament eventually assembled on 2 June, a young M.P., Mr Allan Savory, who had recently resigned from the Rhodesian Front and now sits as an Independent, placed a delicate finger on a subject which has been of increasing concern to the press and a few individuals.

Mr Savory: Mr Speaker, the last few months have seen a very vital stage in Rhodesia's history, and it is disturbing to hear speakers like the one immediately prior to me standing up to say how pleased he is that the Prime Minister permitted a debate in Parliament on this report. I hope that it will not be too long before Parliament is automatically entitled to debate items as vital as settlement proposals and reports of this nature——
(*The Prime Minister:* Inaudible interjection.) (Hansard. 6 June 1972.)

But many Members of Parliament themselves were not interested in rational debate and cabinet ministers led the way in barracking and vilifying African members, shouting them down when they suggested compromise and consultation between whites and Africans.

Mr J. B. Hove, M.P. had a rough passage when, replying to allegations that wide-spread intimidation had been practised by Africans, he tried to give some picture of what had been happening in the Belingwe District. He said that after police had ordered one meeting to disperse the people had said they were only discussing the proposals and a chief present said he was in charge of the meeting and he would control it. The police arrested the chief and carried him away in their van. When Pearce commissioners visited his area, Mr Hove said, some of the chiefs were locked up in the District Commissioner's office to prevent them from meeting the Commission with their people in the tribal trust lands. '. . . the people were told at the start that they could go out and discuss the proposals as they liked but immediately when people started to organize themselves to discuss the proposals they were followed by policemen and soldiers with guns and——(*Hon. Members:* "Nonsense.").' (Hansard. 7 June.)

Senator Morris, not fully recovered from the fact that he had not been able to 'guide' the procedures of the Pearce Commission, flayed their report.

'It is my opinion that many of the views in this report amount to nothing more than cant, claptrap and hypocrisy,' he said. But he paid tribute to the four commissioners, two from Victoria Province and two from Matabeleland North who had differed from their fellow-commissioners in their findings (the only four to do so) 'for their courage in giving the conclusions they did'. Their conclusions were that the level of intimidation was too high and the level of comprehension too low for them to be able to report.

A meeting that the Victoria Commissioners had held in Fort Victoria has been discussed in the last chapter, but the first time that the Matabeleland North Commissioners leapt to my attention was when I read the Pearce Report. It is not in the least surprising that they found themselves the recipients of Senator Morris's congratulations judging by a section of their report printed on page 200 of the Pearce Report.

Our impression throughout the Province was that pressured persuasion, in varying degree, was a major factor at all save private interviews. Such persuasion was almost entirely by African on Africans:

On each of the first five days, in the Bubi and Nyamandhlovu Districts, we saw the same faces of cheerleaders and ex-detainees at every meeting. The atmosphere was more or less hostile and tense, and the 'show' invariably organized. Overt acts were not always observable, but at each venue we were informed by witnesses in private of previous threats of house burnings, etc. to secure a publicly shouted 'no'. European farmers told us that their labour was too afraid to come and see us. The events of '61–64 seemed imprinted on tribal memory . . .

At Nyamandhlovu, on 24 January, our interpreters told us that an unidentified voice in the crowd had threatened to stone any of a gang of PWD road labour who dared to see us privately. The European overseer finally persuaded them to file past us one by one. All said 'No', with eyes downcast, although up to the reputed threat we had had several 'Ayes' interspersed with 'Noes'.

This report was worthy of the pen of the Rhodesian Ministry of Internal Affairs . . . 'the same faces of cheerleaders and ex-detainees . . .' (what does an ex-detainee look like? I would like to know as one day I hope to be an ex-detainee myself) . . . 'the "show" invariably organized . . .' '. . . tribal memory . . .' 'Overt acts were not always observable . . .' But conceding that style and language are not always important, the last sentence of the report is, in itself, breathtaking and throws some doubt on the level of comprehension of the two commissioners themselves.

'. . . up to the reputed threat we had had several "Ayes" interspersed with "Noes".'

Nyamandhlovu is a Sindebele speaking area. The word for 'No' in Sindebele is *Ai*, or *Ayi* (pronounced Aye). Ayi is a clear and definite No. The English word 'Aye' is scarcely used in Rhodesia except perhaps by a few elderly whites, and in the House of Assembly.

The hostile reaction of the Rhodesian authorities to the Pearce Report was to be expected. The reaction of the British Foreign and Commonwealth Secretary, Sir Alec Douglas-Home, was astounding and could not have been expected except, perhaps, by his worst detractors.

It is clearly laid down in the five principles that 'the British Government would need to be satisfied that any basis proposed for independence was acceptable to the people of Rhodesia as a whole.' Sir Alec is the author of those principles and has repeated them so often that he must by now know them by heart.

In the simplified version of the settlement proposals put out by the Pearce Commission, with the full authority of Her Majesty's Government behind them, the situation facing the people of Rhodesia was clearly explained.

We, who are members of the British Government's Commission, wish to tell you about the proposals for the future government of your country. After telling you what these are, we shall ask you whether you accept them. If you do accept, then the present dispute will end and Britain will declare to all the world that your country is now independent. If you do not accept, then things will continue as they are at present and how this will turn out no one can easily say. We will explain this all more clearly so that you can understand and decide. It is for you, the people of Rhodesia, to say whether you accept or reject the proposals. Britain will agree to what the people of Rhodesia as a whole may decide.

These are the proposals.

Rhodesia will become an independent country.

The British Government will give up its claim to make laws for your country.

By saying NO the African people demonstrated that they did not want Rhodesia to become an independent country – yet. They did not want the British Government to give up its claims to make laws for Rhodesia.

But Sir Alec Douglas-Home would not accept a 'No' as an answer.

It was to have been expected that the Rhodesian regime would renege on any aspects of the settlement proposals when it had been legalized and sanctions had been lifted, unless all aspects of the settlement proposals were powerfully guaranteed, externally.

It was not to have been expected that, because he had been given a 'No' when he wanted a 'Yes', Sir Alec would attempt to renege not only on the five principles, but on the findings of the Pearce Commission.

Mr Howman, Rhodesia's Minister of Foreign Affairs who, with Mr Ian Smith and Mr Desmond Lardner-Burke, took part in the final negotiations with Sir Alec and the British team, was on record as saying that he and his colleagues did not intend to honour the terms of any settlement reached with Britain. In June 1969, he spoke of past negotiations with the British Labour government and of the concessions that the Rhodesian regime had been prepared to make in return for the recognition of Rhodesia's independence. 'We made these offers always with this understanding that we would change the constitution as we saw fit.'

Unlike Mr Howman, Sir Alec had initially given every impression that he would abide by the findings of the Pearce Commission.

The Pearce Report stated that one of the main reasons for the rejection of the settlement proposals was that of the overriding distrust of the Smith regime by the African people. There was ample reason to distrust the regime. As Mr Pat Bashford, leader of Rhodesia's tiny, moderate Centre Party, had said in his evidence to the Commission: the Centre Party accepted the proposals despite the fact that –

'We know only too well the political dangers inseparable from conferring legality upon those who have shown such little regard for the rule of law.

'We fully realize the dubious value of solemn assurances uttered by men to whom oaths of allegiance are but scraps of paper to be torn up at will . . .'

The fact that Her Majesty's Government were trying to reach an agreement with such men was cynical enough. Sir Alec's reaction to the pronounced failure of the settlement attempt was the pure essence of cynicism.

He naturally paid tribute to the Pearce Commission for their 'independence' and 'devotion' in completing their difficult task. The tribute was rather cooler than the one he had paid on the announcement of the proposed terms of settlement when he had said: 'For this result I am greatly indebted to the Lord Goodman and to the team of negotiators, who have worked so hard and made my visit possible . . .'

Sir Alec was not indebted to the Pearce Commission. Their findings had been a political embarrassment. He was appalled by the 'No' verdict. And so, in the weeks ahead, he vented his embarrassment and his cold, carefully restrained anger on the African people of Rhodesia.

'Britain will agree to what the people of Rhodesia as a whole may decide,' Lord Pearce had said. In his honesty, had he known what Sir Alec's reaction to a 'No' was going to be, he would probably have had to add: '. . . if you say "Yes"'.

In the very same statement in which he announced the findings of the Pearce Commission to the House of Commons, Sir Alec said:

When honourable members have read the report *I hope that they will study once again the terms of the proposed settlement.*

Although the proposals have failed to gain acceptance *they still represent* a genuine attempt to find a sensible, *and in all the circumstances,* a just solution of Rhodesia's special social and political problems.

It will be apparent to honourable members that the negotiations of November followed by the Pearce Report have created a situation in which many new ideas will be current and in which positions, which hitherto have been inflexible, could become more fluid. [As there was no sign that the inflexible racist doctrines of the Rhodesian Front had become any more fluid since the publication of the Pearce Report – on the contrary – it looked as though any proposed fluidity would be on the British side.]

It is clear, therefore, that in these circumstances there must be time for reflection, particularly by Rhodesians, for the problems of Rhodesia can essentially only be solved by Rhodesians themselves.

Her Majesty's Government feel that plenty of time should be given in which the position can be clarified and that meanwhile no door should be closed . . .

Britain will agree to what the people of Rhodesia as a whole may decide . . .

If so, the settlement proposals should have been withdrawn immediately by the honourable Secretary for Foreign and Commonwealth Affairs, and scrapped. The proposals had been found completely unsatisfactory as a basis for independence.

Sir Alec warned in a B.B.C. interview, taped shortly after he had announced the findings of the Pearce Commission, that without this settlement there would be no justiciable Bill of Rights, no majority rule within sight, no money for the development of the Tribal Trust Lands.

Under his settlement proposals the justiciable Bill of Rights wasn't worth the paper it was written on; majority rule was no more in sight under the continuing government of the Rhodesian Front than it had ever been, and the money offered for the development of Tribal Trust Lands would simply have been a further step towards laying a foundation of apartheid in Rhodesian society. The managing director of Tilcor (Tribal Trust Land Development Corporation), which would have played a major part in the administration of the British money had said in March 1972 that any money coming from Britain would be used firstly to 'create an infrastructure along community lines'; secondly for the establishment of factories in the Tribal Trust Lands and, as he said, lastly for education. This is apartheid . . . the development of different areas for different racial groups.

This was all bad enough, but then on 15 June the Rhodesian press reported that so far as Sir Alec was concerned, the settlement proposals were still 'on the table'. He was reported as saying that despite the Pearce verdict he thought that a settlement 'with Rhodesia' was still possible. He said that Mr Smith had 'neither discarded nor modified' the agreed terms since the Pearce Report was published.

'In that sense, I regard them as still being on the table.' He thought there 'must still be an outside chance' of reaching an agreement with Rhodesia, adding: 'It still can't be very difficult to get a settlement with Mr Smith.' He said that there were two extremes in Rhodesia –

the right-wing pressure for 'complete racial separation' and the African view that 'you must fight it out'.

'Somewhere between the two you are going to find a sensible compromise. You have got to compromise . . .'

This was malfeasance on a scale comparable to that of the Smith regime. He had deliberately, according to the press report, misinterpreted the findings of the Pearce Commission who did *not* report that the African view was that 'you must fight it out'. In his evidence to the Pearce Commission, the African leader Mr Joshua Nkomo had stated:

. . . we unreservedly reject these proposals because they do not satisfy universally accepted conditions of independence and self determination for all our people; they are racial and discriminatory, and we believe that if implemented, they will engender feelings of hostility between black and white citizens of our country and bring about bloodshed and untold human suffering. This must not be allowed to happen. We therefore appeal to you, Lord Pearce, to impress upon the British Government to abandon these proposals and summon a constitutional conference at which leaders of all sections of our population will take part. We know there are formidable problems to be encountered but we believe that with goodwill by all of us, they can be overcome.

We on our part are prepared to work resolutely for a constitutional settlement that will give peace and security to all citizens of our country irrespective of colour.

The whole tenor of the report in discussing African attitudes was in direct contradiction to Sir Alec's statement that the African view was 'you must fight it out'.

Worse was to follow.

Rhodesia's *Chronicle* headlined more thoughts of Sir Alec on 16 June 1972.

THINK AGAIN, PLEADS SIR ALEC
EXAMPLE OF 'LEADERSHIP FAILURE' BY A.N.C.
EVIDENCE OF TERMS NOT BEING FULLY UNDERSTOOD

The report read:

A strong appeal to all the people of Rhodesia, particularly the Africans, to think again about the settlement proposals was made in Parliament today (15/6) by the Foreign Secretary, Sir Alec

Douglas-Home. He said there was evidence that the proposals had not been fully understood. He asked all Rhodesians, particularly Africans, to study the advantages obtained for them in the proposals, not against an ideal situation but against the indefinite continuation of the present Constitution, which meant racial confrontation . . .

Sir Alec said he believed the time required for the Rhodesians to adjust their minds again to the prospect of a settlement would be after next November – when sanctions come up for their annual legislative renewal. The Foreign Secretary said he could not tell how long sanctions would last.

'If at some future date we decide sanctions have finally failed in their purpose, or evasions are so widespread that they are intolerable, we should not act in some hole-in-the-corner way. We should come to this House and go to the United Nations and state the case plainly for a change of policy.'

. . . There was evidence that the proposals were not fully understood. A member of an A.N.C. delegation which had recently met him had been quite unaware that there was any blocking mechanism in the proposals.

Sir Alec was interrupted by Labour Members who pointed out that Lord Pearce had found the proposals well understood. Sir Alec said he accepted Lord Pearce's judgement, but the instance he mentioned did constitute a failure in leadership.

He said he also had a duty to ask the Africans to look at what they had rejected as there was so much evidence throughout the Pearce Report that the only alternative to the proposed settlement was confrontation and violence . . . [He gave no references.]

He emphasized that there were no better terms he could negotiate for the Africans . . .

Eventually Sir Alec moved that the Commons 'take note' of the Pearce Report. He did not ask that the report be accepted.

It was by now apparent that Sir Alec was not interested in the wishes or decisions of the people of Rhodesia as a whole. He still wanted to settle with Mr Smith. He had joined the current attempt by the Rhodesian authorities to belittle and denigrate not only the African National Council, but the African people of Rhodesia as a whole. He had hinted that sanctions might be lifted. He did not respect the findings of the Pearce Report. He misinterpreted it – or tried to – and sometimes gave the impression that he did not fully understand the findings. He spoke of a 'failure in leadership' demonstrated by *a* member of *an* A.N.C. delegation he had recently seen, not being aware of one of the hundreds of facets in the settlement proposals. He was blissfully unaware of his own grave shortcomings in leadership and honour – so far as Rhodesia was concerned.

CHAPTER FOURTEEN

Dignity, Justice and Fair Opportunities

I know that the great tragedies of history often fascinate men with approaching horror. Paralysed, they cannot make up their minds to do anything but wait. So they wait, and one day the Gorgon devours them.

Albert Camus

LOOKING back 150 years it is almost inconceivable to us today that any person or interest in the United Kingdom could have supported the slave trade, let alone endeavoured to justify it on moral grounds.

It will not take many more years to bring similar, retrospective clarity of mind to shock people that as late as 1972 Her Majesty's Government paid so much more attention to the racist, selfish wishes of a quarter of a million whites in Rhodesia than to the expressed desires of the five million subjected Africans for whom Britain had declared herself responsible.

'The general impression we received,' reported Lord Pearce, 'was that Africans, given the opportunity of expressing their views, rejected proposals which they held did not accord them dignity, justice or fair opportunities, and which did not accord them the parity of recognition which was as important to them as parity of representation.'

Sir Alec Douglas-Home may speak of the seven years since U.D.I. as 'past history' – as if that period was a cancelled cheque to be cast aside, dead and without meaning or value. But November 1965 to the present day is a vital, important chapter at the beginning of which Mr Smith was dismissed from office and clearly recognized as a man in rebellion and a usurper of power.

'It was argued,' writes Lord Pearce, 'that Britain should not recognize Rhodesian independence by treating with an illegal Government. Many expressed dismay that the United Kingdom Government had negotiated with a rebel regime, or as one witness put it: "Britain seems to be punishing Africans instead of the Rhodesian Government." Or, as another person said: "Africans were not a party to

U.D.I. and we won't be used as pawns to legitimize Mr Smith and his regime".'

There has been no transformation in Mr Smith or his supporters since U.D.I. But what has happened to Her Majesty's Government, as represented in this context by Sir Alec Douglas-Home, to transform them into men ready and willing to shake hands with Mr Smith on a deal which left five million people at the mercy of the Rhodesian Front?

It was argued by Africans rejecting the terms, states Lord Pearce, that:

> British involvement in the future of the Africans of Rhodesia should continue and ties with Britain should not be broken. Those who argued this did not wish Britain at present to surrender its claim to be able to influence affairs in Rhodesia. A few recognized the limitations of Britain's actual power but still thought it would be a mistake for the Africans to agree that this tenuous support be withdrawn. We ourselves observed – and all but one team of Commissioners commented to the same effect – that Africans in general retained a loyalty to the Crown and belief in Britain's ability to influence events in Rhodesia. One Commissioner commented that dismay, concern and anger had often been expressed in one way or another that the British Government appeared to be willing to abandon the African. He had gained the impression that, had Britain been able to retain a meaningful presence and exert authority to ensure that the proposals were implemented, there would have been many more 'Yes' votes.

Since Ghana achieved her independence in 1957 there has been a surge of freedom from colonial rule down the continent of Africa. In the fifteen years that have passed there has been great suffering as well as happiness, but despite the heavy cost of freedom (which those who live in Europe should be the first to acknowledge) what people would be willing to return to colonial status? The greatest benefits independence brought were psychological, spiritual, but there was also the continuing urge to achieve a viable, flourishing economy and full nationhood.

'Rhodesia' also desires independence and the right to establish herself as a nation amongst nations. A number of her friends argue: 'Why not, when other countries in Africa have been granted their freedom by the colonial power? Why should Rhodesia be denied what other countries have sought and obtained?'

Of course if 'Rhodesia' wanted what other countries have fought for, then she should have it – power given to all the people to choose their own government, their own way of life. But this is exactly what 'Rhodesia' does not want. To ensure that power was kept out of the hands of the people Mr Smith declared his U.D.I. and has risked the lives of his fellows and seriously damaged the Rhodesian economy in what was the racial gamble of the century. What 'Rhodesia' wants is what South Africa was given in 1910. Nothing less than exclusive power for the white elite so that they, as the new 'colonial power', can exploit for their own gain the labour potential of five million people, the entire mining potential throughout the 100 million acres of Rhodesia and the agricultural potential of 45 million acres. In return, the whites are prepared to 'share' on an apartheid basis (blacks here and whites there) 8 million acres of parks and reserves and allow the Africans the remaining 45 million acres of land on which to lead a tribal existence.

Under white rule the average wage of a white is ten times that of an African. Under white rule R$16 million a year is spent on the education of white children and R$17 million on African children – which works out on the relative enrollments as ten times for each white pupil as for each African. But if it should be suggested that the white child is only ten times favoured then no account is being taken of the fact that the great majority of African children get only five years of schooling and while there are 700,000 African children in primary schools fewer than 500 are enrolled in the university. Every white child can obtain without difficulty all education desired.

This is the situation which British shareholders in Rhodesia are helping to perpetuate. Unfortunately, as has been observed before, statistics do not bleed.

The Smith regime were prepared to inflict enormous damage on the Rhodesian economy in their bid to maintain power but eventually their hearts quailed when they contemplated the continuing erosive effect of sanctions. So they agreed to negotiate with Britain once more and Britain was prepared to connive with them in order on the one hand to gain, on the other to grant legal independence based on a racial, unjust and authoritarian constitution.

Despite this Africans remained amazingly tolerant.

Many criticized the lack of effective consultation with African leaders. No African had been involved in the negotiations: they were therefore not a party to them. If their national leaders had been involved and said they should accept, that would have been different. Some said that for this reason earlier British proposals would also have been unacceptable to Africans. It was also argued that the issue was essentially one between the Europeans and Africans in Rhodesia, or between the Rhodesian Government and the Africans; it was not between the British and Rhodesian Governments; it had to be settled in Rhodesia. Because no African was present or consulted some suspected that the present agreement was designed to benefit the European but not the African. Some thought that better terms could have been obtained if Africans had been present; others believed that there was something to hide. All who raised this point asserted that the African had a right to be consulted and that neither Government appreciated African aspirations; Africans should no longer be thought to be incapable of expressing their own needs. (Pearce Report. Paragraph 313.)

However much tolerance was demonstrated the brutal fact remained that the Smith regime were criminals who not only had committed treason but had contravened many of Rhodesia's own laws, notably the Preservation of Constitutional Government Act which has been conveniently forgotten since U.D.I. While Her Majesty's Government were apparently prepared to forgive and forget, the Africans could not and would not forget, however forgiving they were prepared to be. Lord Goodman had said that the negotiators were prepared to take certain political risks. The negotiators did not have to suffer the consequences. The Africans did. The Pearce Report states:

Mistrust of the intentions and motives of the Government transcended all other considerations. Apprehension for the future stemmed from resentment at what they felt to be the humiliations of the past and at the limitations of policies on land, education, and personal advancement. One summed it up in saying 'We do not reject the Proposals, we reject the Government.' This was the dominant motivation of African rejection at all levels and in all areas. Few could bring themselves to believe that the Government had changed its policies or that the European electorate on whom it depended was prepared to change its attitudes or its way of life. Most refused to see advantages in the Proposals. Those who did doubted whether the Government would ever implement them. These people thought that as soon as Independence was recognized and sanctions revoked, a Government which had torn up previous constitutions could do so again; and even if the Government kept faith, the white electorate would turn them out and replace them by representatives and parties not committed to the present terms. A majority of Africans were convinced that the present governing party was committed to the perpetuation of white supremacy in Rhodesia. They argued that the Government had not sought the support of the African in the past, and were not likely to do so now. If the Government believed that the Proposals were in Rhodesia's best interest, why, they asked, had Ministers not said so unequivocally? Why had no gesture of goodwill been made towards the African people? Why had no indication been given that there were to be any changes except in the distant future?

It was also thought that for Sir Alec Douglas-Home and others to be deceived by Hitler was forgivable. But to make the same kind of mistake twice and to allow a compromise with Smith in 1972 was inexcusable.

In Rhodesia the people as a whole should be ready for independence on the same basis – majority rule – as was required in other countries; or if the people as a whole are not ready for independence the colonial tie should be maintained.

One of the most important consequences of the test of acceptability was the formation of the African National Council (A.N.C.) under the leadership of the president, Bishop Abel Muzorewa and the vice-president, the Rev. Canaan Banana. The A.N.C. was inaugurated on 16 December 1971, in their own words, to 'explain and expose the dangers of accepting the settlement proposals' and to co-ordinate the campaign for rejection. It called for a 'non-violent rejection of the settlement terms.' After the test of acceptability it was decided to prolong the existence of the A.N.C. as a vehicle from which to strive for a just society.

I first became aware of the Rev. Canaan Banana towards the end of 1970 when I saw a picture in the *Chronicle* of a garlanded Methodist minister being carried shoulder-high by scores of singing members of his congregation after his return to Bulawayo from an overseas trip. I remember thinking at the time that this must be a very special man. Not many ministers are met at airports by singing congregations. A few weeks later I met Mr Banana and found that he was indeed a very special person. He is one of the very few people I have met in my life who somehow manages to generate love and liking in those around him, for those around him.

Like Bishop Muzorewa, Mr Banana is a small man physically. He is quiet and unassuming, but fearless in stating his beliefs. 'I have a conviction that the Gospel of Jesus Christ I preach is a Gospel of total redemption. It seeks to redeem the total man. It does not compartmentalize man as some religious fanatics do. It is a gospel that seeks to heal the bleeding wounds of moral, economic, social and political ills of our time.'

During 1971 we became friends. On one occasion the subject of when he was born came up.

'1936,' he said.

'You're not very much older than I am then,' I said.

'Oh yes I am.'

'Well, seven years. That's not a great deal.'

'It is,' he said. 'When you were born I was old enough to look after you.'

Few whites had heard of Bishop Muzorewa and the Rev. Banana before the A.N.C. was formed and successfully opposed the settlement proposals. They are now classed amongst the bitterest enemies of the Rhodesian Front. In 1970 Bishop Muzorewa was banned from entering the Tribal Trust Lands (where members of his family live) and both men are now the subjects of vicious and often childish attacks in Rhodesia's Parliament.

Mr Newington: . . . It seems that nothing the Rev. Banana touches turns out to be more than tainted fruit. – (*An Hon. Member:* Fruit salad.) (Hansard 7 June 1972) – and Hon. Members roared with mirth at allusions to slipping on Banana skins.

Bishop Abel Tendekayi Muzorewa was born in April 1925 of peasant parents, the eldest in a family of six boys and three girls. He was, he says, a typical African boy of around forty years ago. He was a herd-boy for a long time before going to school and 'found pride in that profession', especially in driving the cattle to the dip-tank. He completed his Standard Six at the Old Umtali Mission, and soon after that took up teaching without professional training, like so many of his fellow-teachers in those years.

While he was a teacher he decided to 'answer the call' to enter the ministry of the church and he completed his theological training in 1953 at the Hartzell Theological Seminary, Old Umtali. In 1955 he was ordained a deacon of the United Methodist Church and in 1957 he was ordained an elder, which is a full minister of the United Methodist Church.

In 1958 he set off for academic studies in the United States and was there during the flowering of the civil rights campaign. First he gained a B.A. degree at the Central Methodist College in Fayette, Missouri and then he studied for and achieved an M.A. degree in Nashville, Tennessee. After ten years abroad he returned to Rhodesia.

In September 1968 he was ordained bishop for the Rhodesian

Area of the United Methodist Church and in 1972, in recognition of his courage in giving leadership to his people in their struggle for liberation, he was elected president of the All-Africa Conference of Churches.

He is married and has five children. His eldest son, Blessing Tendekayi is studying in the United States as are two of the bishop's brothers. A third is a lecturer in economics at the University of Lesotho, Botswana and Swaziland.

When I first met Bishop Muzorewa he was electrifying congregations in various Rhodesian centres with Ezekiel, Chapter 37, on the valley of dry bones. For as Ezekiel preached in what seemed a cemetery of bones, a situation with no hope, he called on the four winds to breathe upon the bones that they might live. 'So I preached as he commanded me, and the breath came unto them, and they lived, and stood up upon their feet, an exceeding great army.'

Bishop Muzorewa is above all a preacher. 'My invitation to become chairman of the A.N.C. came as a total surprise to me,' he told the *Sunday Mail* (27 February 1972). 'I was astonished that so many people of different denominations, different organizations and different political views should come forward and ask me to be their leader. I considered their request for three weeks before deciding to go along with them.'

He stated, in this interview, that he found the material benefits offered under the settlement proposals secondary to the moral question involved. 'One hears a lot about the "benefits" of the settlement deal. I don't want something that will benefit Africans, something that will benefit whites, or something that will benefit any particular section of Rhodesian society. My only desire is for a settlement that is just. If there is justice for all men in the proposals, that's fine. If there is not, then they must be rejected.'

The interviewer asked if the Bishop hated whites.

'I was a premature baby and my life was saved by a white missionary nurse,' the Bishop replied. 'I have grown up among white teachers and clergy. My congregation and my church – which has 50,000 members in Rhodesia – includes whites. I have many white friends and I know many whites who support the A.N.C. Africans do not hate whites; they hate the laws which have caused animosity between the races.

'Just recently I had trouble with my car. While it was being repaired at a garage I got into conversation with the European manager. He knew who I was and we chatted about various things. I told him I was late for an appointment, and he offered to give me a lift there.

'Afterwards I said to my wife: "You would not think that there was this kind of person in Rhodesia." But of course there are plenty. It's just that they are hidden away by the laws that keep us apart. That is the tragedy of Rhodesia.'

Canaan Banana was born of Christian parents in the little centre of Essexvale, thirty-six years ago. He was educated at Mzinyathi Methodist Mission and went on to do teacher training at Tegwani. In 1960 he embarked on a two-year theological training course at Epworth College, Salisbury, and was then ordained into the Methodist ministry. Bishop Muzorewa's United Methodist Church is America-based. Mr Banana was ordained into the Methodist Church of the United Kingdom.

He has an exceptionally wide knowledge of Rhodesia, having served in many different centres over the years. In 1970 he underwent training in an Urban Industrial Mission course which was held in south-east Asia.

In January 1971 he resigned from the Methodist ministry in protest against attacks being made by the leadership of his church on the World Council of Churches for their grants to liberation movements. 'I felt the church distorted the World Council position and failed to appreciate the need for the Christian church to respond to human suffering.'

But at the end of 1971 he was invited back into the ministry and is now involved in the lay training department of the Methodist Church. He is married and has three sons but, like Bishop Muzorewa, he and his family face a grim future in which every particle of their courage, faith and long-suffering will be called upon.

'No sane person can be blind to the political cataclysm now engulfing our country . . . We daily witness organized and legalized robbery by those who today wield economic power through the immorality of the maldistribution of land.' Mr Banana speaks of the 'semi-slavery of the mass labour force – a constant reservoir of cheap labour, who are more or less like tools for production and economic profit.

'Remember, these are people for whom Jesus died. He said "I come that they may have life and have it more abundantly." '

When the findings of the Pearce Commission were announced the African National Council called for a national convention. 'It is expected that this convention will pass a resolution calling upon the British Government, the Rhodesian Government, the African leaders and leaders of other recognized parties to bring about a constitutional conference,' the A.N.C. stated.

This was the first positive action to be taken by anyone involved after the Pearce Report was published. The A.N.C. said that it would invite representatives from the Rhodesian Front, other Rhodesian political parties, trade unions and employers' associations, organized commerce and industry, the churches, local authorities, chiefs and the judiciary.

The press asked Mr Ian Smith for a reaction. He said he would have nothing to do with the A.N.C. or any national convention called by the A.N.C. 'As far as Muzorewa and company are concerned, they set themselves up to oppose the settlement terms and stated that once that was over their task would be over. Their behaviour during the campaign left a lot to be desired, I think. A lot of lawlessness connected with the campaign – according to my security reports – was attributed to them.'

This allegation was laughable, as had Mr Smith any shred of evidence against the A.N.C. he would have proceeded post-haste to have the A.N.C. leaders prosecuted.

'I would say,' he continued, 'they present to me a picture of a bunch of unscrupulous politicians who have hoodwinked the poor African into going in a direction which may be to the advantage of these few politicians but obviously to the disadvantage of the African.

'They would have to prove themselves a lot more responsible and show that they do speak on behalf of the African people before I will have any truck with them.'

Mr Smith went on to say that his government would not sponsor any dialogue, but he said that neither he nor his government was devoid of new ideas on the settlement issue.

'I have always said that I am prepared to speak to people in this world as long as I am satisfied that the talks are going to be constructive.' He also said that it would be foolish of Rhodesians to rule out the possibility of having to tighten their belts. In times of economic pressure many countries had to do this, he said.

His government banned the sale of membership cards by the A.N.C. which was intended to raise money. It then declared the A.N.C. to be a political party, thus paving the way for the eventual bannings and imprisonments that undoubtedly lie ahead. Then it declared that it would be illegal for the A.N.C. to receive money from abroad.

Sir Alec has called for black and white Rhodesians to get together in Rhodesia and has said that the solution to Rhodesia's problems really lies in the hands of the people within Rhodesia.

This is a truth which should have been accepted before any deal was attempted with Mr Smith. Until black and white agree there cannot be a settlement worth the name. Any agreement must warrant and include the assent of the African people. At this point the Africans are still ready to negotiate, but Mr Smith refuses to walk the only road that can lead to settlement.

There is no doubt that Africans still wish to talk to whites. This was made clear throughout the Pearce Report. 'What they now wanted, Africans said, was a national convention, or a constitutional conference, or a meeting together of Rhodesian Africans and Europeans under some independent chairman when these issues could be discussed and progress made towards their resolution.'

But the Smith regime would not countenance negotiations with the African people. This, together with the fact that Sir Alec had left the rejected proposals on the table, had stated that Rhodesian officials were free to visit London, had asked the Commons to have another look at the proposals, had said it could not be all that difficult to get an agreement 'with Mr Smith' led to the greatest of unease amongst the African people.

This unease was increased by what was happening in Rhodesia itself. On 28 June the *Chronicle* published a report from the A.N.C. that the Rhodesian Government was conducting a desperate campaign to reverse the African 'No' to the proposals. An A.N.C. statement said the Government was sending forms to prominent Africans, and chiefs were being summoned to meetings addressed by officials and Government Ministers.

'The campaign is intended to make the chiefs and Africans in non-A.N.C. leadership declare that they and their people were deceived by the A.N.C. and that after reflecting the situation they and their people are now in favour of the proposals . . .'

No comment from the government was available.

This wouldn't have alarmed many people had Sir Alec not spoken of a failure in A.N.C. leadership; had he not asked Africans to reconsider the terms; had he not said that the method of testing acceptability would have to be re-examined. But his statements tied in all too well with what was actually happening in Rhodesia.

If Her Majesty's Government truly believe that some future settlement can be arrived at with the Smith regime and without *representative* African participation they are wrong. If Her Majesty's Government believes that it will be enough to get a certain number of Africans to accept the rejected settlement proposals which will then be implemented by both governments, then they are willing violence on to Rhodesia with a cruel irresponsibility.

It may well be that there is no alternative to violence. But while there remains a desire for peaceful, constitutional change, Her Majesty's Government should be obliged to do everything in its power to explore all avenues of peaceful change.

Sanctions should not only remain in force. They should be strengthened. The Monday Club/Beaverbrook Press argument that sanctions have either failed or are harming Africans more than whites should be dismissed with the contempt it so patently deserves.

It is clear to any impartial observer that the pressure of sanctions – and nothing else – forced the Smith regime to the negotiating table. It is equally clear that the argument that sanctions should be lifted because only Africans are being harmed is a wicked, self-interested lie perpetrated by those who care least of all for Africans.

'Many said that sanctions should not be lifted,' writes Lord Pearce, 'until the Government had demonstrated its determination to change course and to implement the Proposals in the spirit as well as the letter; sanctions might affect the African more seriously than Europeans, but this was a price they were prepared to pay.'

Sir Alec has stated that Britain is the only country effectively observing sanctions. This is not true. He says that there are wide-scale evasions of the sanctions policy. Undoubtedly this is true of some but not all countries. But the British Government should find little comfort in lamenting the fact that Rhodesian police are charging about Rhodesia on Yamaha motorbikes. The British Government should be fulfilling its duty in concert with the United Nations in endeavouring to plug any sanctions leak. The sanctions policy will not be reinforced by polite, irrelevant conversations with South Africa and Portugal. It is time for some very hard talking with South Africa and with Portugal, the 'friends' of Her Majesty's Government who have sabotaged, at every turn, British Government policy.

The sanctions policy will not be reinforced by maintaining a reluctant blockade of Beira (for the sole reason that Russia may be invited to take over should Britain withdraw) when Rhodesia's oil and petroleum comes in through Lourenço Marques.

Sanctions, blockades and all the misery engendered by white Rhodesia which has embittered the relationship of white Rhodesia with the United Kingdom and with the rest of the world is super-ficially negative, unproductive and regrettable. We have all suffered to some extent.

But what was the necessity for it all? What could Mr Smith not have achieved if he had kept within the law and attempted to foster a spirit of trust and co-operation with the United Kingdom? Why did the Smith government decide to rebel if it was not given its own way?

The answer to that is that everything, friendship, trade, financial investment, a thriving economy – all, all were available. What was not on offer was the readiness to go along with merciless racial oppression designed to maintain white supremacy.

That alone was forbidden. But to the leaders of the white Rhodesians that was the fruit above all others they desired, for it had been theirs, surreptitiously perhaps, throughout the years.

The lives of many people, black and white, are at stake, and this is not a time for soft words and meaningless platitudes. Rhodesia is not just a topic for conversation, debate and speeches. Rhodesia is teetering on the brink of tragedy and we need strength and help from Her Majesty's Government – and from the rest of the world. The very last thing that Rhodesia needs is a new chapter of British appeasement, a 'settlement' between Her Majesty's Government and Mr Ian Smith. If the Africans of Rhodesia cannot look for support, for integrity, honesty and an unswerving devotion to the ultimate goal of justice in Rhodesia from Her Majesty's Government then of course they will look elsewhere for help. There is so much at stake. There are so many lives visibly hanging in the balance.

The separation between the Smith regime and Her Majesty's Government should be a matter of high principle. But Her Majesty's Government blinks at this and speaks of the realities of power, of the inevitable. What Her Majesty's Government should affirm is that principle will not be forsaken again, policies will be drafted which are realistic and far-sighted and which not only take account of the fact that Rhodesia will move towards majority rule but will help to facilitate the training of people for positions in the new government.

The consequences of standing firmly on principle should not be dreaded as inevitable but should be saluted as incalculable. The only hope of peace, justice and safety in Rhodesia lies in the hands of the African people, not in the hands of the Smith regime. This is the basic fact which should be recognized by Her Majesty's Government in any future dealings with Rhodesia.

Hokonui Ranch
Dadaya
July 1972

Postscript

I have always said there would be a 'Yes' and I still believe there will be a 'Yes'.

Rhodesian Minister of Internal Affairs, Mr Lance Smith.

July 1972

11 November 1972 marked Rhodesia's seventh year of isolation. That night the annual 'Independence Ball' was held in Salisbury and, at midnight, Mr Ian Smith rang the bronze 'Liberty Bell' to mark the seventh year of 'independence' — an independence unrecognized by any country in the world. Those sipping 'whisky' at the Independence Ball where the Liberty Bell was rung were in fact drinking a Bulawayo product of cane spirit, ionized water, and flavouring. As 1972 drew to a close the shortage of foreign currency was becoming desperate. The book trade was importing between twenty and twenty-five per cent of the books normally bought before U.D.I. Approximately sixty per cent of Rhodesia's white farmers had made a loss in three out of the past four years. The tobacco burley market had collapsed. Shortage of transport was becoming acute. The bottom had dropped out of the second-hand car market as fewer second-hand cars became available and those that did had done enormous mileages. Sanctions were having an increasing impact and some Rhodesian Front leaders seemed to be recognizing the need to meet some African leaders in a bid to find a solution to lead to a settlement and the ending of sanctions.

At the very moment when the effect of sanctions was becoming obvious to all, Sir Alec Douglas-Home, in an effort to placate supporters of Mr Ian Smith on the right wing of Britain's ruling Conservative Party, announced that it was his view that the previous Labour Government 'ought never to have internationalized the problem by taking it to the United Nations and asking for mandatory sanctions. But mandatory sanctions are a fact of life which we have to face'. On that day, 9 November 1972, Sir Alec moved in the House of Commons that the sanctions policy be extended another year. He seemed to do so with considerable reluctance and used the opportunity to introduce a number of small relaxations in the sanctions policy against Rhodesia which were intended, he said, to ease individual hardship. It was significant that the relaxations primarily benefitted white Rhodesians, particularly one which would allow those in need of medical treatment to obtain a British passport so that overseas treatment could be obtained, even if that treatment was available in South Africa. Bishop Muzorewa, who has been seriously ill in the second half of 1972 and who needs overseas medical treatment, has had his passport seized by the Rhodesian authorities, as had the Rev. Canaan Banana. The new passport relaxation announced by Sir Alec meant in reality that the Rhodesian authorities alone would have the right to say who should and who should not be able to use a British passport, and the way was cleared, perhaps unintentionally, for any Rhodesian Front doctor to have the ability to furnish Rhodesian sanctions-busters with a medical certificate stating overseas treatment to be necessary.

In the same debate Sir Alec said that if the sanctions policy was found to have failed: 'I may be compelled by events to come to the House and to go to the United Nations and to state the case plainly for a change of policy. In that event I should have to mobilize a good case to the House and to the United Nations. In the event of failure, however, as I have said before, that would be the straightforward thing to do — to say straight that the policy had failed.'

But Sir Alec had missed the point. If the sanctions policy was at any stage to be lifted, the people he would have to explain himself to would not primarily have to be the House of Commons or the United Nations. The people with every right to any explanation were the African people of Rhodesia who had themselves, through Lord Pearce, authorized the continuing policy of sanctions.

While Sir Alec was speaking in the House of Commons, the Minister of State for Foreign and Commonwealth Affairs, Lady Tweedsmuir, was putting the government case for the extension of sanctions for another year in the House of Lords. During her speech she said: 'It is said that we are the only country that carries out sanctions. We are not the only country, but I believe that we are the most thorough. There have been various proposals to strengthen sanctions. Our representative at the United Nations has instructions to consider these proposals in the Supervisory Committee, which is due to meet shortly at the United Nations. But our own view is that the most important action that can be taken by other nations is to make existing sanctions more effective . . .'

The sanctions policy against Rhodesia had already been seriously breached by the decision of the United States Government to allow

the importation of chrome and other strategic minerals from
Rhodesia the preceding year, despite the fact that the United States
Office of Emergency Preparedness had estimated that the chrome
ore stockpile in the United States was over one million tons in excess
of United States security requirements.

Britain did not protest about that major sanctions-busting
decision made by the United States. Indeed, when Sir Alec flew out
to Rhodesia to sign the settlement proposals with Mr Smith, he
used this sanction of the United States as an argument as to why
there must be a settlement with the Smith regime as, he said, the
sanctions policy was irreparably harmed. There was an uneasy
feeling abroad that, far from being dismayed, Her Majesty's Government was grateful for the American decision as it made available
another argument for dropping the sanctions policy. It is difficult
to believe that the United States would have started re-importing
chrome and other minerals from Rhodesia had the British government lodged a protest in strong terms.

On 17 November 1972 it was announced in Salisbury that new
legislation was to be introduced in Rhodesia under which every
African over the age of sixteen would have to carry a 'pass' — an
identity certificate — at all times. Mr Ian Smith said that the
proposed legislation, modelled on that pass-system of South Africa,
would not impede the still proposed settlement, the terms of which
were still lying 'on the table'. The new pass system would be enacted
under existing legislation, he said, and this did not conflict with the
proposed settlement terms.

This new development naturally confirmed all the suspicions
opponents of the settlement terms had ever had. The road along
which the Rhodesian Front were preparing to drag Rhodesia was
clearly marked 'apartheid'. Any settlement with the Rhodesian
Front regime would simply strengthen them in their avowed
intention of creating a racially segregated society.

Under the proposed new legislation any African, be he a Member
of Parliament, a Chief, a member of the Senate, or anyone else,
will have to apply for a permit should he wish to leave the country
for a visit. Rhodesia has become one vast detention camp with the
whites the captors, the blacks the captives. There will be many
arguments about the way eventual freedom will be achieved. But
one thing is certain. At the present moment the two most important
political bargaining weapons Africans have within Rhodesia are the
continued sanctions policy against Rhodesia and the continued
isolation of the illegal Smith regime from the rest of the world. If
the sanctions policy is shattered and the Smith regime recognized

the Africans will have to turn away from their stated desire for a constitutional conference involving all groups in Rhodesia, under the chairmanship of Britain or an impartial judge of international standing. The possibility of peaceful change in Rhodesia is remote, but it is there. If the weapon of sanctions is removed the Africans will have to turn to other friends for help and other means for change.

London
November 1972

Index